"This look at true self and false self is a thoughtful examination that carefully weaves in biblical truth and psychology in a way that is sure to help the reader find freedom in their true self."

—AMY MATTIA
Director, Karis House

"Brett's teaching on the true self and false self is not merely an intellectual exercise for him, but more so an expression of his commitment to pursue God and his truth. Brett exemplifies key qualities of an effective teacher and solid thinker. What he teaches emerges out of his own life experience, rooted in humility and authenticity. It is a pleasure to witness how he manifests these qualities in service to the body of Christ."

—BOB HUDSON
Founder, The Cross Ministry Group

"In this stimulating work, Vaden explores the self by examining the Scriptures, some key figures in Christian tradition, and secular psychologists. Nor is this simply a patchwork of different perspectives. Vaden evaluates and considers Christian theologians and psychologists with the standard of God's word. We can be grateful for this careful study on a theme that concerns both Christians and those who don't confess the faith."

—THOMAS R. SCHREINER
Southern Seminary

"It is a delight to see this kind of thoughtful work being done in the area of Christian psychology. Vaden's book is a model of the kind of soul-honest and biblically rooted writing that we need to understand the complex journey of the human and Christian life."

—JONATHAN T. PENNINGTON
Southern Seminary

"Vaden's careful contemplation and discernment are displayed through-out this work, which pushes beyond simply aligning psychology and theology. Vaden offers a perspective on the self that is saturated in a biblical worldview, while equipping the reader with practical responses that can be offered to a culture in need of the self-awareness, social relations, and active practices of which he speaks."

—PAUL LOOSEMORE
Covenant Theological Seminary

"Vaden believes we know ourselves better . . . in dialogue—between fallen human beings and a holy God, between Christian and secular understandings of human nature, and between self and other. Dialogue is our best and only means of seeing past the withered fig leaves of our myriad false selves . . . Where Vaden excels is in his dialogical synthesis of biblical, historical, and contemporary perspectives. This is psychologically informed, pastorally sensitive work. We do well to listen, and reflect, with care."

—JONATHAN P. BADGETT
The Southern Baptist Theological Seminary

The True Self and False Self

The True Self and False Self

A Christian Perspective

Matthew Brett Vaden

Foreword by Eric L. Johnson

PICKWICK *Publications* · Eugene, Oregon

THE TRUE SELF AND FALSE SELF
A Christian Perspective

Pickwick Publications
An Imprint of Wipf and Stock Publishers
199 W. 8th Ave., Suite 3
Eugene, OR 97401

www.wipfandstock.com

PAPERBACK ISBN: 978-1-7252-9269-7
HARDCOVER ISBN: 978-1-7252-9270-3
EBOOK ISBN: 978-1-7252-9271-0

Cataloguing-in-Publication data:

Names: Vaden, Matthew Brett [author]. | Johnson, Eric L., 1956– [foreword writer]

Title: The true self and the false self : a Christian perspective / Matthew Brett Vaden.

Description: Eugene, OR: Pickwick Publications, 2022 | Includes bibliographical references and index.

Identifiers: ISBN 978-1-7252-9269-7 (paperback) | ISBN 978-1-7252-9270-3 (hardcover) | ISBN 978-1-7252-9271-0 (ebook)

Subjects: LCSH: Christianity—Psychology | Self-knowledge, Theory of | Self | Self (Philosophy) | Identity (Psychology) | Theology, Practical | Psychology, Religious

Classification: BR110 V33 2022 (print) | BR110 (ebook)

12/16/21

To Rachael Elaine Vaden

Contents

Foreword

How important is self-understanding in Christianity? Augustine, Calvin, Pascal, and Kierkegaard believed it was foundational. Yet, the supreme importance of God in Christianity; some common misunderstandings of Scripture; and our contemporary, secular cultural context, in which the Self looms much larger than God, have made it difficult for Christians to approach the subject in organically Christian ways.

At the same time, we could say that some degree of self-understanding, even if only implicit, is one of many inevitable constituents of human life. From womb to tomb, humans are continuously learning about themselves (initially, indirectly, in how others respond to them; and ideally, increasingly, through their own intentional activity). This makes the construction of a contemporary Christian model of self-understanding quite urgent.

But what would distinguish such a model? Should it derive all of its elements from the Bible? Should it be focused only on one's union with Christ or the quality of one's Christian life? Should it be marked by a distinction between the religious aspects of one's life and the more mundane? Perhaps Christian self-understanding should be characterized by comprehensiveness, encompassing all the aspects of a Christian's self, since God is related to all of them, in one or more ways.

Christians probably won't all agree on an answer. But the lack of unanimity does not mean there is no distinctive Christian model of self-understanding, at least in the mind and heart of God. Indeed, multiple perspectives on such a complex topic is usually a sign that a rich, complex

ix

model that brings them altogether awaits development. In the meantime, the identification of some fruitful distinctions in the Christian self would be a useful step towards a comprehensive model, and the false self and true self is one such, especially valuable, distinction.

It is a curious fact of twentieth-century Western psychology that Thomas Merton and Donald Winnicott came up with these same terms, around the same time, apparently independently of each other, and understood them from very different worldview standpoints. This book builds on their contributions, but goes much further by considering relevant biblical material (in Proverbs, Jesus's teachings, and Paul's epistles), wisdom from some giants of the Christian tradition (Augustine, Luther, and Kierkegaard, in addition to Merton), and the research program of a contemporary social-cognitive-developmental psychologist, Susan Harter, as well as Winnicott's more clinical texts.

However, we could summarize the project of this book as an attempt to understand the true-self/false-self constructs that Merton and Winnicott first identified, according to a fundamentally Christian interpretive framework, while also incorporating the insights and findings of two modern psychologists. The Christian tradition provides a theocentric view of the true and false selves, specifically one in which their meaning is disclosed ultimately in Christ; whereas Winnicott and Harter have focused on the developmental dynamics that occur in a fallen/created world that contribute to their formation, though they wrote, of course, as secularists. Placing their secular insights and findings within a Christian interpretive framework might be considered a gross category mistake to some, but it simply reflects the recognition of the deep unity of psychological knowledge that exists in Christ, according to biblical worldview assumptions (John 1:9; Col 1:15; 2:3). This work consequently serves as a marvelous example of Christian psychology academic scholarship. The author does not attempt to baptize Winnicott and Harter's contributions, like so many Christians do in psychology, by uncritically appropriating them, in order to show how a scientific perspective can complement a religious perspective, as if Winnicott's and Harter's writings were themselves free of worldview assumptions. Instead, he appropriates the contributions of the modern psychologists only after interrogating it according to Christian assumptions, noting some of the distortions and lacunae. Such critical appropriation is a necessary step in the Christian translation of the contributions of secular models to begin to show how Christian theological and psychological understandings of human development, psychopathology, and adult self-understanding actually essentially co-here, and lead to a more comprehensive model than Merton himself proposed and modern psychology could ever develop, given its neo-positivist assumptions.

Before concluding the Foreword, however, I would be remiss if I did not also bring to light Brett's personal journey with respect to the book's central themes. As someone who has known him for most of his adult life, I am a witness of the growth in his self-understanding regarding his own false and true selves. He mentions in the Introduction a ministry that has benefitted both of us, called Men at the Cross (that also works with women!), founded by Bob Hudson, that introduced him to this pair of self-concepts, and to which he has given himself as a volunteer and a leader, as a part of this quest. In addition, I have known him to be generally honest and humble about himself, receptive to the feedback of God and others, and hungry for more of God's reality, in spite of the pain such openness entails. The objective value of this book, I think, is self-evident. The observations I conclude with provide some indication of the personal authenticity that ought to coincide a book such as this.

May God enliven the insights and integrity of this book, so that they germinate and grow in all those who read it.

Eric L. Johnson
Professor of Christian Psychology
Gideon Institute of Christian Psychology & Counseling
Houston Baptist University

Preface

In November 2008, I attended a weekend event called Men at the Cross. There the concepts of the false self and true self came to have deep personal meaning for me. Through Men at the Cross and through my relationships as a husband, father, and friend, I have come to see some of the effects of living out of the false self. I write this book, then, out of more than academic interest; the beginning and basis of the work has been my own journey as a follower of Christ.

I have had many partners in this work, and I am grateful for them all. Some of the people who have directly contributed to this book are my doctoral committee, headed by my doctoral supervisor, Eric Johnson, with Jonathan Pennington, Greg Allison, and Earl Bland. Thanks to Bob Hudson, creator of Men at the Cross. Thanks to friends who have encouraged me, including Daniel Vaden, Jordan and Sharla Goings, Michael and Melissa Spalione, and Brent and Courtney Moore. Thanks to my parents and my wife's parents for their gracious and constant support: Larry and Laura Vaden, and Greg and Libby Bozeman.

I owe my wife, Rachael, the most gratitude. I honor her for her faith, hope, and love, which have inspired me to persevere in scholarship and sanctification. Lastly, I thank our children, Story, Arrow, and Harmony, who in their own way are helping me discern the truth about myself.

This work is primarily intended for Christian researchers, teachers, and practitioners in the fields of psychology, theology, and counseling. I especially hope it will fall into the hands of those wanting to enlarge the scope and depth of psychology and theology by understanding the two fields together. The flow of the book will appeal to Christian readers because it starts with what is probably most familiar (Christian viewpoints) and proceeds to less familiar perspectives by modern psychologists. Although this is a scholarly work, I aim for a personal and clear style.

Brett Vaden
St. Louis, Missouri
February 2021

1

Introduction

The True Self and False Self

Two personal experiences drew me to this subject. The first was a weekend retreat called Men at the Cross, where I received the gospel in a fresh way. I had heard the gospel preached and explained countless times growing up. I had studied the gospel in Bible college and seminary. And so I knew that, as the Apostle John puts it, "God so loved the world that he gave his one and only son, that whoever believes in him shall not perish, but have eternal life" (John 3:16 NIV). I had followed and known the Lord Jesus Christ for many years. But I had not known myself very well. I had not known, or at least had resisted knowing, the parts of me that were more pretense than truth. And though I thought myself sincere and honest, the whole truth about me scared me more than I cared to acknowledge. I kept that door closed as much as possible. At this men's retreat, however, my truth and falsehood confronted me. Rather, I confronted them, because others helped me to do so with the gospel. The impact on me was life-changing. For one thing, my sense of self was shaken. I realized I had based my identity in false selves like the "performer" and "good boy." I was disillusioned and humbled. On the other hand, being knocked off my center of gravity opened up space in my heart to be re-centered in Christ. The door I had kept closed was now ajar.

My second experience was reading Thomas Merton's *New Seeds of Contemplation*. Merton's poetic teaching about the false self and true self gripped me. Here was another Christian, albeit outside my tradition, who

1

was nevertheless powerfully articulating what I was learning about the gospel and myself. Merton's words clearly and movingly described how profoundly entwined sin is with the false self. Though I had read Genesis 3 again and again through the years, I had never quite reckoned with how integral the false self is to the story of Adam and Eve, and thus to the story of all their descendants. As a result of sin, we all hide from God and cover our nakedness with "fig leaves." Though God created us to know him and be known by him and others, we have exchanged our "naked and unashamed" existence for sin, shame, and the falsehood we use to hide. In Adam, all now enter life with his same aversion to being known, as well as with his same proclivity to concealment and self-protection. Thus, Merton writes, "To say I was born in sin is to say I came into the world with a false self. I was born in a mask. I came into existence under a sign of contradiction, being someone that I was never intended to be and therefore a denial of what I am supposed to be."[1] The false self that people wear is a denial of their humanity and their calling. Yet, though the true self is hidden, we may still attain it through grace: "The secret of my identity is hidden in the love and mercy of God."[2] Though lost because of sin, we can regain our true selves through the love of God and union with his Son.

These experiences awakened my desire to put off my old, false self and put on the true self. But I was also intrigued by how relevant and applicable the subject is in our day. Many people are trying to discover their true self. Many are aware of a lack of authenticity in others, and sometimes they feel the lack in themselves. This is true of Christians as well as non-Christians, and both have tried to address the problem. While unbelievers have many resources, without Christianity they lack the real diagnosis and cure. On the other hand, Christian psychologists and counselors could learn much from the work of secular psychology. I want to help both sides, but especially Christian counselors and pastors, who may be tempted to either utilize secular techniques and theories *carte blanch* without reorienting them to Christianity, or to read their Bibles and apply their counsel in isolation from outside wisdom.

As to my aim, I am proposing a Christian theory of the false self and true self that is informed by both modern and ancient scholarship. Since at least the 1950s, secular psychologists have been talking about

1. Merton, *New Seeds of Contemplation*, 33–34.
2. Merton, *New Seeds of Contemplation*, 35.

the true and false self. They have often described the false self as an internal saboteur that blocks people from feeling authentic or real.[3] The true self, however, means "being and feeling real" and belongs "essentially to health."[4] But this conversation goes back much further than the twentieth century. From ancient times, thinkers have written about true self and false self behavior. I'm particularly interested in the Judeo-Christian perspective on these phenomena, and so will give special attention to what the Bible has to say.

For those interested in my methodology, let me explain a few principles guiding my work. First, I believe that the best way to produce a robust definition of the true self and false self is to listen to many voices, even if they disagree. In the absence of dialogue between different perspectives, we won't have a full understanding. Yet, second, because I am a follower of Jesus Christ, I believe Christianity provides the most accurate and complete worldview. And so, in this book I will privilege the Bible over all other sources of knowledge.

In this regard, I intend this book to be a work of Christian psychology.[5] One of the main tasks of Christian psychology is to interpret the discoveries and assertions of secular psychology from the standpoint of Christianity. Secular psychology can be a helpful source of knowledge, and it is appropriate and imperative for Christians to wisely and faithfully utilize it in their research and practice. But the Bible has authority over all other sources of knowledge and is the primary source of knowledge about the nature, psychopathology, and psychological healing of individual human beings. Thus, an adequate Christian articulation of any concept from secular psychology must be guided and ruled by the teaching of Scripture. My hope is to do just that.

To adequately define the false self and true self, I believe we need to answer four questions: (1) Why do people reflect on themselves? (2) Why do they understand themselves wrongly? (i.e., constructing a false self) (3) What does true self-understanding entail? And (4) What interventions can foster true self-understanding?[6] Let me briefly explain each of these questions.

3. Masterson, *The Search for the Real Self.*

4. Winnicott et al., *Home is Where We Start From*, 35.

5. See Johnson, *Foundations for Soul Care.*

6. I'm working off of Jones' and Butman's four categories for analyzing modern psychotherapies: model of personality, model of abnormality, model of health, and model of psychotherapy. Jones and Butman, *Modern Psychotherapies.*

Why Do People Reflect on Themselves?

According to both Christian and secular theories, people naturally develop the ability to reflect on themselves, i.e., to make themselves the object of their own observation, description, and evaluation. All the various psychological constructs, processes, and phenomena that have the word "self" attached depend upon this capacity (e.g., self-regulation, self-determination, self-esteem). William James proposed two particularly important concepts we need to understand for our study: the Me-self and the I-self.[7] The Me-self is what people perceive, describe, or evaluate when they reflect on themselves. By analogy, think of the image you see in a mirror as your Me-self. The I-self, on the other hand, is the one who perceives, describes, and evaluates. The I-self is the one who looks into the mirror. In other words, the I-self is the knower, observer, or experiencing subject, whereas the Me-self is the thing known, observed, or believed about oneself. Human beings acquire the I-self capacity to observe the Me-self through the course of normal human development; as we grow in our ability to speak and use language, we talk about ourselves, describing ourselves, often in more and more nuanced ways.[8] With each stage of life, from infancy to adulthood, people's cognitive abilities and facility with language increase, allowing them to construct a more and more integrated or global understanding of themselves.

Christian and secular perspectives align in many respects about humanity's capacity for self-understanding, but in other significant respects they are at odds, particularly concerning the ultimate reason or purpose for employing this capacity. We will explore all this more fully later.

Why Do People Construct a False Self?

Many theorists also disagree about why people view themselves wrongly, even within the secular ranks. Some secular theorists think it's possible to use false self behavior adaptively to maximize psychological health.[9] To these theorists, the false self is a natural result of normal human development, because it enables people to adapt and succeed in life (e.g., by promoting higher self-esteem and self-confidence).

---

7. James, "The Principles of Psychology."
8. See chapter 2 of Harter, *The Construction of the Self*.
9. Taylor and Brown, "Illusion and Well-Being," 43–66.

Other secular theorists consider false self behavior abnormal and think that it is ultimately unhealthy and destructive, though it may bring short-term gains.[10] According to these theorists, false self behavior is a sign of pathological psychological development for two main reasons. First, false self behavior consists of deceiving others, resulting in problems with cultivating and maintaining positive social relationships. Second, it consists of deceiving oneself, resulting in negative psychological experiences related to self-worth, depression, narcissism, blindness to one's shortcomings, and other intrapersonal problems.

Christian theorists can affirm that false self behavior brings both interpersonal and intrapersonal suffering. However, Christians should insist on a third reason that the false self is unhealthy: as a manifestation of humanity's sin, it abets human beings' descent into spiritual death, or separation from God. The false self enables people to deceive themselves about spiritual realities—which go beyond the social and psychological spheres—so that they believe life, happiness, and salvation are up to themselves. To live under this pretense is to live in what the apostle Paul calls "the flesh" (Phil 3:3–11; Gal 5:16–17), which is the human condition in its fallenness, apart from God.[11] Life in the flesh is characterized by self-deception, because although the truth about God is revealed to people, they suppress that knowledge and believe a lie (Rom 1:18–20, 25). This state of self-deception—of knowing the truth while at the same time denying it—means that one is a divided person who lacks integrity or wholeness.[12] In such people (which is in fact all human beings) there is a disconnection, a split between their conscious awareness and their unconscious or suppressed knowledge. In the Gospel of Matthew, the term "hypocrite" denotes this kind of person. Hypocrites are marked by the inability to discern the truth about themselves, even though they may observe it in other people (Matt 7:1–3). When hypocrites look at their lives, they do not see the true self, which they have suppressed from conscious awareness, but the false self. Eventually, if this state of self-deception is not rectified, people trapped in the false self will be eternally separated from God, and so without hope of ever attaining wholeness or salvation (Matt 7:21–23). While this basic Christian theory of the false self shares

10. Leary, *The Curse of the Self*; Harter, *The Construction of the Self*.

11. Moo, "'Flesh' in Romans," 366–67. Moo delineates five senses of "flesh" used by Paul: (1) material covering human bones, (2) human body as a whole, (3) human being generally, (4) human state or condition, and (5) human condition in its fallenness.

12. Via, *Self-Deception and Wholeness in Paul and Matthew*.

similarities with secular viewpoints, it goes beyond the temporal human plane to the eternal.

What Is True Self-Understanding?

Just as theorists disagree about what constitutes abnormality and pathology in human development, they also differ about what constitutes psychological wellbeing, wholeness, or salvation. Secular theorists who think the true self is a sign of healthy psychological development do so for two main reasons, as we have said: the true self enables positive social relationships and positive psychological experiences. Christians affirm these benefits, but they add a third: as a manifestation of salvation and faith, true self behavior reflects a positive, right relationship with God. Christians believe that people who are cut off from God are also cut off from themselves, while those who know him also know themselves. Knowledge of God and knowledge of self are intertwined.[13] That is because human beings are more than psychological or social beings; they are also spiritual beings, created by God. Unhindered access to the true self is possible only with God.

What Interventions Foster the True Self?

Regarding interventions that foster the true self, secular theorists point to people's need for self-reflection in the context of supportive, validating social environments. People grow up best in good homes and strong communities, where they can learn to see themselves more and more accurately, judging and evaluating themselves based on what is really true about them. True self-understanding is fostered when people learn to base their self-worth and happiness on realistic standards, so that they do not need to deceive themselves or others about their accomplishments in order to have stable positive emotions. From a secular viewpoint, the happiest people are those who focus on creating "true" or "optimal" self-esteem that is based on self-determined standards, rather than self-esteem based solely on others' standards.[14]

13. For example, Calvin, *Institutes of the Christian Religion*, 4.

14. Harter, *The Construction of the Self*; see also Deci and Ryan, *Intrinsic Motivation and Self-Determination in Human Behavior*; Kernis et al., "Master of One's Psychological Domain?" 1297–305.

Christians can affirm much about the secular emphasis on supportive, non-coercive social experiences. For example, in his letter to the Corinthians, Paul teaches that it is immature or "weak" for a person to go against his or her own internal standards, or conscience, in order to conform to someone else's standards (1 Cor 8:9–11).[15] Human wellbeing and wholeness depend upon living out what one's own beliefs, desires, and values, rather than going against conscience by conforming to the expectations or pressures of other people.[16] However, because Christians believe all psychological problems are fundamentally the result of a spiritual problem, they think that the most important interventions for fostering health are spiritual in nature, having to do primarily with human beings' relationship with God.

Delimitations and Suppositions

If you want to know what I'm *not* trying to do in this book, as well as what some of my assumptions are, read below. Otherwise, skip to the next section.

This book is not an attempt to produce empirical research. I hope, however, that this work will lay the foundation for future empirical studies. By articulating a psychological theory of the false self and true self that is uniquely Christian, I hope to enable researchers to design instruments and methodologies to study the false self and true self with a higher degree of "tradition validity" than those that are not equipped to measure the theory as it is uniquely expressed from a Christian perspective.[17]

I am not going to directly engage related topics in the history of philosophy. For example, the concepts of the self, consciousness, and self-deception have received ample attention from philosophers, resulting in varying theories.[18] The intricacies of these discussions, while interesting,

15. See Via, *Self-Deception and Wholeness in Paul and Matthew*, 52.

16. In contrast to secular theorists, however, Christians maintain that while healthy, whole people live out their own beliefs, desires, emotions, and so on, they do so in conformity to God's will and design.

17. For a helpful overview of what "tradition validity" in Christian psychology entails, see Roberts and Watson, "A Christian Psychology View," in Johnson, *Psychology and Christianity*.

18. See Taylor, *Sources of the Self*; Rosenthal, "XV—Unity of Consciousness and the Self," 325–52; Fingarette, *Self-Deception*; Crites, "The Aesthetics of Self-Deception," 114–18; McLaughlin and Rorty, *Perspectives on Self-Deception*.

would take me far afield from my purpose, which is to propose a Christian theory of the false self and true self through dialogue with secular theories.

Lastly, by attempting to bring together the ideas of Christians and secular psychologists on the true self and false self, I am undertaking a task too large for this book alone. Since it is unfeasible to adequately consider the particular insights of every person who has written about these ideas, many worthy representatives from these two groups were excluded. Among secular psychologists, I will interact with representatives who have specifically used the language of "true self" and "false self."[19] Among Christian theorists, the discussion will be limited to individuals whose writings have shaped the discourse of the Christian tradition, even though most did not use the language of "true self" and "false self." Many relevant works must be omitted due to the limitations of space and time.[20]

Now let me share some of my assumptions. I am approaching my subject in a way meant to be *canonical* and *dialogical*. First, canonical, in that the Bible is presupposed to be the primary, authoritative text for psychology. Holy Scripture trumps every other source of knowledge about individual human beings, including discoveries ascertained by reason and empirical science. The Bible is especially valuable for understanding the concepts of the false self and true self as they have been used in secular psychology, because the Bible provides us with the ultimate disciplinary matrix, or worldview, for interpreting all data and theory.[21] The Bible, therefore, provides the paradigm by which the concepts of the false self and true self are evaluated, translated, and transposed in order to grasp their greatest import, meaning, and usefulness. Therefore, I will attempt to consider these concepts under the guidance and rule of Scripture.

We will also consider extrabiblical texts, however, because other sources of knowledge exist in addition to the Bible, and it is through harmonizing these sources that greater knowledge can be attained. The first set of texts belong to the Christian tradition, which offer reflection on ideas pertaining to the false self and true self in light of the Christian faith. The second set of texts belong to secular psychology, in which these

19. Specifically, Winnicott, *The Maturational Processes and the Facilitating Environment*; Harter, *The Construction of the Self*.

20. For example, there are many influential works written by early Christian writers—such as those by Origen of Alexandria and Maximus the Confessor—that could be considered, but the present study will focus on the thought of Augustine of Hippo as representative for that time period.

21. Johnson, *Foundations for Soul Care*, 153–65.

terms are defined according to a secular worldview. Secular psychologists in the twentieth century have asked certain questions about human beings—psychological questions—that have led them to formulate the concepts of the false self and true self. The research that has been accomplished is insightful and even profound.

The conceptualizations of the false self and true self in secular psychology, however, have not adequately taken God's special revelation in Scripture into account, and so they are incomplete and distorted. To the degree that secular psychology's conceptions diverge from God's revelation about human beings and Scripture's teaching, these formulations are fallacious and do not correspond with reality. On the other hand, because of the inquiries and research accomplished by secular psychology, new ways of understanding human beings have been broached, and it is possible for both secular psychology and Christian soul care to benefit from this understanding.

Thus, I am bringing the texts of two discursive communities—Christian psychologists and secular psychologists—into a kind of dialogue, but I do so under the auspices of Holy Scripture, informed by what Christians throughout history have understood. The discourse of secular psychology is not identical to that of Christian psychology, and the differences between them are analogous to two dialects. Secular discourse shares many concepts with Christian discourse, but not all.[22] Often the problem with secular ideas is that they are too thin, limited as they are to descriptions of empirically verifiable phenomena. While psychology should be scientific, Christian discourse cannot limit itself to what humans can rationally ascertain through observation and testing. Secular theorists have not sufficiently understood what people need in order to know their true self, because their criterion for the true self and false self is limited to subjective self-reflection.

To relate the discourses of secular psychologists and Christians, I will present them in their own distinct dialects: the Christian dialect in chapters two and three, and the secular dialect in chapter four. I will relate these dialects to enrich them both, but also to reconfigure the conceptions

---

22. For example, Christians and secularists can easily share concepts with relatively little ethicospiritual freight like "neuroplasticity," "systematic desensitization," and even "transference." More value-laden concepts, however, cannot be shared, because they are based on conflicting worldview assumptions. Thus, the following secular concepts betray a materialistic, mechanistic, de-spiritualized view of reality that cannot be directly carried over into Christian discourse: "defense mechanisms," "self-actualization," and "unconditional positive regard."

of secular discourse and harmonize them with Christianity. I will identify the inadequacies of the secular perspective, so that commensurate elements can be integrated within a Christian perspective of the false self and true self. In this way, I am operating under the direction of Johnson's proposal to "translate" the discourse of secular psychology for the sake of benefiting the theory and practice of Christian soul care.[23] This is no easy task, and even done well it will never be totally complete (in this world), yet it is hoped that this work will promote further dialogue between the secular and Christian communities for the good of both.

Outline

The aim of this study is to synthesize insights from Christianity and secular psychology in order to answer four questions: (1) Why do people reflect on themselves? (2) Why do they understand themselves wrongly? (i.e., constructing a false self) (3) What does true self-understanding entail? And (4) What interventions can foster true self-understanding?

In chapter 2, I present a biblical response to these questions, with specific focus on passages from Proverbs, Matthew's Gospel, and Paul's letters. We will first look to the Bible, since it is the epistemological foundation for a Christian understanding of the false self and true self. Regarding the self, the authors of Scripture do not describe how the human capacity for self-reflective processes develop, but they do assume this ability is present and that it has a purpose: we have the ability to reflect on ourselves, primarily because doing so enables spiritual and ethical well-being. Ethicospiritual (i.e., ethical and spiritual) self-understanding enables us to participate in loving communion with God and other people. However, Scripture reveals that, due to sin, the function of self-reflection has been corrupted, so that we cannot know ourselves rightly, as God intended for us, without his gracious help. The Bible describes sinful human understanding in severe terms: foolish, hypocritical, and unspiritual or "fleshly." Fallen humanity possesses a distorted ethicospiritual vision that prevents us from attaining whole, authentic self-understanding; in the flesh, sinners depend upon themselves to find their true self—apart from faith in Christ—making their efforts ultimately futile. Scripture is meant to disclose the self-knowledge people have repressed, so that they may know and internalize the truth about themselves and become whole.

23. See chapters 6 and 7 of Johnson, *Foundations for Soul Care*.

This occurs through the proclamation of the gospel, which is the message of reconciliation in the cross of Jesus Christ. Several gospel interventions that promote true self-understanding will be considered from Matthew's Gospel and Paul's letters.

In chapter 3, we will retrieve relevant contributions from four Christian thinkers, beginning with arguably the most influential theological anthropologist in the early church, Augustine of Hippo. Augustine believed that the source of life and real being is God, and in order to find God, people must turn inward, leaving the external sensible world and entering the realm of intelligible things and the "inner self." Augustine presents a philosophically rich Christian perspective on how true self-understanding is an integral aspect of salvation and wellbeing. Next we look to Martin Luther, who said that every human being is called to participate in a personal one-on-one relationship with God, through which they receive their most fundamental identity: child of God. Complementing Augustine's more ethereal psychology, Luther's theology of sin, the cross, and "gospel signs" provides a gritty and grounded contribution to how we understand the false self and true self. Following in Luther's wake, we will find Søren Kierkegaard, who defined the self in terms of relationship, and whose psychological insight anticipated modern formulations, particularly in terms of developmental psychology.[24] Framing his conclusions within the Christian worldview, Kierkegaard said that in order for people to experience full selfhood, they must leave behind lesser ideals and reach the highest criterion possible: God.[25] As we will see, Kierkegaard's works were largely an attempt to help people come to this point of decision, so that they might become Christians and "rest transparently" in God with true self-understanding. Chapter 3 will end by examining the thought of Thomas Merton, who used the terms true self and false self frequently in his writings, teaching that humanity has refused their calling to be their true selves, exchanging a life of dependence on God and concurrence with his will for a life of falsity, insecurity, exile, and sin.

In chapter 4 we look to the insights of two secular psychologists who have devoted significant attention to the false self and true self. The first theorist is Donald W. Winnicott, a seminal representative of object-relations psychology and one of the first modern psychologists to

---

24. See chapters 3 and 7 in Evans, *Søren Kierkegaard's Christian Psychology*.

25. Søren Kierkegaard, *The Sickness unto Death*, 79.

extensively treat this subject. Winnicott's theory focuses on the foundation of the false self and true self in infancy, pointing to the influence of a mother's early care, who provides the first "facilitating environment" for psychological maturation. Winnicott's overall theory of the false self and his strategies for remedying it are fascinating. The second theorist is Susan Harter, a developmental psychologist who is widely recognized for her research on self-esteem, the construction of multiple selves, and false self behavior. Harter identifies the cognitive and social factors that determine how a person forms the false self in the stages of childhood, adolescence, and adulthood.

I will do my best to honor what Harter and Winnicott have accomplished in their work, retrieving their insights and discoveries, amplifying their voice for our ears, while remaining aware of their secular bias and critiquing their viewpoints according to any blind spots I notice.

The fifth chapter draws together the insights from previous chapters, proposing a Christian theory on the false self and true self, answering the main questions of the study. The self, false self, and true self are defined according to their final, formal, and efficient causes. The content of each type of self-knowledge, that is, the information people know about themselves in each type, will also be described. Finally, intervention strategies for fostering the true self will be considered.

2

A Scriptural Perspective

The Self in the Bible

As explained in the introduction, when I talk about the "self" in this book, I am referring to the "Me-self"—what one perceives, describes, and evaluates when one is the object of one's own reflection—and what important uses it has for human wellbeing. In this section I will show that, according to the Bible, the two most important uses for understanding oneself are spiritual and ethical in nature.

First, self-understanding is *spiritually* useful, because it helps us give and receive love with God and others, participating in the life of God's loving communion, for which we were created. According to the Bible, God designed us to be the pinnacle of his creation, because unlike other creatures he made humans in his image: "Then God said, 'Let us make man in our image, after our likeness'" (Gen 1:26a). Created to be like God, humans are equipped for communion with him.

Christians have conceived various views of how the image of God (Latin, *imago Dei*) is a reflection of God; among the most common and developed are the structural, relational, and functional views.[1] The structural aspect refers to the human psychological structures that reflect analogous structures in God's being. These include: "reason, memory, will, emotions, language ability, an immaterial spirit, creativity and freedom,

1. See Cortez, *Theological Anthropology*; Grenz, *The Social God and the Relational Self*. These three views are sometimes taken together as three mutually inclusive aspects of the *imago Dei* that show how human beings resemble their Creator in various ways. To this grouping, Johnson adds a fourth aspect, "holiness" or "ethicospiritual resemblance."

personality, relationality, self-consciousness, joy, and morality, culminating in the emergence of personal agency with good character."[2] One of the
structural capacities that humans share with God is self-consciousness,
which allows people to reflect on themselves, form opinions and judgments about themselves, and eventually formulate a multi-faceted understanding of the Me-self. This *imago Dei* capacity is spiritually useful,
because communion with God greatly depends on it. Our ability to understand who and what we are enables us to know God. As Calvin asserts,
"Every person . . . on coming to the knowledge of himself, is not only
urged to seek God, but is also led as by the hand to find him."[3]

For this purpose, Scripture helps people to understand themselves.
Although the Bible is God's revelation of himself, it is also his revelation of humanity. The Bible reveals humanity's origin and purpose in its
first two chapters, and thereafter it chronicles what Christians have considered the most important events of human history: Adam and Eve's
disobedience and exile from Eden; the dispersion of the nations; God's
judgment in the flood; the selection of Abraham as the father of God's
chosen people Israel; Israel's rise and fall; the life, death, resurrection, and
ascension of Jesus Christ; and the beginning of the Church. Referring to
some of Scripture's specific narratives, Paul says that they were "written
down for our instruction" (1 Cor 10:11). While the Bible informs people
about themselves in various respects, it is primarily aimed at revealing
spiritual truths that lead them to fulfill their spiritual design; the Bible
is a book that teaches us about our nature as spiritual beings, that is, as
beings who are created to know and love God and to enjoy his fellowship
with other like spiritual beings. Scripture fosters this self-understanding
primarily in order to achieve these spiritual goals.

Second, the capacity for self-understanding is also *ethically* useful,
according to Scripture, for people must have a certain degree of self-
awareness in order to obey God's greatest commands. In Deuteronomy
6:4–5 the people of God are called to love God "with all their heart, soul,
and strength." This command assumes the ability to regard and consider
oneself in specific ways, and without this self-understanding the command could not be fulfilled.[4] The command inevitably prompts individ-

2. Johnson, *God and Soul Care*.

3. Calvin, *Institutes of the Christian Religion*, 4.

4. Johnson, *Foundations for Soul Care*, 416–17.

uals to ask themselves, "How much of my heart is loving God?"[5] Thus, the command requires people to reflect on themselves, particularly on how wholeheartedly they love God. For the individual Israelite, such a posture of self-reflection was expected to be the daily *modus operandi*, as necessary on a regular basis as any other life-sustaining activity:

> And these words, that I command you today, shall be on your heart. You shall teach them diligently to your children, and shall talk of them when you sit in your house, and when you walk by the way, and when you lie down, and when you rise. You shall bind them as a sign on your hand, and they shall be as frontlets between your eyes. You shall write them on the doorposts of your house and on your gates. (Deut 6:6–9)

Jesus would later say that the command to love God with all one's heart, soul, mind, and strength is the greatest commandment (Matt 22:38; Mark 12:29–30; see Luke 10:25–28). To fulfill it, one must achieve at least some degree of self-understanding regarding one's love for God.

In a similar way, the second greatest commandment requires people to reflect on how well they are loving their neighbor:

> You shall not hate your brother in your heart, but you shall reason frankly with your neighbor, lest you incur sin because of him. You shall not take vengeance or bear a grudge against the sons of your own people, but you shall love your neighbor as yourself: I am the LORD. (Lev 19:17–19)

This text from Leviticus partially reveals why self-reflection is so essential to God's greatest commands. Loving one's neighbor is a matter that primarily concerns one's "heart" (Hebrew, *leb*), which is the "inner, middle, or central part" of the person and the "seat of emotions and passions."[6] The opposite of obeying the command would be to hate one's neighbor in the heart. Hating and loving are accomplished both internally and externally, but the emphasis of the command is first placed on one's internal disposition. The command prompts me to ask, "Am I loving my neighbor from the inner depths of my being?"

The two great commandments are confirmed in the writings of the New Testament. The Gospel of Matthew records an incident in which a lawyer (i.e., an expert in Jewish law) asked Jesus to name the greatest commandment. Jesus answered that it was the command to love God,

5. Johnson, *Foundations for Soul Care*, 416.

6. Gesenius, *A Hebrew and English Lexicon of the Old Testament*, 523–24.

followed by the command to love one's neighbor (Matt 22:35–39). Jesus then added, "On these two commandments depend the whole Law and the Prophets," by which he meant that these commands state the true end of the Torah.[7] And so, Jesus affirms that if people want to fulfill the purpose of God's Law, they must obey these two great commands—commands which require self-understanding. Jesus taught that obeying God's law involves the inner life of a person, and he directed people seeking righteousness to an internal self-examination; to be sure that one is an ethically righteous person, one must be "pure in heart" (Matt 5:8; see 5:28, 6:21; 12:34–35).

In summary, the Bible affirms that we were made to know ourselves, and such knowing is good, because it is spiritually and ethically useful. The Bible informs us, however, that this is not the whole story, for we no longer know ourselves as we ought.

The False Self in the Bible

Because of sin, humanity's capacity for self-understanding has been seriously corrupted. Human beings can no longer come to know themselves with complete accuracy, barring the gracious intervention of God. Under the dominion of sin, people's self-understanding is distorted.

The Bible does not use the term "false self" or any exact equivalents. Indeed, the Bible does not have a synonym for the "self," which developed its modern usage over many centuries.[8] Consequently, the following discussion will be limited to biblical terms that denote certain attributes of fallen humanity linked with false self-understanding. These terms are "foolishness," "hypocrisy," and the "flesh."

Foolishness

In the Book of Proverbs, the fool is a person who is severely morally and spiritually compromised and whose conduct and character are marked by a significant lack of discernment. Waltke's definition captures the idea communicated by two Hebrew words used in Proverbs:

---

7. Davies and Allison, *Gospel according to Saint Matthew*, 246.

8. Taylor, *Sources of the Self*.

> The two derogatory words glossed "fool," *ˀwîl* and *kᵉsîl*, refer to people with morally deficient characters that prompt their irrational behavior. They are blockheads because, deaf to wisdom, from their distorted moral vision, of which they are cocksure, they delight in twisting values that benefit the community.[9]

The fool conducts his or her life in an irrational way, but the wisdom literature of the Bible reveals that this conduct is inextricably related to a "distorted moral vision." In Proverbs 1:7, we see the classic Hebraic understanding of wisdom, in which moral discernment and moral uprightness are intimately connected. The wise person begins to truly walk in wisdom by fearing the Lord. The fool, however, refuses to listen to the Lord or to choose what is right.[10] To be foolish is to be bent or inclined towards godlessness and evil.

Moreover, the more foolish a person is, the more wicked. Proverbs correlates folly with moral culpability: to the extent that I choose folly and iniquity over wisdom and righteousness, to that I extent have I become more culpable for my actions. The types of fools described in Proverbs fall upon a range, spanning from pliable naivety on one end, to deliberate hardened wickedness on the other.[11]

The least foolish and evil is the simple person, the *petî*, who naively gives no thought to his or her ways (Prov 14:15).[12] Proverbs classifies the *petî* alongside fools rather than the wise because they have not developed wisdom or proven it through experience. While naïve people are classed with fools, such people are not inherently culpable because they are essentially characterized by a lack of experience, both in wisdom and virtue as well as folly and vice. Outside of Proverbs, the simple are never described in terms of moral deviance, but are the special recipients of God's protection (Ps 116:6) and instruction (Pss 19:8; 119:130).[13] The *petî* is parallel, if not synonymous, with the young (*naʿar*). As people who are inexperienced in both wickedness and righteousness, the young and simple have the greatest potential for development, and their malleability and openness to advice make them the primary target of the sage; thus, the intended audience of Proverbs is first and foremost the *petî* and the

9. Waltke, *The Book of Proverbs*, 112.

10. Fox, *Proverbs 1–9*, 40.

11. "We can arrange the types of fools on a continuum from ingrained moral defect and unchangeability to relative innocence and improvability." Fox, *Proverbs 1–9*, 38–39.

12. Fox, *Proverbs 1–9*, 42–43.

13. Fox, *Proverbs 1–9*, 43.

naʿar (Prov 1:4).[14] As they have great potential for turning to wisdom, they may also become intractable fools.[15] The simple person's lack of self-awareness and self-control render him or her liable to foolish decisions and speech patterns, which—without correction and rehabilitation—will inevitably solidify into an ingrained disposition.[16] The innocent naivety and callowness of the simple person may eventually become a willful, culpable choice to turn away from wisdom (Prov 1:22, 32) and inherit folly (Prov 14:18).[17]

The second stage on the path of folly is doltishness or stupidity (*kᵉsîlût*). This person manifests the same types of behavior as the ignorant *petî*, but the cause is different: rather than acting more innocently out of ignorance and inexperience as young and naïve people do, the dolt's behavior flows from smugness.[18] These people have begun to trust implicitly in their decisions and ways of acting, without hesitating or considering much whether they may be wrong. Like the *petî*, the smug betray their foolishness by reckless and impulsive actions (Prov 14:16; 21:20). The key difference between a naïve youth and a person who has slipped into *kᵉsîlût* is the latter's unquestioning confidence that they are right. The "smug mental sloth," complacency, and obtuseness of these people blind them to their mistakes, closing them off from outside correction or teaching.[19] The imminent danger and certain destructiveness of folly is hardly imaginable to the *kᵉsîl*; in fact, folly has become a joy to return to habitually for pleasure and amusement (Prov 10:22; 15:21; 26:11). On the other hand, the idea of repenting is repulsive and abominable (Prov 13:19). People characterized by *kᵉsîlût* are so deformed in their character that they have come to love their folly, treasuring it and resisting attacks against it, seeking confirmation from their companions or "tribe," hardening their hearts and closing their minds to anyone or any group that disagrees with their beliefs or behaviors. This type of fool will not easily be dissuaded, not even by a hundred blows (Prov 17:10).

Given enough time and habituation, the perversity towards which the *kᵉsîl* gravitates eventually becomes the only possible way to live.

---

14. Fox, *Proverbs 1–9*, 43; Pemberton, "It's a Fool's Life," 213–24.

15. Pemberton, "It's a Fool's Life," 218.

16. Pemberton, "It's a Fool's Life," 216–19.

17. Fox, *Proverbs 1–9*, 43.

18. Fox, *Proverbs 1–9*, 42.

19. Fox, *Proverbs 1–9*, 41.

People at this point have become fools in the worst sense, the *ewîl*, fools who no longer even make the choice between good and evil because all they know is wickedness, having become severely incapacitated in terms of moral, spiritual, and psychological health.[20] The *ewîl* employs all his or her reasoning powers according to the warped moral values that have become ingrained. Such people are completely deaf to wisdom, so that no amount of remedial punishment cures them: "Crush a fool [*ewîl*] in a mortar with a pestle along with crushed grain, yet his folly will not depart from him" (Prov 27:22). As with the *kᵉsîl*, the folly of the *ewîl* seems like wisdom, and true wisdom seems like foolishness. Yet, Proverbs differentiates the *kᵉsîl* and *ewîl*, characterizing the *ewîl* as clever, crafty, perhaps highly intelligent, and aware of what he or she is doing. While such people are unskilled or foolish with regard to goodness, they are "wise" and skillful in evil.[21] Such experts in evil have cut off their minds from God so that no beneficial knowledge of him is available to their comprehension:

> For my people are foolish;
> they know me not;
> they are stupid children;
> they have no understanding.
> They are "wise"—in doing evil!
> But how to do good they know not. (Jer 4:22)

What is most striking about the final stage of folly is how easily it can be mistaken for true wisdom. These fools are wise in one sense but utterly foolish in another. The *ewîl* has gained a limited species of wisdom, or masterful understanding (*hokmâ*).[22] This kind of wisdom, however, does not flow from God but is set against him. The expertise of the *ewîl* is not true wisdom because it produces evil, yet it is an expression of mastery and the fruit of training and experience. The *ewîl* uses knowledge skillfully and appears wise, but this wisdom is proven false by his or her evil deeds.

There are two ways in which a fool's wisdom is false. First, the fool's seeming wisdom lacks a right understanding of the ethical and spiritual dimensions of life; fools do not know the true God, and thus true wisdom is beyond their grasp. What most distinguishes Proverbs from other wisdom texts of the ancient Near East is that the wisdom of Proverbs is grounded in the moral and spiritual orders defined by Yahweh. Whereas

20. Fox writes, "'*iwwelet* is essentially a moral pathology." Fox, *Proverbs 1–9*, 40.

21. Fox, *Proverbs 1–9*, 40.

22. See Sæbø, "Ḥkm," 423–24.

writings like those of Amenemope could be easily transferred and shared among a variety of religious contexts, Proverbs is uniquely oriented to the God of Israel and inextricably tied to the other books of the Old Testament by "sharing the same Lord, cultus, faith, hope, anthropology, and epistemology, speaking with the same authority, and making similar religious and ethical demands on their hearers."[23] To be truly wise, according to Proverbs, one must come to know the Lord and fear him (Prov 1:7). While one may amass knowledge and expertise in certain areas—for example, temple construction (Exod 28–36), waging war (Isa 10:13), and political advising (Isa 47:10)—wisdom cannot be reduced to human skills or professional capabilities, since it is fundamentally ethical and spiritual and derives its potency for coping with life from the God of Israel.[24] No matter how much of other kinds of knowledge one attains, the person who cordons off the ethicospiritual knowledge revealed by God is stupid:

> Surely I am too stupid to be a man.
> I have not the understanding of a man.
> I have not learned wisdom,
> nor have I knowledge of the Holy One. (Prov 30:2–3)

Commenting on these words of Agur the sage, Waltke says that without comprehensive knowledge, which includes ethicospiritual knowledge given by God, a person cannot perceive or evaluate anything in a way that demonstrates wisdom:

> Human beings destroy the environment because they understand its ecology only in parts. Likewise, apart from comprehensive knowledge, the skillful art of living is impossible. . . . Apart from revelation of the Holy One, even Agur, who studied wisdom, is nothing more than a brute beast living by his imperfect senses.[25]

The second way in which a fool's wisdom is false concerns the limited means through which the fool attains knowledge. As seen from Agur above, the gaping lacuna of knowledge concerning the ethical and spiritual orders of human life renders the fool's knowledge so sub-par that he or she is like a brute beast. Likewise, the fool's means of getting knowledge is also brutish. In Proverbs, people become wise first and

23. Waltke, *The Book of Proverbs*, 67.

24. Sæbø, "Ḥkm," 423.

25. Waltke, *The Book of Proverbs*, 79.

foremost by heeding the counsel of authorities outside themselves (10:8; 12:15; 18:2; 19:20); for example, wisdom may come from parents (Prov 2:1; 3:1; 13:1; 15:5). Ultimately, however, God gives wisdom to those who seek him and listen (Prov 2:4–6; 3:5–7; 9:10; 28:5). Truly wise people do not attribute knowledge to their efforts, but to the Lord. The sage calls the young and simple to become wise through faith: "Trust in the Lord with all your heart, and lean not on your own understanding" (Prov 3:5). To put confidence in God's counsel rather than oneself characterizes wise people; they are not wise in their own eyes, but instead fear the Lord (Prov 3:7). Fools, on the other hand, depend on their own understanding and disdain outside instruction (Prov 1:7b; 12:5). Conceited in their own presumed wisdom and smugly aloof from God's counsel, wise fools think they can attain *ḥokmâ* through their own experience of the world and through their rational powers of discovery, apart from divine insight. Yet, this path to wisdom is inherently false. According to Proverbs, true wisdom is a gift of God and cannot be culled merely from the natural world through training or experience.

The dilemma of human understanding versus divine understanding lies at the nexus of the false self and the fool. The fool is a person who depends on human understanding alone and rejects God's help, and in so doing the fool becomes confined to a constricted perspective on the world and himself. The fool has decided to reject God's comprehensive perspective as a source of knowledge in favor of discovering everything, including himself, from a merely human point of view. According to Proverbs, however, the fool's understanding will never be adequate apart from God's insight. People may think they know themselves, but only the Lord knows them completely (Prov 16:2).[26] For this reason, even the clever fool (*ewîl*) only has an incomplete, and therefore distorted, self-understanding. Fools will construct a false self as long as they lean solely on their own understanding.

To summarize, Proverbs presents a nuanced and graded picture of foolishness. First, the fool's character devolves gradually along a continuum beginning in ignorance and innocence (*petî*), moving to smug

26. Commenting on Prov 16:2, Fox says, "What God examines is human sincerity in its depths, even beneath a person's delusive opinions of himself. A person who thinks that his behavior is righteous may realize, deep down, that it is not. He may even deny that knowledge to himself. God, however, will ferret out hypocrisy and hold the hypocrite fully responsible for his misdeeds, knowing that they were done not in innocent error but willfully. One cannot hide from God and must not hide from himself." Fox, *Proverbs 10–31*, 608–9.

self-confidence and complacency (kᵉsil), and ending in hardened, wicked expertise (ewîl). Second, whatever knowledge or mastery fools achieve cannot amount to true wisdom because they depend on their own understanding, not God's, and consequently they cannot understand the ethical and spiritual dimensions of life. Finally, by refusing the knowledge of the ethicospiritual realm, fools confine themselves to a compartmentalized knowledge not only of God but also themselves. Thus, foolishness impedes true self-understanding.

As an attribute of fallen human beings, foolishness denotes a contributing factor to false self-understanding. A fool's self-understanding will always be false to some degree, because his or her perspective is incomplete, being grounded in human understanding alone, which the fool presumes to be the most credible, authoritative standard of knowledge. By describing the fool, Proverbs partially explains why human beings conceive a false view of themselves: they resist receiving knowledge about themselves from God. Having declined God's wisdom, they are unable to know themselves as wisely as they might.

Foolishness is sometimes hard to recognize in fallen human beings, because many foolish people appear good, wise, and even godly. We can see this phenomenon more fully explained in Matthew's Gospel, where Jesus exposes the false wisdom and piety of the "hypocrite."

Hypocrisy

The Greek noun translated "hypocrite" was first used for actors in ancient Greek culture, but its use developed and was applied in other contexts besides the theater:

> The Greek verb originally meant "to give a judgment on a question," in other words, "to give a reply." . . . But the corresponding noun came to be used of an actor who conveys a part in a play by word and gesture. Using the term in this way thus came to express the idea of a person acting in a role that was not his or her own. Then the term was used more generally to refer to a person who pretended to be what he or she was not and to convey the idea of hypocrisy or dissimulation. Thus hypocrisy is a lie that gives a false impression regarding oneself.[27]

27. Marshall, "Who Is a Hypocrite?" 132.

In the Greek language, "hypocrite" commonly referred to either a theatrical actor or a person who pretended to be what he or she was not. However, the term hypocrite takes on a specialized meaning in the Gospels, a meaning that captures the psychological nature of the hypocrite.

Hypocrisy is chiefly characterized by inconsistency.[28] In the Gospels, the concept is applied to the Pharisees and scribes. The Gospel of Mark records how the Pharisees once confronted Jesus, asking him why his disciples neglected certain hand-washing traditions that the Pharisees strictly observed. Jesus responded:

> Well did Isaiah prophesy of you hypocrites, as it is written, "This people honors me with their lips, but their heart is far from me; in vain do they worship me, teaching as doctrines the commandments of men." You leave the commandment of God and hold to the tradition of men. (Mark 7:6–8)

What characterizes the Pharisees as hypocrites is the inconsistency between their speech which honors God, and their hearts which are far from God.[29] Thus Jesus calls people "hypocrite" who outwardly behave in ways that contradict their inner intentions.

To the degree people recognize the inconsistency between their behavior and intention, they are more or less aware of their hypocrisy. We will call the least aware hypocrite "Hypocrite A" and the most aware "Hypocrite B." For an example of Hypocrite B, consider an occasion in which the Pharisees were maliciously trying to entrap Jesus in his words. They said to him, "Teacher, we know that you are true and teach the way of God truthfully, and you do not care about anyone's opinion, for you are not swayed by appearances" (Matt 22:16). They then asked him their question, seeming to be genuine, but inwardly hoping his answer would condemn him in some way. Aware of their malice and duplicity, Jesus exposed them: "Why put me to the test, you hypocrites?" (Matt 22:18). In this case, "hypocrite" refers to a person who is aware that his or her behavior does not correspond with his or her actual desire.[30] "A hypocrite may be a play actor who consciously feigns piety to cloak an inner godlessness . . . In this case, the hypocrite is more aware of the hypocrisy than anyone else."[31]

28. Marshall, "Who Is a Hypocrite?" 144–45.

29. Marshall, "Who Is a Hypocrite?" 135–36.

30. Marshall, "Who Is a Hypocrite?" 135.

31. Garland, *Reading Matthew*, 77.

By contrast, Hypocrite A is marked by a lack of conscious awareness. Hypocrite A is self-deceived, so that, "the discrepancy is not between what others think about a person and the inner reality but what
the hypocrite thinks of himself or herself and what God thinks.... In this
case, others are sometimes more aware of hypocrisy than the hypocrite."[32]
Perhaps this kind of hypocrite was who Jesus had in mind in the Sermon
on the Mount when he exposed the behavior of one who judges others,
seeing the "speck" in one's brother's eye, but who misses the "log" in one's
own eye (Matt 7:1–5). Addressing this kind of hypocrite, Jesus says, "You
hypocrite, first take the log out of your own eye, and then you will see
clearly to take the speck out of your brother's eye" (Matt 7:5). In this context, Jesus is referring to a hypocrite who does not recognize his or her
own faults.[33] Hypocrite A, therefore, is less aware of his or her hypocrisy
than Hypocrite B.

While there seems to be a range of awareness among hypocrites, all
hypocrisy is characterized by a mixture of conscious and unconscious elements. To see this mixture, consider when Jesus describes the Pharisees
in Matthew 23, portraying them as both partially aware of their inconsistency, yet partially unaware:

> But woe to you, scribes and Pharisees, hypocrites! For you shut
> the kingdom of heaven in people's faces. For you neither enter
> yourselves nor allow those who would enter to go in. Woe to
> you, scribes and Pharisees, hypocrites! For you travel across sea
> and land to make a single proselyte, and when he becomes a
> proselyte, you make him twice as much a child of hell as your-
> selves. Woe to you, blind guides.... You blind fools!... For you
> are whitewashed tombs, which outwardly appear beautiful, but
> within are full of dead people's bones and all uncleanness. (Matt
> 23:13–17, 27)

On the one hand, in this passage we can clearly see the conscious
side of hypocrisy when Jesus calls these hypocrites "whitewashed tombs,"
who keep up a good appearance to mask their inward corruption.[34] On
the other hand, we can see the unconscious side of hypocrisy as Jesus
repeatedly calls these hypocrites "blind" (vv. 16–17, 19, 24, 26), suggesting that the Pharisees were not aware of their inconsistencies, at least in

---

32. Garland, *Reading Matthew*, 77.

33. Davies and Allison, *Matthew*, 105.

34. Marshall, "Who Is a Hypocrite?" 141–42.

some respects.[35] While hiding their sinfulness from others, they were also hiding it from themselves, blinding themselves to the point of missing God's kingdom, forfeiting their own salvation, and zealously assimilating people into a way of life without realizing the hellish people they and their proselytes were becoming.[36] Hypocrites differ in how conscious they are of their inconsistency.[37] The hypocrite is both aware and unaware of some personal inconsistencies, and this means the hypocrite is always in some degree self-deceived. In a variety of ways, hypocrites hide and ignore their inconsistencies.

In the Gospel according to Matthew, hypocrisy is just as much about self-deception as it is about inconsistency.[38] To be a hypocrite is to be "blind" to one's actual ethical and spiritual condition (Matt 23:16–17, 19, 24, 26). Hypocrites are self-deceived because they think they have met God's standard of righteousness.[39] Hypocrites are so convinced of their righteousness that they expect God's approval and acceptance, but Jesus reveals their folly and disastrous lack of awareness:

> Not everyone who says to me, "Lord, Lord," will enter the kingdom of heaven, but the one who does the will of my Father who is in heaven. On that day many will say to me, "Lord, Lord, did we not prophesy in your name, and cast out demons in your name, and do many mighty works in your name?" And then I will declare to them, "I never knew you; depart from me your workers of lawlessness." (Matt 7:21–23)

Hypocrites are (at least partially) unconscious about their actual moral status. They have deceived themselves into adopting a false standard of righteousness that is based on outward appearances. They deceive themselves into believing that as long as they and other people consider their outward deeds righteous, then they are truly righteous.

---

35. Marshall, "Who Is a Hypocrite?" 142.

36. Hiding one's sinfulness from oneself would seem to be impossible, at least on an overt or conscious level, since it would seem that one can only hide something from one's conscious awareness intentionally or consciously; self-deception is a paradox that defies a simplistic explanation. For this reason, it must be understood as an action that can only be unconsciously or perhaps semi-consciously done, and without one's full awareness.

37. Marshall, "Who Is a Hypocrite?" 150.

38. Via, *Self-Deception and Wholeness in Paul and Matthew*, 92.

39. Via, *Self-Deception and Wholeness in Paul and Matthew*, 95.

What passes for true piety to human beings, however, does not necessarily meet God's standards. Jesus calls his followers to distinguish between apparent and actual righteous deeds, as we can see in his description of two kinds of alms-giving (Matt 6:2–4), two kinds of prayer (6:5–6), and two kinds of fasting (6:16–18). According to Jesus, a truly pious person would have a heart that is consistent with his or her life. Falsely pious persons, on the other hand, merely don a façade of pious deeds that hides an impious heart. Hypocrites like the Pharisees Jesus exposed base their righteousness only on an outward performance of God's law, not discerning the inconsistency between their performance and their motives, nor even seriously questioning whether or not those motives were pure. Jesus intensifies and sharpens the demands of God's law by addressing people's inner emotions, thoughts, and desires (Matt 5:21–30). It is clear that the Pharisees failed to meet these standards: "For I tell you, unless your righteousness exceeds that of the scribes and Pharisees, you will never enter the kingdom of heaven" (Matt 5:20). They also failed to recognize this truth about themselves. They are "bad trees" who deceive themselves by thinking they are producing good fruit, and this is the nature of the hypocrisy Jesus seeks to expose and rectify: "Either make the tree good and its fruit good, or make the tree bad and its fruit bad, for the tree is known by its fruit" (Matt 12:33). In calling hypocrites to acknowledge their hypocrisy, Jesus is also calling them to accept that the law is narrow and hard (Matt 7:13–14), and that true righteousness entails inner and outer integrity or "wholeness."[40] This fact should be no surprise, as it is what God has commanded all along:

> You shall love the Lord your God *with all your heart and with all your soul and with all your mind.* This is the great and first commandment. And a second is like it: You shall love your neighbor as yourself. On these two commandments depend all the Law and the Prophets. (Matt 22:37–40, my italics)

Jesus makes clear that the law has always required people's whole-hearted obedience, calling us to love God and neighbor wholly, with good deeds that stem from good motives.[41] By exposing their hypocrisy, Jesus attempts to help people recognize the hard truth about themselves, that they are actually not whole and that outward deeds alone cannot make them whole.

---

40. Via, *Self-Deception and Wholeness in Paul and Matthew*, 95–96.

41. In the command to love God and neighbor whole-heartedly, Israel was called to "mirror God's moral and spiritual oneness." Janzen, "The Claim of the Shema," 245.

How do these ideas relate to the false self? Hypocrites profess to be righteous and to know God, but they are not actually righteous, since they only possess the appearance of righteousness and piety based on seemingly pious deeds. Hypocrites are actually fools who do not know God and are not truly righteous, though they convince themselves otherwise. Hypocrites are fools who will eventually meet a tragic fate, in which God declares their actual nature—to their shock and horror—as workers of lawlessness who neither do God's will nor receive his approval (Matt 7:21–23). The person they thought they were is a charade. Relating this discussion to the false self, we may say that hypocrites are people who base their achievement of God's will—and thus, their righteousness and wholeness—on an external view of themselves, and who avoid evaluating their heart. Therefore, by definition, hypocrites have a distorted understanding of themselves.

Hypocrites ignore the truth in order to avoid their actual state of unrighteousness before God: "The hypocrite is blind to her own depth because she does not want to give her whole heart, her depth."[42] According to Dan Via's reading of Matthew, the self-deception of hypocrites involves two false "cover stories": the more conscious and positive story is that they have attained righteousness because they are praised for their deeds, and the less conscious negative story is that they must zealously expand their righteous reputation and influence by winning more adherents or converts.[43] Yet deeper than these cover stories is the hard truth, which hypocrites have blocked from their conscious awareness:

> We see an indication in the Gospel that in the self-deceived hypocrite there is a veiled awareness of the rebellion within (negative real story) that disturbs the tranquility of believing oneself righteous (positive cover story). This awareness generates a negative cover story, less conscious than the sense of righteousness, which is seen in the zeal of the self-deceived to win converts. . . . The negative real story (wickedness), concealed but still operant, challenges the positive cover story (righteousness) and generates the negative cover story (anxious zeal to win proselytes).[44]

42. Via, *Self-Deception and Wholeness in Paul and Matthew*, 96.

43. Via, *Self-Deception and Wholeness in Paul and Matthew*, 96–98.

44. Via, *Self-Deception and Wholeness in Paul and Matthew*, 97.

Deep down, hypocrites have buried the truth of their unrighteousness. Under the guise of zeal and superficial righteousness, they have hidden from themselves the awful reality of their sin.

Along with Proverbs, Matthew's Gospel teaches that people can be more or less aware of themselves and their alignment with the truth. However, in Matthew we see Jesus raise the stakes. We might imagine that the Pharisees, studying the Scriptures and claiming to fear the Lord, would have been the most wise and whole people. In fact, they were "blind fools." Jesus reveals that, ironically, the people who thought they were leading others to God were really dragging themselves and others to hell. Even those who claimed to follow Jesus could be self-deceived. Thus, going beyond Proverbs, Jesus teaches that merely aligning oneself with God and claiming to fear him is not enough to avoid foolishness or hypocrisy.

To more fully understand how deeply and pervasively foolishness and hypocrisy affect human beings, we will consider Paul's concepts of "the flesh" and "the old self."

The Flesh

Here I will show that, in light of Paul's teaching, false self-understanding is ultimately caused by a spiritual problem, which Paul describes as "living according to the flesh." Life in the flesh is characterized by serving sin and abusing God's law, leading to death.

The Law

Paul taught that the purpose of the law is to elicit faith and promote life (Romans 7:10; 8:3–4; 9:31–32).[45] God gave the law to Israel in order to lead them to faith in Christ for salvation (Rom 10:1–4). Paul calls the law holy, righteous, good, and spiritual (Rom 7:12, 14). God intended the law and faith to be complementary, not antithetical. Far from deterring people from faith, the law was meant to elicit people's trust in God. Paul makes clear that people should not trust merely in the law, but in God who gave the law. The end or goal of the law is not salvation through dependence on the law, but through faith in Christ (Rom 10:4).[46] God gave

---

45. Via, *Self-Deception and Wholeness in Paul and Matthew*, 23.

46. Seifrid, "Romans 7," 133.

the law to help his people Israel, intending it to function like a "guardian" (Greek, *paidagōgós*) over a child "until Christ came" (Gal 3:24).

Why then does Paul say that the law increased people's trespasses (Rom 5:20), aroused the sinful passions (Rom 7:5), and ended in spiritual death (Rom 7:10)? People might blame the law as the cause of sin—and thereby the cause of death—because as soon as they come into contact with (i.e., "know") the law they are led not into faith but "all kinds of covetousness" (Rom 7:7–8). Paul rejects that train of thought, however, and argues that the primary cause of death is not the law but sin:

> Did that which is good [i.e., the law], then, bring death to me? By no means! It was sin, producing death in me through that which is good, in order that sin might be shown to be sin, and through the commandment might become sinful beyond measure. (Rom 7:13)

The law does not cause death, but sin causes death by means of the law: "Sin is the *ultimate* cause of death. The law is the *instrumental* cause, but it is not itself blameworthy, for it is inherently good."[47]

How is the law the instrument of sin? In the first place, it is by means of the law that sin becomes a conscious possibility. When people perceive the law (i.e., when the law "comes"), sin "comes alive" in their awareness (Rom 7:9). Paul points to the specific sin of coveting as an example:

> Yet if it had not been for the law, I would not have known sin. I would not have known what it is to covet if the law had not said, "You shall not covet." But sin, seizing an opportunity through the commandment, produced in me all kinds of covetousness. (Rom 7:7b–8a)

Knowing that the sin of coveting is a possibility—and subsequently knowingly (and culpably) committing the sin of coveting—proceeds from the realization that the law forbids it. In this way the law becomes "an opportunity" for sin. As the positive indicator of what is good, the law is also negatively the indicator of what is evil. It is through this dialectic within the law that sin becomes known; inherent in the law is the opposition between good and evil, and thus by implication the law makes people aware of the possibility of sin. By teaching what sin is, the law teaches *that* sin is. Thus, the law becomes the instrument of sin, in the first place, by making it a conscious possibility.

47. Schreiner, *Romans*, 372.

In the second place, by revealing the possibility of sin, the law also becomes the occasion for actualizing sin. In Romans 7:8, Paul makes this idea explicit: "But sin, seizing an opportunity through the commandment, produced in me *all kinds of covetousness*" (my italics). Sin is realized or "produced" through the law when the law makes it known *and* people opt for it. The law enables consciousness of sin, which in turn gives rise to actual sins. And so, the law is the instrument of sin in two respects: first, sin becomes a possibility when people perceive through the law that sin *can* be, and second, it becomes an actuality when they *consent* for it to be.

By observing the logic of Rom 7:7–8, it is clear that the law is not responsible for people's sin, because it only makes sin a conscious possibility. For sin to become actual, people must not just assent to sin but consent to it. That is, for sin to be "produced" in a person, he or she must go beyond seeing it as a possibility to seeing it as an expediency. The law cannot be charged for making sin to appear expedient, for it does just the opposite by condemning sin and threatening God's punishment against it (Rom 1:18, 32).[48] When the law is transgressed, it makes good on these threats and shows its own goodness and sin's sinfulness (Rom 7:13). While the law does indeed bring the awareness of sin, it by no means tempts people to sin and it bears no blame when they do sin: "So the law is holy, and the commandment is holy and righteous and good" (Rom 7:12).

If the law does not make sin appear good or beneficial, then why do people consent to it? The answer is that they have been deceived. "For sin, seizing an opportunity through the commandment, *deceived* me and through it killed me" (Rom 7:11, my italics). People are rightly made aware of sin through the law, but they are deceived into believing sin is an expediency. Perhaps people suppose that because sin is possible it must also be expedient, as another means to life in addition to what God had prescribed. (Here it must be understood that Paul considers sin to be "an offense against God" and the "disruption of a right relationship with God."[49] When people believe sin is expedient, they are assuming that life is possible outside of communion and trust in God. Of course, this flatly contradicts what the law says.) The thinking proceeds like this: "If it is possible to sin and cut off my relationship with God, then sin must be

---

48. Paul no doubt had in mind texts like Deuteronomy 28:15–68, in which the curses for disobeying God's law are spelled out to Israel.

49. Morris, "Sin, Guilt," 877.

another means to live and thrive." Based on an erroneous assumption, people (consciously or unconsciously) choose to believe a life without God can be just as truly good as life with God. Why do people make this assumption? Again, they are deceived by sin. It becomes difficult to probe much farther, because choosing to make this assumption cannot be explained as a process of reasoning, since choosing sin over God is not rational; otherwise the sin could be attributed to faulty reasoning.[50] Paul depicts his own sin as something that defies his comprehension: "I do not understand my own actions. For I do not do what I want, but I do the very thing I hate" (Rom 7:15). People under sin's deception do not comprehend why they do what they do.[51] Sin is so entrenched that Paul is unable to fathom its pervasive, controlling influence over him. He describes his state as slavery: "For I do not do the good I want, but the evil I do not want is what I keep doing. Now if I do what I do not want, it is no longer I who do it, but sin that dwells within me" (7:20). Sin's enslaving power confounds people's ability to comprehend it. Therefore, while we cannot ultimately explain why people consent to sin, Paul makes clear that people have been deceived.

Furthermore, Paul describes this state of deception, wherein one believes that sin is an expediency to life, and he reveals its real end: "For to set the mind on the flesh is death" (Rom 8:6a). Five senses of "the flesh" can be distinguished in Paul's writings: (1) the material covering human bones, (2) the human body as a whole, (3) human beings generally, (4) the human state or condition, and (5) the human condition in its fallenness.[52] In Romans 7, Paul uses the last sense of flesh, referring to the bent in humanity (and in himself) that, dominated by sin, opposes God.[53] Paul says that even though he wishes to do good (i.e., what the law bids), "nothing good dwells in me, that is, in my flesh" (Rom 7:8). The deception of sin has gotten such a hold on humanity that it has become a defining aspect of our existence—sin has made us into beings "of the flesh": "I am of the flesh, sold under sin" (Rom 7:14b). Sin is a slave master that overrules one's personal desire and free will: "For I have the desire to do what is right, but not the ability to carry it out" (Rom 7:18b). The

50. Seifrid, "Romans 7," 147–48.

51. Schreiner argues that this ignorance does not equate to being unconscious or unaware of one's actions, but being unable to comprehend sin's power or depth in oneself. Schreiner, *Romans*, 373.

52. Moo, "'Flesh' in Romans," 366–67.

53. Schreiner, *Romans*, 354.

analogy to slavery coincides with how Paul has depicted sin as an agentic power, especially one that deceives (Rom 7:11). Sin enslaves people by deceiving them with a mendacious promise of life, and it eventually pays its slaves with "the wages of death" (Rom 6:23). To "set the mind on the flesh" means believing sin's lie—that life can be gotten apart from God— rather than recognizing that the flesh inevitably leads to death.

Sin and the Flesh

"The flesh" is a very apt term for what Paul seeks to describe about fallen human beings, and it proves to be crucial for understanding the solution to humanity's sinful condition. Without this term we might suppose that people could approach sin as an ethical problem, trying to mend it themselves, living a better life, and this supposition is not without reason. If sin boils down to a person transgressing God's commands and thereby impinging his or her relationship with him (i.e., an ethical problem), then would not the solution consist in striving to obey the law instead (i.e., an ethical solution)? Paul clearly answers "no," and for several reasons. For one, Paul states that forgiveness of transgression and justification with God are impossible through attempting to keep the law's commands: "For by works of the law no human being will be justified in his sight, since through the law comes knowledge of sin" (Rom 3:20). A second reason, therefore, is that trying to keep the law by "works of the law" only leads to sin. This is because, thirdly, sin does *not* boil down merely to transgressing God's commands (i.e., ethical infractions, or sins). Rather, fundamentally, sin means rejecting God as the Creator and Sustainer of one's life, accepting *oneself* as the creator and sustainer of one's life (see Rom 1:18–21). Sin is at bottom not an ethical problem but a spiritual one: humans have been deceived into conceiving themselves capable of attaining the good life apart from God, deceived into believing that living in the flesh is more expedient than living in the Spirit. This is the lie of sin: that people can attain true and whole life *in themselves*, rather than in communion with God. For Paul, existing in the flesh means seeking to provide for our own security instead of depending on God for it.[54]

Thus, what might seem to solve the problem—going back to the law and consenting to one's own righteousness as the true expedient for life— fails miserably, because that would be to live in the flesh (i.e., "believing

---

54. Via, *Self-Deception and Wholeness in Paul and Matthew*, 26.

that I can create life for myself by my own righteousness").[55] Depending on oneself to gain God's favor is one of the surest ways to forfeit one's salvation, because what is really necessary is absolute dependence on God, yet,

> Humanity resents that utter reliance on God; men and women want at least to cooperate with God in saving their lives—but that is the very way to lose their lives for by that very process sin is not really acknowledged, and its judgment and condemnation in the flesh are not really accepted.[56]

The law of God should show people their rebellion and God's opposition to their sin, but a fleshly (i.e., self-reliant) orientation renders the law impotent to perform its truth-revealing effect. By living in the flesh people abstract the law from God, and they use it as a "buffer" and an "independent authority" to escape God and refuse creaturely dependence.[57] By trusting in their own ability to find life, and by strengthening this fleshly confidence with a distorted view of the law, they are deceived about their sin and their dependence on God.

Paul's concept of the flesh clarifies that sin is not merely an ethical problem but a spiritual one, because sin does not just describe one's actions but one's being: human existence is "in the flesh." Sin has come *inside* people and made them predominantly fleshly beings without spiritual life: "So now it is no longer I who do it but sin that dwells within me. For I know that nothing good dwells in me, that is, in my flesh" (Rom 7:17–18). Sin dwells within us as something that deceives us and causes us to repress the truth about ourselves, particularly the fact that we are sinners; because sin is internal, the depth and degree of our sinful condition is largely unconscious to us. Thus, we are deceived and ignorant about our sin. Indwelling sin can be likened to a narcotic drug that, once inside a person's body, severely compromises one's self-awareness and self-control. Once the person *takes in* the drug, the drug partially *takes over* the person. People are responsible for indwelling sin: it is not just the master (sin) that bears the responsibility but also the slave who consented to slavery (sinner). Despite being responsible, however, human beings in the flesh are incapable of solving the problem on their own: "For the mind that is set on the flesh is hostile to God, for it does not submit to God's law; indeed, it cannot" (Rom 8:7). Furthermore, all attempts to do

---

55. Via, *Self-Deception and Wholeness in Paul and Matthew*, 26.

56. Torrance, *Incarnation*, 72.

57. Torrance, *Atonement*, 113.

so are simply disguised manifestations of the life of the flesh; one way many Jews presumed to be righteous was through circumcision, but Paul exposed their hypocrisy:

> For no one is a Jew who is merely one outwardly, nor is circumcision outward and physical. But a Jew is one inwardly, and circumcision is a matter of the heart, by the Spirit, not by the letter. His praise is not from man but God. (Rom 2:28–29)

When used as a way to attain righteousness, the ethical life is also the fleshly life. The reason being that the problem is not ethical but spiritual, and as long as we approach it from an ethical standpoint the problem will remain, cloaked through hypocrisy.

People might take the opposite route and resign themselves to lawlessness rather than ethical striving. They might reject such striving as characteristic of hypocrites and instead favor outright debauchery. They might mistake God's grace as a license to lawlessness, embracing a kind of antinomianism that Paul was accused of teaching, summarized as, "Why not do evil that good may come?" (Rom 3:8a). Paul strongly denies this charge, asserting that to "continue in sin" leads to death (Rom 6:15–16, 20–21, 23), arguing against "lawlessness leading to more lawlessness" (Rom 6:19).

In Paul's thinking about sin, neither one's ethical righteousness (i.e., "works of the law" [Rom 3:20]) nor lawlessness (i.e., "continuing in sin") are expedient solutions, for both are manifestations of the flesh—that "self-centeredness which expresses itself both in rebellion against God and in zeal for religion"—and both lead to death.[58] The only true expedient for life, according to Paul, is faith, or "the mind set on the Spirit" (Rom 8:6b). The problem of sin is a spiritual problem, in which people are confronted with two options: either to live "according to the flesh" or "according to the Spirit" (Rom 8:5). Living according to the Spirit means consenting to life grounded in God, that is, believing that "the glory and the basis of the *human* spirit is established and directed by the *Holy* Spirit."[59] In Paul's understanding, Christians are to live a spiritual life by continually recapitulating the same trust in "God's own presence by the Spirit" that they experienced when they first believed.[60] It is in this

---

58. Chamblin, "Psychology," 767; see Bultmann, *Theology of the New Testament*, 1.232–46.

59. Meye, "Spirituality," 907.

60. Fee, "Some Reflections on Pauline Spirituality," 99.

sense that faith in Christ is a "Yes to God."[61] Faith means saying "Yes" to relational trust and communion with God, which he originally offered to humanity in the beginning before sin, and which he graciously re-offered in various ways throughout salvation history, culminating finally and definitively in Jesus Christ. By describing Christians as those who "walk not according to the flesh but according to the Spirit" (Rom 8:4), Paul demonstrates that Christianity is not fundamentally concerned with people's moral conduct (i.e., ethics), but with the power that animates and upholds their whole existence.[62] The only real solution to the problem of sin, according to Paul, is to discover what this power is and to denounce all other confidences for the sake of depending on that power alone. Paul believes that power lies outside of people (i.e., *not* in the flesh), revealed in the gospel of Jesus Christ, which is "the power of God" (Rom 1:16).

The Old Self

That the gospel is the "power of God for salvation" means that, according to Paul, the true source of life and the only solution to sin is found in consenting to what God has done in Christ. Christians are those who have renounced their confidence in themselves (i.e., the flesh) and instead trusted in another person, Jesus Christ. At the same time, this is a struggle for believers, who are not yet completely liberated from their "bondage in corruption" but who hope for what they "do not see" (Rom 8:21, 25). The gospel is both the proclamation of the completed accomplishments of Christ and the hoped-for fulfillment of his work in the lives of believers, who have just begun to experience their redemption in Christ:

> The new life of believers, just because it consists in participation in Christ's life, has on the one hand the character of having passed over into the world of the new creation; on the other hand, because this life is hidden and awaits its revelation, it has the character of life in the flesh by faith (Gal 2:20) . . . or life in and through the Spirit.[63]

---

61. Barth, *The Christian Life*, 133, 144.

62. This includes the ethical life, and the conflict between flesh and Spirit has ethical ramifications along with others: "Spirit stands for the divine life and power as manifested to men. Its end is to bring men to God, to give rise to virtues, and to impart eternal life." Stacey, *The Pauline View of Man*, 178.

63. Ridderbos, *Paul*, 214.

From his Christian vantage point, Paul perceives the conflict between life in the flesh and life in the Spirit as the result of living simultaneously in two different epochs of human history, the "old" and the "new."

Paul describes humanity belonging to the first epoch as "the old self" (Greek, *ho palaios anthrōpos*). The old age began with the sin of the archetypal old self, Adam, and it extends to all those who are in "solidarity with Adam" and who are, therefore, "dominated by the power of sin."[64] "The "old" points to everything connected with the fall of humanity and with the subjection to the distress and death of a transitory life, separated from God."[65] The old age began with Adam because sin and death came through him: "sin came into the world through one man, and death through sin" (Rom 5:12).

The new age began with Christ, the archetypal "new self" (Greek, *ho kainon anthrōpos*) (see Eph 2:15). "Christ and Adam stand over against one another as the great representatives of the two aeons, that of life and that of death."[66] In pitting the old against the new, Paul reveals more specifically just how these ages began: "Therefore, as one trespass led to condemnation for all men, so one act of righteousness leads to justification and life for all men. For as by the one man's disobedience the many were made sinners, so by the one man's obedience the many will be made righteous" (Rom 5:18–19). Sinners belong to the age that began with sin. Christ inaugurated the new age, however, with "one act of righteousness" or "one man's obedience."

Believers enter into the new age and put on the new self at baptism, at which point they are given "the divinely appointed sign and seal of the fact that by God's gracious decision the old person was, in God's sight, crucified with Christ on Golgotha."[67] As the symbol of a person's solidarity with Christ, baptism for the Christian is the "demonstrative line of demarcation between the old and the new, and faith in the gospel means a self-judgment, that of being dead to sin and alive to God."[68] Paul's use of the term new self, therefore, "denotes the unity between baptized believers and the person of Christ himself in his redemptive action."[69]

---

64. Dunn, *Romans 1–8*, 332.

65. Dockery, "New Nature and Old Nature," 628.

66. Ridderbos, *Paul*, 57.

67. Dockery, "New Nature and Old Nature," 628.

68. Ridderbos, *Paul*, 214.

69. Dockery, "New Nature and Old Nature," 628–29.

Through union with Christ, who is "the firstborn" of the new age (Rom 8:29), those who trust in him are initiated into the new age and become part of the "new creation" (2 Cor 5:17; Gal 6:15) as people being remade to be like Christ (Eph 4:23–24; Rom 8:29). Yet, this transformation is not instantaneous, because believers exist in the overlap of ages, and they only experience the "firstfruits" of their salvation:

> For we know that the whole creation has been groaning together in the pains of childbirth until now. And not only the creation, but we ourselves, who have the firstfruits of the Spirit, grown inwardly as we wait eagerly for adoption as sons, the redemption of our bodies. For in this hope we are saved. Now hope that is seen is not hope. For who hopes for what he sees? But if we hope for what we do not see, we wait for it with patience. (Rom 8:23–25)

Christians are still in the process of attaining their hope, because Christ's redemption of humanity from the old age has not been completed. Christians face "the suffering of this present time" until the "revealing of the sons of God" (Rom 8:18, 19). The old age and the new age are intermingled in the life of the believer.

While Paul's concept of the "old self" helps explain the historical cause (i.e., Adam's sin) behind humanity's fleshly condition by which "the many were made sinners" (Rom 5:19), it also demonstrates that one of the most basic differences between Christians and non-Christians concerns their understanding of history and their place within it: Christians are enabled to see human history as a grand narrative that began with Eden and communion with God; next it fell into an age of sin and death and separation from God, in which he nevertheless continued to pursue and rescue humanity; and then, at the climax, history underwent an amazing reversal when God became human and, through his death on the cross and subsequent resurrection, reconciled humanity back to himself. In light of this view of history, Christians should understand themselves as persons whose destiny is totally dependent on what Jesus Christ has done for them. Because they must continue to "put off the old self" and "put on the new" (Eph 4:22–24), they experience an "already/not-yet" existence, which is marked by the struggle between the flesh and the Spirit.[70] Only

---

70. Some commentators translate the imperatives of Eph 4:22–24 as indicatives, so that rather than exhorting believers to continually put off the old self and put on the new, Paul simply reminds them of what has already been done. Even if this apparently forced reading of the text is correct, it does not negate the similar exhortations Paul gives in Romans to "present one's members" to God rather than sin (Rom 6:13) and to

Christians can consciously experience the conflict between the life of the flesh and that of the Spirit, because only they live in both ages. The struggle of living in the Spirit (i.e., to "put to death the deeds of the body" [Rom 8:13]) is peculiar to Christians by virtue of their "spiritual life," in which they have access to God despite their fallen condition:

> Christians live spiritually as and to the extent that they live ec-centrically. What are they in and of themselves but poor, weak, and foolish sinners who have fallen victim to death? They can only look beyond themselves, clinging to God himself, and to God only in Jesus Christ, and this only as they are freed to do so, and continually freed to do so, by the Holy Spirit. This is, of course, their plight—the plight of Christians alone. . . . This life in this happy plight is their spiritual life.[71]

Non-Christians, however, do not experience history in this light, nor do they see themselves in relation to Christ (or Adam) like Christians do. They do not recognize either the old age or the new, and so the conflict between the flesh and the Spirit remains outside their experience. Because non-Christians do not have the Spirit, they live according to the flesh and cannot comprehend "the things of the Spirit of God," which appear to them as "folly" (1 Cor 2:14).

What is most befuddling to unbelievers is the proclamation of Christ's crucifixion: "For the word of the cross is folly to those who are perishing" (1 Cor 1:18a). For believers, however, Paul goes on to say that the cross is "the power of God" and the "wisdom of God" (1 Cor 1:18b, 24; 2:5). For Christians who have been "baptized into Christ Jesus," the cross marks the death of the old self (Rom 6:3, 6), and as it is followed by Christ's resurrection, the cross marks the beginning of new life in the new age: "For if we have been united with him in a death like his, we shall certainly be united with him in a resurrection like his. . . . So you also must consider yourselves dead to sin and alive to God in Christ Jesus" (Rom 6:5, 11). While finding one's hope and identity in a crucified Messiah may appear absurd, it is really a mark of divine wisdom. That unbelievers think it folly demonstrates that they are blinded to the truth about God and themselves.

"put to death the deeds of the body" (Rom 8:13). For an example of the former view see Murray, *Principles of Conduct*, 211–19; Schreiner interprets the imperatives in Eph 4:22–24 as commands calling for continued obedience. Schreiner, *Romans*, 315–18.

71. Barth, *The Christian Life*, 94.

Thus, from a Christian perspective, because non-Christians misunderstand human history—especially its climax in Christ—they have a false self-understanding primarily as it concerns their spiritual condition, that is, that they are sinners who live in the flesh and therefore separate from God, and as it concerns Christ's relevance for their situation and the solution to their spiritual problem. This false (spiritual) self-understanding also has effects on how they see themselves ethically: they may assume that they are righteous in themselves, that their good conduct can earn righteousness, or that good conduct does not matter and they can behave however they please. Unbelievers do not recognize or experience the division of ages because they are blind to God's eschatological inbreaking through Christ (2 Cor 4:4), living according to the old age and the old self, which has no access to life in the Spirit but is solely characterized by confidence in the flesh.

To summarize the previous two sections, from a Pauline perspective, a false self-understanding principally means not seeing oneself in relation to Christ nor seeing one's true situation in human history, the focal point of which is the cross and resurrection of Christ. This ignorance is due to setting one's mind on the flesh, or refusing (consciously or unconsciously) to trust in God for life and salvation, attempting to attain life in one's own, self-determined, self-empowered way. Because of the deception of sin, fallen humanity is enslaved to life in the flesh and its false self-understanding. Knowing God's law cannot set them free, because the flesh "weakens" the law and twists it into a fleshly means of earning one's own righteousness, which is "hostile to God" (Rom 8:3, 7–8).[72] Rather than breaking people out of sin's deception, the law becomes entangled in it, increasing and empowering sin (1 Cor 15:56; Rom 5:20). While people who intentionally pursue "works of the law" may seem to be righteous and spiritual, they are really only masking their fleshly life, leading to the same end as the less disguised path of lawlessness. Neither legalism nor antinomianism can solve the problem of sin, because the solution can never be attained through fleshly means but only through Christ. To live as if this were not the case belies a false self-understanding.

---

72. See Fitzmyer, *Romans*, 484.

The False Self in the Bible

Let us draw a few key parallels between Proverbs' notion of foolishness, Matthew's depiction of hypocrisy, and Paul's concept of the flesh. First, all three concepts denote a distorted ethicospiritual vision: fools lack true wisdom, because they reject the ethicospiritual knowledge that comes from fearing and trusting the Lord, and they depend on their own understanding (Prov 1:7; 3:5); hypocrites are blind to their actual ethical and spiritual condition, because they base their righteousness on the outward performance of God's law (Matt 23:23–24); and everyone who lives according to the flesh misunderstands what is really expedient for attaining the good life, because their fleshly nature impedes them from realizing that the solution is outside themselves (i.e., not in their legalism or lawlessness). A second parallel, then, is that the authors emphasize the necessity of outside help. The problems presented by foolishness, hypocrisy, or the flesh require outside intervention. Furthermore, as a third parallel, that outside intervention must be fundamentally spiritual: wisdom, righteousness, and the good life can only be found by looking to God in Christ.

Following upon this last parallel, we may note how these concepts differ and together demonstrate a developmental unfolding of the precise nature of humanity's problem and the kind of help required to solve it. Proverbs reveals that the problem of folly is not merely intellectual but ethical; foolishness is coextensive with wickedness, just as wisdom is with righteousness. Furthermore, Proverbs calls people to become wise and righteous through trusting Yahweh instead of relying merely on "one's own understanding" (Prov 3:5). As starkly unique as this philosophy stands in comparison with others of the ancient Near East, the sages of Proverbs only anticipate the further revelations that later came through Matthew and Paul. In the concept of hypocrisy, it becomes much more clear how deeply people can deceive themselves and others into seeming to have found the solution: for it is not just the Gentile or ignorant Jew that may fail to become wise, but even the Pharisee who claims (and presumes) to know God's law and keep it. Matthew reveals that even a person who appears to "fear" and "trust" the Lord, as Proverbs prescribes, can end up as a ruinous fool who "built his house on sand" (Matt 7:26). The truth that Proverbs 3:5 hints at, which is that people must trust in God *wholly*, is one that Matthew expounds and clarifies by conveying Jesus' emphasis on the heart and its relation to outward deeds. However, a much greater development in both Matthew and Paul is the revelation that the solution required for folly and hypocrisy is found in Jesus; to fear and trust in Yahweh equates with fearing and trusting in Jesus. Paul goes beyond Matthew by more fully explaining just how greatly people need Jesus' help. Although Matthew works to accomplish the same purpose, he does so through a more inductive or implicit procedure. Paul, however, emphasizes that human beings are enslaved to sin and have no hope of attaining salvation through their own works. Paul's point in using the concept of the flesh is to lump all the futile ways people try to attain salvation into one category (i.e., "living according to the flesh"), so as to distinguish these from the one expedient solution, which is "living according to the Spirit" through faith in Christ. Along with this contrast, Paul also reveals the contrast between a Christian and non-Christian view of history. In Christianity the events of Jesus' time on earth are considered the center of human history. To ascribe ultimate historical importance to a Jewish man crucified in a minor province of ancient Rome is puzzling to many non-Christians, who have not been taught about the new age that Christ inaugurated—a teaching that Paul expects maturing Christians to know (Eph 4:21–24). Furthermore, Christians have related themselves to Christ in a way that anyone who has not realized his significance would consider strange. What sage of Proverbs would have been able to understand "the word of the cross" as wisdom (1 Cor 1:18), or who among Jesus' twelve disciples would have considered themselves "baptized into Christ Jesus" (Rom 6:3) unless the "mystery" of the gospel had been revealed to them (Rom 16:25; Eph 1:9–10; Col 1:25–26)? From a Christian and particularly Pauline perspective, being "in Christ" grants access to a new way of living in history and understanding one's place within it, enabling people to understand the spiritual nature of their fallen human condition, revealing that the solution is not gained through "confidence in the flesh" but in Christ: "For we are the real circumcision, who worship by the Spirit of God and glory in Christ Jesus and put no confidence in the flesh" (Phil 3:3).

In light of the parallels and developments regarding the biblical concepts of foolishness, hypocrisy, and the flesh, a scriptural perspective on the false self calls us to appreciate humanity's distorted ethicospiritual vision and the impossibility of solving this problem apart from absolute dependence on God in Christ. A definition of the false self that takes this perspective into account should, therefore, attribute false self-understanding in part to what Paul calls living in the flesh, or fallen humanity's attempt to attain life apart from faith in Christ.

The True Self in the Bible

Now to another important question: How does true self-understanding correlate with human flourishing? According to the Bible, people's well-being depends on having true *spiritual* self-understanding. While there are truths about a person besides spiritual truths, spiritual self-understanding (i.e., how we stand in relation to God) is the most important kind of self-knowledge. When people realize the truth about themselves, they become more whole, true, and flourishing human beings.

The True Self in Proverbs

In the prologue of Proverbs, we are told that these proverbs are for knowing "wisdom and instruction," providing the simple (*petî*) with prudence, knowledge, and discretion (Prov 1:1–7). In the first nine chapters, readers hear several speeches urging them to pursue wisdom, describing the rewards and pitfalls associated with wisdom and folly. In short, "the complacency of fools destroys them; but whoever listens to me will dwell secure and will be at ease, without dread of disaster" (1:32–33). We have seen that false self-understanding is bound up with folly, and how fools devolve into worse states of ethico-spiritual self-deception as they reject God's ways, leading to their destruction. But what about the true self?

Wisdom and True Self-Understanding

Proverbs ties true self-understanding to wisdom, and so to goodness and health. This wisdom is not an arbitrary kind, slanted merely toward a certain (i.e., Israelite) perspective of the world, offering a limited angle by which to navigate life's challenges. Rather, Proverbs claims to offer universal wisdom, the same wisdom by which the universe was made. The good sense offered here is the logic of creation, the wisdom of the God who made all things: "Blessed is the one who finds wisdom, and the one who gets understanding. . . . The Lord by wisdom founded the earth; by understanding he established the heavens" (3:13, 19). It follows that, if people pursue this wisdom, they will discover a knowledge and way of life that is not just practical, but true; Proverbs shows a path to life that is indeed pragmatic, but in the best and surest kind of pragmatism, one that guides wisdom-seekers towards truth and reality, teaching them not just how to survive on the street, but how to work with the grain of the universe.

Living in contradiction to the wisdom of reality is likened to a man traveling a path to death (9:13–18; cf. 5:3–5; 7:25–27). Traveling this path leads to increasing darkness and delusion: "The way of the wicked is like deep darkness; they do not know over what they stumble" (4:19). In contrast, Proverbs describes wise people walking a path that becomes more visible as it goes: "But the path of the righteous is like the light of dawn, which shines brighter and brighter until full day" (4:18). By following the ways of Yahweh, according to the wisdom that made all things, the wise progress toward greater and truer understanding of reality, including themselves. As they heed their parents' commands and teaching, they ensure safety, because "the commandment is a lamp and the teaching a light" (6:25a).

The wise also differ from the foolish because they discern the difference between what is good for them and what is evil, perceiving their "steps" and the ends to which they are heading. Fools heedlessly head into destruction, unable to see that they are jeopardizing themselves (7:6–27). Fools are like animals unaware that they are about to be slaughtered (7:22–23). Fools don't realize that they are doing evil to themselves: "these men lie in wait for their own blood; they set an ambush for their own lives" (1:18). Doing evil, disobeying God's ways, shows blindness and lack of self-knowledge. "Such are the ways of everyone who is greedy for unjust gain; it takes away the life of its possessors" (1:19). The wise, however, see the danger of evil, understanding that the Lord's ways lead to their flourishing (3:7–8, 13–26). Whoever finds wisdom "finds life and obtains favor from the Lord, but he who fails to find me injures himself; all who hate me love death" (8:35–36). Wisdom enlightens people, revealing their state and the way toward goodness and health, unlike folly which obscures how the fool hurts himself, deceiving him so fully that he enjoys it: "Stolen water is sweet, and bread eaten in secret is pleasant. But he does not know that the dead are there, that her guests are in the depths of Sheol" (9:17–18; cf. 13:19; 15:14). In contrast, wise people delight in wisdom and take righteousness seriously, knowing what's good for them (10:23). Wise people "hate falsehood" (13:5), and "discern their way" (14:8). A fool "despises" his way, not caring to see himself truly, but the wise evaluate themselves against God's law (19:16). If folly corresponds to self-delusion, wisdom is linked to self-understanding. The more people seek wisdom and righteousness, the more they rightly understand themselves and discern their way (14:8).

The Source of True Self-Understanding: Yahweh

Proverbs, however, sets a limit on how much even the wise can know, subordinating people's capacity for self-knowledge to the Lord (20:24). Even wise people can be deluded, thinking they are right when they are wrong: "Every way of a man is right in his own eyes, but the Lord weighs the heart" (21:2). "Whoever trusts in his own mind is a fool, but he who walks in wisdom will be delivered" (28:26). The wise don't trust in themselves as the source of wisdom, because that would lead them astray. The wise realize their limits, not depending on their perspective to know or judge themselves. Rather, they trust in the Lord (3:5).

Proverbs clearly identifies Yahweh as the source of wisdom and understanding. By searching for wisdom "like silver" and "hidden treasure," people's search will inevitably lead to "the fear of the Lord" and "the knowledge of God," since "the Lord gives wisdom; from his mouth come knowledge and understanding" (2:4–6). The "beginning of knowledge" is the fear of Yahweh (1:7), and all progress in becoming wise requires being humble, teachable, and obedient before God, acknowledging him in all one's ways, trusting in him wholeheartedly, not being "wise in your own eyes" (3:5–7).

The True Self in Matthew

As we move onward from Proverbs to Matthew's Gospel, we see Matthew affirm that true self-understanding entails whole-hearted trust in Yahweh, but we also get a fuller picture of the true self: true self-understanding requires trusting in the Lord as he is revealed in the Gospel of Jesus Christ.

The Source of True Self-Understanding: The Gospel of Jesus Christ

In Matthew, "the gospel" refers to Jesus' message that in him the kingdom of God has come. Jesus demonstrates this message by delivering people from various kinds of evil. The gospel is the "good news" of the "restoration and healing of the helpless."[73] Matthew often uses the term "gospel" to refer to deliverance from some physical infirmity, as when Jesus heals people who are sick or impaired, or to deliverance from spiritual captivity, as when he frees people who are demonically oppressed.

Specific instances of "gospel" in Matthew do not bear the same semantic freight as in the Pauline corpus, but when taken as a whole literary work, the "'Gospel according to Matthew' (*euangelion kata Mattaion*) presents the same proclamation that Paul and the other apostles preached: the "message of God's saving work in Christ."[74] Matthew does not tease out the Christological and soteriological aspects of the gospel like Paul does, but instead he provides a written "eyewitness testimony" of Christ's life, death, and resurrection.[75] Thus, along with Mark, Luke, and John, Matthew preserves a record of what Christ said and did—the historical facts upon which Paul and the other apostles' based their teaching. Matthew's eyewitness testimony complements Paul's theological instruction, because it provides "the narrative bedrock" needed in order to accomplish "theological reflection on the person of Christ."[76]

Of course, Matthew and the other gospel writers record not only narrative but also discourse. Without the four Gospels, "the circumstances surrounding [Jesus'] life, ministry, death, and resurrection would be lost to history, *as would be the substance of his teachings*" (emphasis mine).[77] Along with all the other acts Jesus did, Matthew considered Christ's teaching to be an essential part of the gospel, or the message of Christ's saving work. Christ's teaching holds the same power that the gospel holds: the power to save. Peter affirms as much in John 6:68, saying, "Lord, to whom shall we go? You have the words of eternal life."

As Proverbs directs readers to seek the wisdom of Yahweh, Matthew directs readers to seek to the wisdom of Jesus, for they are one and the same. Trusting in Yahweh means trusting in Jesus' teaching. His words lead to the very same life that the Proverbs invite people to find: a life of righteousness, wisdom, flourishing, and, in particular, a life of true self-understanding.

73. Broyles, "Gospel (Good News)," 282–86.

74. Luter, "Gospel," 369.

75. Bauckham, *Jesus and the Eyewitnesses*.

76. Perrin, "Gospels," 265.

77. Perrin, "Gospels," 264.

Wholeness of Heart and Deed

As I said in the previous discussion on the false self in Matthew, a crucial problem Jesus addressed in his teaching was hypocrisy, or the inconsistency between people's motives and behavior. The solution that Jesus brings is wholeness of heart and deed, which he initiates by redirecting people's gaze from their outward behavior to the inner state of their heart.[78] Hypocrites gaze outwardly to the praise of others for confirmation of their righteousness (Matt 6:2, 6, 16; 23:5), and they take the wide, easy way to salvation in which they appear to keep the law by their outward deeds (7:13). Those who look inwardly, however, soon recognize that the real demand of the law is much higher: in a truly righteous person, good outward deeds are supposed to match and flow from an inwardly good heart. Jesus calls people to acknowledge this inward dimension of the law and consent to it as the narrow, hard, and true way to life (Matt 7:14). Jesus invites people to recognize that their life's outcome will only be as good as the place on which they have set their hearts (6:19–21), or the sights on which their eyes have gazed (6:22–23), or the master they have served (6:24).[79] Jesus' teaching is that godliness, righteousness, and all the qualities that constitute "the good life" depend upon wholeness of heart and deed.

Recognizing Lack of Wholeness

Jesus also taught that people ultimately fail to achieve this wholeness on their own, and so they need a savior. The good news he brings is that he has come to heal not only people's physical ailments but also their spiritual sickness. This healing comes to those who accept their helpless

---

78. Perrin, "Gospels," 109.

79. So Hagner says, "Only deeds done for God's glory receive an eschatological reward. This stress is in keeping with the emphasis on the inner obedience to God's commandments, which we encountered in chap. 5. God is concerned with the heart, with the motivation behind a person's deeds, as much as with the external deeds themselves. The application of the passage is clear and timeless in its bearing upon Christians." Hagner, *Matthew 1–13*, 140–41. In contrast, Davies and Allison propose that Matthew is largely concerned with setting out distinguishing characteristics between Christians and unbelievers, not with encouraging Christians to examine themselves. However, this view fails to see that the text is as much a call for Christians to resist hypocrisy in themselves as it is a polemic against unbelievers. Davies and Allison, *Gospel according to Saint Matthew*, 581.

state and admit their need to be transformed in their hearts (Matt 9:12). This transformation is initiated by hearing and understanding what Jesus reveals about one's own heart and deeds.

Jesus tells his disciples, "To you it has been given to know the secrets of the kingdom of heaven" (13:11a). While this understanding is partly intellectual, it must involve more than intellectual knowledge. To believe and understand Jesus' word means his word takes root in one's heart and, from this reformed heart, produces good fruit.[80] Jesus depicts the reformed person as one who has been transformed from being a bad person/tree that produces *seemingly good* fruit/words to becoming a good person/tree who produces *actually good* fruit/words (12:33–35). With this depiction in mind, Jesus then concludes by saying that peoples' words will ultimately justify or condemn them: "I tell you, on the day of judgment people will give account for every careless word they speak, for by your words you will be justified, and by your words you will be condemned" (12:36–37). Jesus wants his hearers to understand that their words will be judged in correspondence with their heart.[81] Jesus delivers people who are captives to hypocrisy by persuading them that they are spiritually empty and need God's power to make them whole. Those who admit their spiritual poverty are blessed (5:3). The Beatitudes are a description of those who have received Jesus' gospel of the kingdom.[82] When we receive the gospel, we become conscious of our unrighteousness and lack of wholeness.[83] Via argues that the first four affirmations in the Beatitudes (5:3–6) describe the emptiness of the person who has recognized his or her spiritual poverty, sorrow, meekness, and need for righteousness; the blessed person sees that he or she is empty.[84] The next

80. Davies and Allison, *Gospel according to Saint Matthew*, 581.

81. Davies and Allison, *Gospel according to Saint Matthew*, 581.

82. Hagner highlights the fact that the kingdom is received, not earned: "The kingdom is declared as a reality apart from any human achievement. Thus the beatitudes are, above all, predicated upon the experience of the grace of God. The recipients are just that, those who receive the good news." Hagner, *Matthew 1–13*, 96.

83. Via, *Self-Deception and Wholeness in Paul and Matthew*, 126–29.

84. Via, *Self-Deception and Wholeness in Paul and Matthew*, 126–27. Likewise, Turner says, "The first four beatitudes show that divine approval means that one has been humbled under God's mighty hand through the kingdom message, so that one admits one's spiritual poverty, mourns over sin and the oppression of God's people, rests in God's care in the face of oppression, and hungers for greater righteousness on earth (5:3–6). Thus humility is the basic trait of authentic kingdom spirituality." Turner, *Matthew*, 152.

four affirmations (5:7–11) demonstrate that the emptiness of the blessed person carries the potential for filling.[85] The person who acknowledges his or her need for righteousness becomes merciful, pure in heart, a peacemaker, and righteous.[86]

Those who recognize their emptiness have a potential for blessed-ness not given to the blind, those who fail to recognize their inner corrup-tion: "You blind guides, straining out a gnat and swallowing a camel! Woe to you, scribes and Pharisees, hypocrites! For you clean the outside of the cup and the plate, but inside they are full of greed and self-indulgence" (23:24–25).[87] The blind are not blessed, because they wrongly base their standard of blessedness only on what can be seen in their external behav-ior. The blind cannot see, because the range of their vision is myopic.[88] Those who see, however, have been enabled to look at the whole picture, which includes their deeds *and* their heart. They are blessed because they recognize and consent to their inner spiritual poverty just as truly as they perceive their outward deeds of good and evil. In light of their awareness, the blessed are filled and empowered for righteous deeds.[89] They not only see, but they act and bear fruit. As a result of recognizing their inner corruption, they actively clean the inside of the cup as well as the outside. According to Matthew, salvation and wholeness comes about through a spiritual reformation wherein people consent to their emptiness and to being filled.

---

85. Via, *Self-Deception and Wholeness in Paul and Matthew*, 126.

86. While the recipients of the kingdom do not merit it through virtue, as recipients they are made virtuous. The second group of Beatitudes demonstrate this virtue-form-ing reality, as Gibbs observes: "The second group of Beatitudes (5:7–12) still describes the disciples of Jesus: the merciful, the pure in heart, and so forth. Those blessings tes-tify that Jesus' call to discipleship begins to transform those who are called. . . . When Jesus joins men, women, and children to himself, that union begins to manifest the life of Christ himself in the lives of his disciples." Gibbs, *Matthew 1:1—11:1*, 255.

87. Via, *Self-Deception and Wholeness in Paul and Matthew*, 126–27.

88. To be blind does not equate to absolute ignorance. The hypocrites with a log in their eye may notice a speck in their brother's eye (Matt 7:3). One's outward vision may be accurate, although insufficient. To most effectively help their brother remove the speck they would do well to first remove the log in their own eye (Matt 7:5). By doing so, their vision is enhanced because it sees both inwardly and outwardly.

89. Via, *Self-Deception and Wholeness in Paul and Matthew*, 128–29.

Consenting to Wholeness

We've seen that Matthew emphasizes the demand of God's law for a pure heart, and that he presents Jesus' message as a call for people to recognize this demand and act accordingly, yet it is clear in Matthew that the action Jesus calls for is *faith*, and that it is through believing in Jesus' power to help them that people are made whole, as he told the woman who touched his clothing, "Take heart, daughter; your faith has made you well" (Matt 9:22; see 8:13; 9:2, 29; 15:28). Matthew's understanding of salvation is in agreement with Paul's, for he also believes that salvation comes through faith, not works. Both writers prioritize grace, rejecting a soteriology of meritorious works.

However, Matthew emphasizes that the gospel is lawful. The gospel rejects licentiousness and reveals how we can keep the law: by receiving God's help through Christ. In other words, whereas Paul highlights the futility of trying to keep the law to be saved—though somehow it must be kept (i.e., justification by faith)—Matthew highlights the necessity of keeping the law to be saved—though to try to keep it apart from Christ's help is futile, like a man who builds his house on sand (Matt 7:26–27).[90]

True self-understanding, therefore, corresponds with neither legalism nor licentiousness. Rather, it means knowing that we are intimately involved in our own salvation. We are not like other creatures—rocks, trees, or other animals—but must consent with heart and deed to the life Jesus calls us to live. We must choose to receive the wholeness Jesus offers us. The true self means understanding that I bear responsibility, that "If you are wise, you are wise for yourself; if you scoff, you alone will bear it" (Prov 9:12). The wise man builds his house on Jesus' words, knowing what he is doing, but the fool, thinking that he has been doing right, comes to the end of his life and realizes too late that he has been deluded (Matt 7:21–27).

---

90. Thus, Via provocatively writes, "for Matthew what God requires and enables as the condition for salvation is acts of obedience that proceed from a heart renewed by understanding. . . . With Matthew it is not a matter of showing that acts of obedience do not count for salvation (as with Paul) but rather of showing that it is only the total obedience of the whole self that counts. For Paul the gospel is that God accepts us without regard for the acceptability of our works. For Matthew the good news is that God makes our works acceptable." Via, *Self-Deception and Wholeness in Paul and Matthew*, 134.

Summary

In summary, true self-understanding in Matthew consists of having an accurate view of one's heart and seeing oneself more completely, both the inside and the outside, both the fruits of the tree and the tree itself. To know their true self, people must recognize their spiritual emptiness and their need for God's gracious power to restore them to wholeness. Furthermore, they must consent to receive wholeness from Jesus.

The True Self in Paul

Now we turn to Paul. Paul describes salvation from two angles: the objective side from which God saves humans, and the subjective side from which humans experience and cooperate with God's saving work. T. F. Torrance captures this distinction in terms of the reconciliation between God and man brought about through salvation:

> If sin is qualified as sin by the personal reaction of God against it, then sin is an objective obstacle that must be taken away. Only God can do that, and only God can remove his wrath from mankind and in that sense reconcile himself to man, and that is what he does in the blood of Christ. But if sin is an act of man going down to the roots of human nature and introducing into the very relation with God which constitutes the human person, a contradiction resulting inevitably in its disintegration . . . then it is in the inner depth of their personal being that humanity must be reconciled to God and we must be healed of our enmity and contradiction to God. Such a double reconciliation, at once objective and subjective, was achieved in the person and work of Christ, in his incarnation, death, and resurrection.[91]

On the one hand, salvation is a work of God that he accomplishes, and it is distinctly objective, outside of the human subject. God justifies sinners through Christ's atonement, and God also delivers them from the demonic powers that held them captive. Although the objective side of God's saving work is essential to Paul's teaching, I will focus mainly on how he treats the subjective side of salvation, where believers experience true self-understanding through the disclosure of their heart. At the same time, this disclosure comes about in part through knowing God's word, so I will offer a partial account of the objective side of God's saving work.

91. Torrance, *Atonement*, 159.

Recognizing the Cover Stories and the Real Story

True self-understanding begins with the disclosure of one's heart, which is brought to light by God's word.[92] Although the full revelation of believers' hearts will be delayed until God's final, eschatological judgment (1 Cor 4:5), the word of God performs a partial disclosure now that anticipates the complete revelation to come (1 Cor 14:25).[93] This work of disclosure is spiritual, wrought by the Holy Spirit, and it involves a mysterious meeting between human spirit and divine Spirit that cannot be expressed in words (Rom 8:16, 26–27).[94] While the mechanism of the disclosure cannot be fully articulated, Paul does describe some of what happens in a person's heart and consciousness.

The word of God, empowered by the Spirit, brings the recognition of two unconscious realities: the less unconscious truth that one is unrighteousness, and the more unconscious truth that one needs grace.[95] The less unconscious truth of one's unrighteousness is that all of one's alleged achievements from which one draws confidence are actually worthless before God, like refuse to be discarded (Phil 3:8). Beneath this truth is the deeper and more unconscious need people have for help and saving grace. As these two realities are brought to consciousness by God's illuminating word, two bogus "cover stories" are debunked: the more conscious cover story that one is righteous in oneself, and the less conscious cover story that one is able to attain righteousness through one's own striving.[96] The word of God exposes the false cover stories and shatters them through the revelation of the hidden real story.

---

92. Via, *Self-Deception and Wholeness in Paul and Matthew*, 48.

93. Via, *Self-Deception and Wholeness in Paul and Matthew*, 48.

94. Via, *Self-Deception and Wholeness in Paul and Matthew*, 49.

95. Via, *Self-Deception and Wholeness in Paul and Matthew*, 49. Although largely adopting Via's model, I have altered the "more unconscious real story," so that instead of categorizing it as an unconsciously known idea (i.e., God graciously loves me) it is expressed as an unconsciously felt need (i.e., I need grace). This change was made, because, contrary to Via's view, Scripture does not indicate that those who live in the flesh believe that God loves them either consciously or unconsciously. Rather, it presents fallen humanity as "unbelievers," who are deeply doubtful of God's good will towards them. This doubt in God, rather than trust, is what sinners have repressed into their unconsciousness. On the other hand, Via is not far off the mark by pointing to God's grace and love, because although the hearts of unbelievers do not perceive it, they do need it.

96. Via, *Self-Deception and Wholeness in Paul and Matthew*, 49.

Paul's letter to the Romans illuminates the hidden real story by revealing four foundational truths. People who know these four truths have true self-understanding.

Created by God for Sonship

In the first chapter of Romans, Paul confronts the bogus cover story that people can be righteous in themselves (i.e., autonomously) by asserting that, despite its repression into unconsciousness, the fact remains that human beings owe God honor and thanks as their creator (Rom 1:18–32). It is evident that God made people, along with everything else, and even though humanity has discarded this knowledge in exchange for futile speculation (Rom 1:21), they cannot undo their nature as creatures no matter how greatly they deny or repress it. Thus, part of knowing ourselves truly means consenting to our nature as God's creatures.

No doubt Paul had the creations accounts of Genesis 1–2 chiefly in mind, in which humanity appears as the most significant creature: "Then God said, "Let us make man in our image, after our likeness. And let him have dominion over the fish of the sea and over the birds of the heavens and over the livestock and over all the earth and over every creeping thing that creeps on the earth" (Gen 1:26). Being made in God's image means that humanity stands in a unique relation to the creator. For one thing, by giving human beings mastery over the earth and dominion over all other creatures, God has exalted them to a position of glory that is analogous with his own, as the psalmist says to God, "You have made him a little lower than the heavenly beings and crowned him with glory and honor. You have given him dominion over the works of your hands; you have put all things under his feet" (Ps 8:5–6). Human beings are God's royal servants, or vice-regents, who represent his authority on earth. Yet the relationship between human beings and God is not just domestic but filial. Human beings are the children of God. Thus, the first human being, Adam, is called "the son of God" (Luke 3:38). Likewise, several passages in the Hebrew Bible refer to God's chosen nation of Israel as God's "sons" (Deut 14:1; Isa 1:2; Jer 3:22; Hos 1:10).[97] As his children, God made human beings not only for service but for a relationship with him as their Father (see Eph 3:14–15).

---

97. Hurtado, "Son of God," 901.

When the unconscious realities of God's grace and of humanity's unrighteousness are revealed, people see the special honor and love that God has given to his image-bearers, his royal children. God cares for humanity and extends grace to them because they are his exalted sons and daughters. His grace is revealed in Fatherly love, the kind of love that forgives rebellious children and makes a way for them to be reconciled.

The human race, however, has forsaken God's gifts and no longer accepts him as Father: "They have dealt corruptly with him; they are no longer his children because they are blemished; they are a crooked and twisted generation" (Deut 32:5). For this reason, Paul usually only speaks about God's fatherhood in reference to believers (Eph 5:1; Phil 2:14–15; Col 1:12), because the father-child relationship is now only possible through "the redemptive activity of God."[98] Yet even believers still await their full adoption as sons and daughters (Rom 8:19–23), and part of being a believer means consenting to one's identity as God's child-in-the-making, who was created once before and is being created anew (Eph 4:24; Col 3:10).

Fallen from Glory

It is clear that in Pauline thinking true self-understanding must also consist in consenting to one's fallen condition. Paul reveals the unconscious real story of human unrighteousness in his teaching about sin, articulated throughout Romans, beginning in chapter 1. Human beings have forsaken their calling as image-bearers and have exchanged it for the worship of idols (Rom 1:23). Consequently, people experience a degraded form of existence that falls short of full humanity (Rom 1:24–32). God did not hinder people's choice but allowed them to dishonor their bodies (Rom 1:24), their passions (Rom 1:26), and their minds, to the point of being filled with self-degrading vices against their nature: unrighteousness, wickedness, greed, evil, envy, murder, strife, deceit, malice, and so on (Rom 1:28–31).

Acknowledging that we are sinners is something everyone must do if they are to have true self-understanding, since, as Paul writes, "all have sinned and fall short of the glory of God" (Rom 3:23). No human being, regardless of his or her heritage, privileges, or accomplishments is exempt from this identification. Paul recognized that some Jews were

98. Guthrie and Martin, "God," 357.

tempted to exempt themselves because of their advantages as God's chosen people, having received the law of Moses; yet, Paul argues that no
advantage can nullify their sinfulness, having broken the law God gave
them (Rom 3:9–20).

This aspect of their identity remains even after sinners believe in
Christ.[99] While believers' former slavery to this identity is annulled, the
presence of sin still influences believers and tempts them to act as sinners; consenting to the true self means recognizing one's old self and its
influence, even as Paul did (Rom 7:14–25; see Phil 3:4; 1 Tim 1:15).[100]
Believers consent to the truth that they are sinners who do the evil they
do not want to do because sin dwells in them (Rom 7:19–20). Believers
recognize their indwelling sin, believing that they are not only sinners,
but that as such they do not yet have the power to completely defeat sin
and must wait for deliverance. Believers recognize that sin is so deep in
them that they cannot plumb its depths and that they are influenced by it
despite their wanting otherwise (Rom 7:14–15).

Loved Graciously in Christ

Just as true self-understanding means identifying as a creature of God
called to be his child, it also means identifying as one who is loved by
God. The real story of God's grace is revealed in the love that God holds
out to sinners, having given his righteous Son to die for them. While
Paul describes people as sinners who practice the same evil they judge
in others (Rom 2:1, 3) and who are under sin (Rom 3:9), they are also
simultaneously loved by God, as Paul declares: "God demonstrates his

99. John Murray argues against the view that the believer can simultaneously possess an old self and a new self, saying instead that believers are completely free of the
old self. Here, I think Murray mistakenly assumes that old self and new self refer to
static ontological natures rather than to two identities that the believer must continually choose between during life on earth. I contend that Murray adopts an overly realized eschatology when interpreting the believer's existence as "new man" and fails to
consider the residual effects of the old man. See Murray, *Principles of Conduct*, 211–19.
I find Schreiner's view more convincing; see Schreiner, *Romans*, 318.

100. Commentators have frequently disagreed about to whom the "I" in Romans
7:14–25 refers. At the heart of the issue is whether Paul is referring to a pre-conversion
experience or post-conversion. For a list of the arguments used for both sides, see Schreiner, *Romans*, 379–90. Dryden captures the essence of this passage, saying, "Paul's
statements about the "I" in 7:14–25 describe the Christian who lives in the antitheses
and tensions that arise from eschatological union with Christ." Dryden, "Romans 7:
Sin, the Self, and Spiritual Formation," 11.

own love toward us, in that while we were yet sinners, Christ died for us" (Rom 5:8). God manifests his love toward humanity by graciously giving them the gift of righteousness by faith in Jesus Christ, apart from works of the law (Rom 3:21–24, 27–28).

This offer is extended and revealed through the proclamation of the gospel, which in Pauline usage is specifically "the message of the cross" (1 Cor 1:17–18) or "the message of reconciliation" (2 Cor 5:19), the content of which focuses especially on Christ's death on the cross (1 Cor 1:23; Gal 3:1) through which he reconciled sinners to God (Rom 5:10). The proclamation of the gospel extends God's gracious love to sinners by asserting that "Christ died for the ungodly" (Rom 5:16) and by declaring that the righteousness of God comes "through faith in Jesus Christ for all who believe (Rom 1:16; 3:22).

The gospel not only conveys the historical facts of what Christ did, but it also makes declarations that enact effects. Because the gospel is God's word, it is "the power of God for salvation to everyone who believes" (Rom 1:16–17).[101] Paul likens those who believe in the gospel's promise to Abraham: "with respect to the promise of God, he [i.e., Abraham] did not waver in unbelief but grew strong in faith, giving glory to God, and being fully assured that what God had promised, he was able to perform. *Therefore it was also credited to him as righteousness*" (Rom 4:20–22, my italics). God's gracious love is not restricted to Abraham or to Israel but extends to all who stand condemned as sinners (Rom 5:6–8, 18). In light of God's love and gift of reconciliation, Paul exults, and he expects believers in Christ to rejoice with him (Rom 5:11). Believers baptized into Christ, Paul maintains, should by default understand themselves to be "alive to God" (Rom 6:11b). Paul describes believers as those who are "beloved of God" and "called as saints" (Rom 1:7). By virtue of their true self-understanding, believers are people who consent to their identity as beloved children of God, who do not fear him but instead trust him, as children trust their loving father (Rom 8:14–16).

Of the four truths we are considering, the reality of God's gracious love in Christ is the most important, because it is the essence of the gospel by which people are justified and made whole. The gospel is about Christ and his "appearance" as the Savior (2 Tim 1:8–10; Titus 3:4–7).

---

101. As the word of God is "living and active" (Heb 4:12), the gospel is a force or power that works, and through it God's salvation and righteousness are revealed in the present. "In this sense it is akin to the biblical notion that God's word is powerful and effective." Luter, "Gospel," 371.

Paul says that God's grace and loving kindness are shown particularly and immeasurably "in Christ" (Eph 2:7). The crux of the gospel's message about Christ concerns his crucifixion, where we see the love of God most clearly. The message of the cross is that "while we were still sinners, Christ died for us" (Rom 5:8). There is no greater demonstration of God's love and grace than Christ's death on the cross, or as Demarest says, "Divine love could do no more for you and me than it did on the cross of Calvary."[102] When the good news of "Christ crucified" is believed, a person is radically changed:

> [O]bjectively, the cross liberates from the power of sin, propitiates God's wrath, washes away the guilt and stain of sin, reconciles believers to God, and achieves a cosmic victory over deadly spiritual foes. . . . Subjectively, Christ's example of suffering on our behalf releases a new moral power that transforms our attitudes, motives, and conduct. At Calvary by faith we see the vileness of our sin and Jesus' loving purposes for our eternal welfare. This paradigm of suffering love incites believers to adopt a new set of values and to pursue a new way of living.[103]

The gospel, or the truth of God's gracious love in Christ, is the only message that can free us to accept the truth about our unrighteousness and expose our cover stories of self-righteousness and autonomy. The kindness of God, Paul says, leads us to repentance (Rom 2:4). God's kindness in the gospel leads us to repent of our false self-understanding.

Incomplete

Finally, throughout Romans Paul recognizes that all human beings, including Christian believers, are incomplete. True self-understanding means knowing that I am not whole but in need of restoration. My cover stories are false. Human beings—my "tribe"—have devolved into sin, and this means that they—and me with them—have fallen from their glorious calling as God's children and become what Paul calls "flesh." This situation applies even to believers—like me—who have recognized their sin and have begun to experience new spiritual life in opposition to their flesh.

When Paul describes believers' union with Christ, he indicates that their experience of new, resurrected life is not yet fully realized but will

102. Demarest, *The Cross and Salvation*, 196.

103. Demarest, *The Cross and Salvation*, 196.

be in the future: "For if we have become united with him in the likeness of his death, certainly we *shall* also be in the likeness of his resurrection" (Rom 6:5, my italics).[104] Believers await their resurrection and the complete restoration of their bodies. One aspect of my incompleteness is that I will continue to suffer physical corruption (e.g., sickness, deformity) and death until my body is transformed and made physically incorruptible.

Likewise, just as believers' bodily existence remains incomplete, their ethicospiritual struggle with sin remains unsettled. By exhorting believers to "not let sin reign in your mortal body" and to "not go on presenting the members of your body to sin," Paul implies that they may still give in to sin's influence and must choose to resist it (Rom 6:12–13).[105] Paul makes this idea more explicit by applying it personally to himself in Romans 7:14–25, confessing that his life is not yet whole or free from sin. He says he is "of flesh, sold into bondage to sin," and that although he desires to do good he does "the very thing I hate" (vv. 14–15). He recognizes a dichotomy in his being: on the one hand, he can refer to himself as the "I" who agrees with the law (v. 16b), who does not want to do evil but good (v. 19), and who serves the law of God (v. 25). This "I" is synonymous with Paul's "inner man" (v. 22) and "mind" (v. 25). On the other hand, he refers to himself as the "I" who is "of flesh" (v. 14), "sold into bondage to sin" (v. 14), and who practices evil (v. 19). This "I" is synonymous with sin or Paul's flesh (v. 18) and the members of his body (v. 23). Paul is presenting himself as a divided person, who simultaneously experiences two opposing influences within himself that are always in conflict. He seems to be describing two aspects of his existence, one that is of the flesh and one that is of God; the former is old and passing away and the latter is new and coming to be (Rom 6:6; see Eph 4:22–24; 2 Cor 5:17). The former part wants to disobey God's ethical requirements and to live spiritually autonomous, but the latter part wants the opposite. Paul points believers to reckon with the reality of this dynamic tension

---

104. As Dunn says, "Here again Paul's readers would recognize that he is not referring to Christ's resurrection in the past as such, but to believers' resurrection which will be just like his. Here again the tense is significant: it is something that will happen in the future. . . . *The whole of this life for the believer is suspended between Christ's death and Christ's resurrection,* or more precisely between the very likeness of Christ's death and that of his resurrection, between the conversion-initiation which began the process and the resurrection of the body which will complete it. Dunn, *Romans. 1–8,* 331, his italics.

105. Schreiner, *Romans,* 324.

within them. True self-understanding means I consent to the lack of my ethicospiritual wholeness.

For these reasons Paul explains that even though believers in Christ experience new life, it is only the "first fruits of the Spirit," and at the same time they also experience groaning because they are not yet redeemed (Rom 8:23). The body is "dead because of sin" and will remain incomplete until it is redeemed (Rom 8:10–11).[106] Likewise believers still face the challenge of having to choose between "walking in the flesh" or "in the spirit" (Rom 8:5–8, 12). In this divided state believers live an already/not-yet existence, located between death and life, flesh and redeemed humanity, the old and new. Therefore, knowing themselves to be in such an incomplete state, they are able to both bemoan their wretchedness due to sin and the flesh, as well as to thank God for his love and redemption (Rom 7:24–25).[107] True self-understanding about our *bioethicospiritual* incompleteness results in both groaning and hoping, because we recognize that we are pressing on toward completion but have not yet attained it (Rom 8:24–25; see Phil 3:12).

In conclusion, according to the Pauline perspective drawn from Romans, knowing one's true self entails consenting to at least four distinct yet simultaneous realities about oneself: that I am a creature in God's image who is intended to be God's child; that I am fallen from glory, indwelt by sin; that I am loved by God in Christ; and that I am incomplete, needing to be made whole bodily, ethically, and spiritually. Since these realities are repressed in the minds of fallen human beings, people can only consent to them through the disclosure of their heart, which

106. So Dunn says, "The Spirit of life has opened believers to a decisively new dimension or age, but the tie to the old age is not yet completely broken. So sin's operations through the body need still to be contested, the sentence of death put into daily effect (v 13); and the rule of death will not be finally ended until the resurrection of the body (v 11)." Dunn, *Romans. 1–8*, 431.

107. Against interpreters who see chapters 7 and 8 neatly divided into pre-conversion versus conversion, Dryden observes how 7:24–25 demonstrates that Paul is referring to the present experience of believers who live in tension between the flesh and the Spirit: "These verses have been a thorn in the side of Pauline interpreters for a very long time, especially since Paul *follows* his thanksgiving in 7:25a with a restatement of his moral impotence in 7:25b: 'So then, I myself serve the law of God with my mind, but with my flesh I serve the law of sin.' . . . [I]n his conclusion of Rom 7 Paul places lament and thanksgiving side-by-side, much to the consternation of interpreters who believe he should have waited until chapter 8 to rejoice. Such facts drive us to recognize that for Paul the 'already' and the 'not yet' are present *in one another* and his theological discourses are illustrative of that dialectic interrelation." Dryden, "Romans 7," 4.

occurs through the proclamation of the gospel; the message of Christ's saving work empowers the conscious recognition of all these realities, especially that of God's gracious love for sinners. Once recognized, the gospel reforms people's identity, so that instead of being deceived by their "cover stories," believers begin to understand themselves truly in light of the ethical and spiritual orders of reality.

Before moving on, I want to emphasize the fact that Paul not only considers God's salvation to bring about a transformation of one's consciousness (i.e., true self-understanding), but also as a change of moral action; ethical behavior is organically related to the disclosure of one's heart.[108] Although not identical, the experience of true self-understanding wrought by God's Spirit correlates with "walking by the Spirit" (Gal 5:16). The Spirit's work of illuminating a person's heart is itself an aspect of being saved, but more follows. Thus, while believers who realize the truth about themselves and God—the real stories of their unrighteousness and God's unmerited grace—already experience a new kind of life, more follows in order to fulfill God's design for salvation. Paul calls believers not only to believe in these truths, but to "work out" their salvation (Phil 2:12).

Interventions in the Bible

According to a biblical perspective, the problem of the false self is that people hide the truth that they are God's and that they have forsaken their true humanity as beings in relation to him. They have repressed this relationship to the point that it has become unconscious. Instead, they are conscious of the fiction they have helped create: that they already possess true humanity and that, even if they were to lack it, they are capable of obtaining it in their own power. This fiction blocks them from consciousness of their true self. They need to hear the truth: that they are neither whole nor able to become so in themselves, but only in relationship with God through faith in Christ. As I have argued, the gospel is the only means of exposing the false cover stories and rendering the reality of human unrighteousness a truth to which people can consent. The gospel is expressed in myriad forms.[109]

---

108. Via, *Self-Deception and Wholeness in Paul and Matthew*, 49.

109. See for example Keller, *Center Church: Doing Balanced, Gospel-Centered Ministry in Your City*, 39–45.

We shall now examine some of the specific ways that the gospel fosters the true self by observing some *gospel interventions* in Proverbs, Matthew's Gospel, and Paul's letters.

Interventions in Proverbs

How does Proverbs intervene to help people grow in true self-understanding? I see three primary ways.

First, Proverbs invites readers into maturity, or wisdom. The book of Proverbs is not a philosophy text for scholars, nor a random assortment of insightful nuggets for the curious. As the prologue expressly tells, the compilers of Proverbs have gifted this book to those who want to grow in wisdom, to the simple and for the wise, to the green youth and for the experienced sage: "to give prudence to the simple, knowledge and discretion to the youth—let the wise hear and increase in learning, and the one who understands obtain guidance" (1:4–5). The book is an invitation to further understanding, and so greater maturity and wholeness. Calling to both the young and old, the simple and sagacious, the writer appeals to readers as a parent to a child, wooing away from ignorance to knowledge, from naivety to shrewdness, from wickedness to righteousness, and, on the whole, from immaturity to maturity.

Although, as I've just tried to emphasize, the invitation is for people at various stages of maturity and wisdom, the naming of the reader as "my son" (e.g., 1:8; 2:1; 3:1; 4:1; 5:1; 6:1; 7:1; 8:32) places us in a certain position, suggesting that we assume the role of learner, novice, or initiate. As readers, we are invited to be sons and daughters who are being led on a journey into adulthood, taught by wise elders and by Wisdom herself (1:20–23; 4:7–9; 8:1–5). We are to hear the invitation not just as a teacher would give to a student, nor as a master to an apprentice, but as a good parent to a beloved child. Guidance is offered here, or better, a rite of passage, leading to our good. By accepting the invitation, we will benefit, as if we were receiving precious jewelry to wear on our head and neck (1:9; 3:3; 4:9; 6:21; 7:3). Ultimately, the invitation comes from Yahweh, from whom parents and Wisdom derive their good teaching. The Lord appeals to readers as his own children, inviting them to accept his guidance and discipline, "for the Lord reproves him whom he loves, as a father the son in whom he delights" (3:12).

Second, in light of their role as children growing toward maturity, Proverbs directs readers to humble themselves, taking the posture of a learner, not a teacher. If we want to go forward, we must start from the right place, not "wise in our own eyes," but fearing Yahweh, opening ourselves to wisdom and instruction (1:7; 3:7). The humble reader should make his "ear attentive to wisdom" and incline his "heart to understanding" (2:2). Moreover, this humble listening and attending must remain; we cannot presume to outgrow this approach, but continually seek to become wiser. "Cease to hear instruction, my son, and you will stray from the words of knowledge" (19:27). This perpetual posture of teachability and open-heartedness ensures growth and flourishing: "Blessed is the one who fears the Lord always, but whoever hardens his heart will fall into calamity" (28:14).

Humility before the Lord, however, does not equate to gullibility. A learner seeking wisdom and a simpleton heading towards folly may both be pliable, but in the former's case, discretion increases. "The simple believes everything, but the prudent gives thought to his steps" (14:15). Proverbs enjoins learners to open themselves to wisdom but shut the door to folly, receptive to the Lord and other wise people but closed to fools: "Whoever walks with the wise becomes wise, but the companion of fools will suffer harm" (13:20); in many situations, it's wise to avoid fools (14:7; 26:4). By and large, the route to wisdom is walked alongside people who are taking the same humble approach, who listen more than they talk (15:28), who aren't reckless but cautious (14:16).[110]

Third, having heard the fatherly invitation to wisdom, having heeded the call to humbly listen and learn, readers are shown the different paths of folly and wisdom, in order to help them discern the difference through comparison, and are called to choose for themselves. To anyone who will take the time and energy required, Proverbs says, "Here are two paths, one leading to death and one to life, and in this book you will find the road signs to help you stay on the right track, but you must stay attentive, using all your wits, or else you may stray. The map is here, but it's up to you to read it correctly." Another analogy that Proverbs uses is of hearing the voices of Lady Wisdom and Lady Folly. These two "women" cry aloud in the street, publicly making their appeal, yet the difference between these two and the ends of listening to one or the other is not obvious, and choosing the right one, Lady Wisdom, requires getting to

110. For a stellar primer on learning and thinking humbly, see Jacobs, *How to Think*.

know her and comparing her with Folly. Lady Wisdom says, "Whoever is simple, let him turn in here!" To him who lacks sense she says, "Come eat of my bread and drink of the wine I have mixed. Leave your simple ways, and live, and walk in the way of insight" (9:4–6). But notice how similarly Lady Folly speaks: "'Whoever is simple, let him turn in here!' And to him who lacks sense she says, 'Stolen water is sweet, and bread eaten in secret is pleasant.' But he does not know that the dead are there, that her guests are in the depths of Sheol" 9:16–18). A key difference between these women lies in what they expect of their guests: Lady Folly invites us to an ignorant bliss of her delicacies; she does not invite thought, caution, or discernment. Wisdom, however, explicitly calls people to get insight. Whereas Folly deludes and deceives, Wisdom promises understanding of the truth. Wisdom enjoins us to have a mind awake: "The beginning of wisdom is this: get wisdom, and whatever you get, get insight" (4:7). Folly welcomes rash, gullible choices, but Wisdom cautions people to choose wisely (14:16). In the main body of Proverbs (chapters 10 and following), everywhere we see the wise contrasted with the foolish, in all kinds of situations and characteristics. For example, take this proverb in 13:11, "Wealth gained hastily will dwindle, but whoever gathers little by little will increase it." In typical fashion, this proverb sets two opposites against each other, inviting readers to discern the difference; at the same time, this proverb, like many others, does not spell out everything; yes, it points out the means and ends of hastily gained wealth versus incremental gain, but it does not say exactly why the former dwindles and the latter increases. So, while it sheds significant light on the issue, it also serves as a riddle, inviting readers to consider more about its meaning and application, e.g., What is it about hasty wealth that makes it liable to dwindle? Part of the pedagogy of Proverbs is to pose truths in a way that welcomes further thought and reflection, so readers can develop their skills and "get wisdom."

In this way, Proverbs promotes readers' agency and responsibility, setting up opportunities for increased understanding, but also greater will. Proverbs' invitation includes both: "Hear, my son, and *be wise*, and *direct your heart* in the way" (23:19, my emphasis). Unlike Lady Folly, who would have her victims deluded and oblivious to their responsibility, Wisdom desires her disciples' consent, not fooling themselves but freely directing their own hearts. Whereas Folly would prefer to avoid the subject of responsibility altogether, Wisdom highlights it, setting up a warning in bright lights for everyone, for the would-be wise and the would-be scoffer: "If you are wise, you are wise for yourself; if you scoff, you alone will bear it" (9:12). Perhaps nothing promotes our agency more than being told this: that we have a choice to make, and that the full weight of the choice falls on us, not someone else. We alone choose for ourself, and we alone will bear it.

Having looked at interventions in Proverbs, let us now return to Matthew.

Interventions in Matthew

Before we get to the interventions I see in Matthew, I want to ensure we understand where Matthew is coming from, expressing the gospel as he does in terms of *wisdom*. Matthew wrote to communicate the gospel of Jesus Christ. Although the four Gospels all aim to record and proclaim in written form the *kergyma*, or the essential message of Jesus Christ, each of them presents the gospel in a unique way, fulfilling certain contextual needs and accomplishing various purposes.[111] Since Matthew presents the gospel in his own unique way, we should expect to see him focus on aspects and expressions of the gospel that other writers, such as Paul, did not.

Matthew portrays the message of Christ in terms of wisdom. His Gospel presents Jesus as the preeminent sage, who disseminates wisdom and is himself the embodiment of wisdom.[112] Jesus is a teacher who gathers learners around him to receive his wisdom, but unlike other sages in Judaism Jesus speaks by his own authority and not of a school or tradition (see 7:28–29). Jesus is *the* teacher, not just a sage among many, and his teaching carries an authority of its own. He surpasses all the sages, even Solomon (12:42).[113] While Jesus upholds much that was already received as conventional wisdom, in particular the teaching of the Torah, Jesus also delivers new wisdom that goes beyond and sometimes even obviates what has already been taught.[114] The Gospel of Matthew assumes the form of a guidebook for those who would learn from Jesus how to rightly understand him and how his teaching relates to what came before

111. Pennington, *Reading the Gospels Wisely*, 31.

112. Witherington, *Jesus the Sage*, 357.

113. Witherington, *Jesus the Sage*, 357; see 201–8.

114. Witherington, *Jesus the Sage*, 360–61.

him, or to help each of Jesus' followers "bring out of his treasure things new and old" (13:52).[115]

In particular, from Matthew's account we see that Jesus taught a revolutionary way of thinking about human wholeness: to be a whole person one's outward behavior must match one's inward motives, and in order to have this consistency people must turn their gaze inward to the part of themselves that only they and God can see. In other words, Matthew shows that by listening to Jesus' wisdom, his disciples can learn how to become whole by undermining hypocrisy and fostering true self-understanding. Recall that the gospel is the primary intervention for these tasks. Matthew delivers the gospel by presenting Jesus and his wise teaching, so that people may become wise and understand themselves better.

Recorded in chapters 6–7 of Matthew's Gospel are some of Jesus' most relevant wisdom teaching on how to undermine hypocrisy and foster true self-understanding. The result of heeding his teaching, says Jesus, is that one will become like a wise man and not a fool (7:24–27). People become wise by reducing their hypocrisy (6:2, 5, 16; 7:5). In 7:21–23, Jesus asserts that many who supposed themselves to have been Christ's followers will ultimately find themselves rejected by him; many who presumed to have a right standing with God will turn out to be self-deceived hypocrites. In contrast to the wise person (see 7:24–25), these people did not hear and apply Jesus' word, despite having thought that they did. Rather, they are like the fool who hears and does not act, resulting in ruin (7:26–27). The reason for the ruin of such people, however, is not that they deliberately decided to be fools, but that they deceived themselves. Not understanding themselves accurately was their folly. At the same time, it was also their disobedience, for by neglecting true self-understanding they were refusing to act on what Jesus taught them. In chapters 6–7, we can discern three gospel interventions from Jesus' teaching.

Practice Secret Piety: Matthew 6:1–18

Jesus tells his disciples, "Beware of practicing your righteousness before other people in order to be seen by them, for then you will have no reward from your Father who is in heaven" (6:1). In other words, if people want to get a reward from God for doing a good deed, then they should do it for that reason alone. Jesus tells us that by seeking other people's

---

115. Witherington, *Jesus the Sage*, 343–47.

attention as a payoff for our piety, we forfeit any reward from God (6:2, 5, 16). If public notice is my goal for performing a good deed, then that is all I should expect to get. On the other hand, Jesus says that if we want a reward from God, we should continue to do good works, but in secrecy. When giving alms, you should "not let your left hand know what your right hand is doing" (6:3); when praying, you should "go into your inner room and shut the door" (6:6); and if fasting, you should "anoint your head and wash your face, that your fasting may not be seen by others but by your Father who is in secret" (6:17–18). In a sense, Jesus is telling his followers to cover up their piety. Rather than practicing piety before people to get their notice, disciples are to hide this part of their life, so that they can reap its true benefits.

Now we must observe that Jesus also tells his disciples to let their light shine before others, so that their good works may be seen and bring glory to God (5:16). Therefore, we should understand that when Jesus advocates secrecy in piety he does not intend absolute secrecy, for then the disciples' light could not be seen, and God would not be glorified by the disciples' righteousness. What kind of secrecy does Jesus mean then if not absolute secrecy? He means enough secrecy to ensure the right motive.[116] As long as people are truly seeking God's reward and not others', then their motive is right and their deeds are truly righteous and worthy of God's reward. The reason Jesus advocates secrecy is that it is the surest way to short-circuit the temptation to seek reward from other people instead of God.

The problem Jesus aims to remedy here is hypocrisy. In all three examples of piety—almsgiving, prayer, and fasting—Jesus contrasts the way disciples should perform them and the way hypocrites do (6:2, 5, 16). Therefore, just as Jesus' instructions aim to ensure that we receive God's reward and not merely people's, they also aim to avert us from becoming hypocrites. As has been seen, hypocrisy and false self-understanding are closely bound together. Because hypocrites evaluate only external appearances and not their inner motives, they neglect to understand their

---

116. It is necessary to observe that there is no contradiction between this passage and Matt 5:16, as Hagner explains: "The deeds of righteousness performed by the Christian will of course be seen by others. According to 5:16, followers of Jesus should let their light shine 'before others [precisely the language of our pericope], so that they may see your good works.' Although this may seem at first to be a contradiction, 5:16 goes on to say 'that they might glorify your Father who is in heaven,' which is in bold contrast to the desire of the hypocrites that 'they might be glorified by others' (v 2)." Hagner, *Matthew 1–13*, 140.

moral and spiritual condition wholly and truly, resulting in false self-understanding. Jesus' direction in Matthew 6:1–18 aims to undermine hypocrisy and so also the false self.

The intervention we are discussing might be stated as a general principle: We should practice piety in secret, in order to expose our true motivations for piety and reform them. Secrecy in piety forces would-be disciples to become conscious of their motivation, particularly regarding whether they are seeking reward from God or from other people. This intervention helps bring to consciousness the moral and spiritual orders of existence, and so can disclose one's heart and its motives. The reason disciples should make their piety a private act between themselves and God, instead of a public exhibition, is that it will lead them into an encounter with their heart and enable them to experience a greater degree of true self-understanding regarding their moral and spiritual state.

Judge Yourself First: Matthew 7:1–5

A second intervention can be discerned in Jesus' teaching about judging others. He instructs his disciples to refrain from judging other people in a hypocritical way. To judge hypocritically would mean that I evaluate and reprove another person without having done the same to myself. Jesus compares this to someone who notices a speck of dust in another person's eye while missing the log that is stuck in his own eye (7:3–4). Jesus then points out the correct process, saying, "You hypocrite, first take the log out of your own eye, and then you will see clearly to take the speck out of your brother's eye" (7:5). While Jesus upholds the legitimacy of evaluating and reproving others, he sets a prerequisite, which is to judge oneself first.

To understand our moral and spiritual condition truly, we need to judge ourselves first whenever we are tempted to judge someone else. Like the former intervention about performing pious works in secret, this one constrains a person to attend to oneself morally and spiritually. Observe the motivation Jesus attaches to the intervention: "Judge not, that you be not judged" (7:1). The judgment Jesus warns his disciples about is God's (see 18:21–35).[117] To judge another person uncharitably because I have neglected to judge myself is to court divine judgment, and as 7:21–23 demonstrates, such neglect may ultimately end in a surprisingly ruinous fate.

---

117. See Hagner, *Matthew 1–13*, 169; Davies and Allison, *Gospel according to Saint Matthew*, 668–69; Nolland, *The Gospel of Matthew*, 318.

This intervention, however, also differs from secret piety, being a more direct assault upon hypocrisy and false self-understanding. It is also different in that it is naturally occasioned by our inclination to judge others. For someone who often experiences the desire to judge others, this intervention could be particularly beneficial.

Beware the Wolf (in You): Matthew 7:15–20

Finally, we can draw out a third intervention in Jesus' warning about false teachers who appear "in sheep's clothing" but who are inwardly "ravenous wolves" (7:15–20). Jesus instructs his disciples how to identify such people, saying, "You will recognize them by their fruits" (7:16a, 20). He explains how a tree's fruit gives evidence of what kind of tree it is: "every healthy tree bears good fruit, but the diseased tree bears bad fruit" (7:17). At first glance, this analogy seems fairly conventional as wisdom teaching goes: it bids us to be watchful for false teachers by judging people based on their outward deeds or "fruit," because the deeds should indicate the goodness or badness of the person. However, Jesus' instruction requires more careful consideration than just a first glance, for like other sages in the sapiential tradition, his speech requires "concentration and rumination to be understood."[118]

Upon reflection we can observe a seeming paradox in Jesus' words here. On the one hand, Jesus says that false teachers are ravenous wolves and bad unhealthy trees. It would seem that we could discern their badness by judging their fruit or deeds. However, it is not that easy, because these false teachers appear as sheep and not the ravenous wolves they actually are. Although they are bad inside, their outward appearance or "fruit" seems good. How then can Jesus expect disciples to apply his instruction? Throughout Matthew's Gospel we can see this theme: that although people's outward actions and appearance should correspond to their motives and heart, this is often not the case. In 12:33–34, Jesus uses the tree/fruit language again to address this inconsistency: "Either make the tree good and its fruit good, or make the tree bad and its fruit bad, for the tree is known by its fruit. You brood of vipers! How can you speak good, when you are evil?" Recognizing the inconsistency between their bad hearts and good words, Jesus tells them to prioritize either one or the other, for even if they were all bad, both in heart and deed, at least then

---

118. Witherington, *Jesus the Sage*, 159.

they would be consistent. *Appearance* is not the thing, but *consistency*, as he later explains to the Pharisees: "Woe to you, scribes and Pharisees, hypocrites! For you clean the outside of the cup and the plate, but inside they are full of greed and self-indulgence. You blind Pharisee! First clean the inside of the cup and the plate, that the outside also may be clean" (23:25–26).

In these teachings, Jesus is pointing out that we can accurately evaluate our righteousness only if we are willing to evaluate our motives, or heart, and not merely our outward actions. For this reason, he instructs us not to expect God's reward for righteous acts unless we do them for the right motives (6:1–18).[119] Only by evaluating our deeds together with the motives behind them can we know our true moral condition. Yet, if our deeds do not always correspond to and reveal our heart, how can the heart be seen or judged?

This question is the same posed above about how disciples can recognize false teachers. To answer it, consider Via's summary comments on the problem:

> Matthew urges his readers to be on their guard against the false prophets, who are wolves in sheep's clothing (7:15). Their righteousness is not real, for it does not correspond to the heart, the inner disposition (7:15b; 23:27–28). These people live in violation of the wholeness that constitutes well-being. But how does Matthew know that the false prophets' hearts are evil since it is also his position that acts can either disclose or conceal the heart and only God really knows what is on the inside (6:4, 6, 18)? The truth is that he cannot know. His theological portrayal of the human condition makes it impossible for him to know whether acts in any particular situation really reveal or conceal the heart. *Matthew urges the reader to discern the falsity of the false prophets, but since that is in the final analysis impossible, the imperative is turned back on the reader.* Beware of the false prophet in you. Are you the ravenous wolf hiding in sheep's clothing, who appears to be righteous but within is full of rebellion? Only about yourself—and not perfectly then, can you discern whether the act was for God's glory and in order to be God's child or was for the sake of human praise.[120]

---

119. Via, *Self-Deception and Wholeness in Paul and Matthew*, 85–86.

120. Via, *Self-Deception and Wholeness in Paul and Matthew*, 92, emphasis mine.

The intervention Jesus offers here is the most subtle and indirect of the three. Instead of plainly telling disciples to beware of the inconsistency or hypocrisy in themselves, he poses the issue as if it were mainly about someone else, that is, "false prophets, who come to you in sheep's clothing" (7:15a).[121] Through a roundabout way, Jesus redirects disciples to consider *themselves* by planting a wrinkle in the logic of his lesson, leading them to ask, "How can I recognize a false prophet if the only sure proof is the tell-tale heart, while the only heart I have access to is my own?" By setting up his disciples in this way, Jesus gives them more ownership of his point. Therein lies the particular effectiveness of this intervention. As an indirect form of instruction, it undermines false self-understanding and fosters true self-understanding quietly, without attracting attention to our hypocrisy until we have discovered it for ourselves. What we discover is that, since the only heart we can access is our own, we should beware our own hypocrisy, inconsistency, and false teaching most of all.

Summary Thoughts on Interventions in Matthew

In these chapters Jesus gives his disciples three interventions to undermine hypocrisy and promote true self-understanding: perform acts of piety in secret before God; judge yourself before judging others; and beware of the false teacher *in yourself*. These three interventions all work to undermine hypocrisy and false self-understanding by directing us to consider our moral and spiritual condition, or to turn our gaze inward and see that true wholeness requires a pure heart in the sight of God. Thus, all three interventions subvert the folly that leads to destruction, and they promote the wisdom that Jesus says will ultimately save a person from ruin (see 7:24–27). While the interventions all work towards this end, there are differences in them.

For example, the first two interventions are direct instructions, but in the third intervention Jesus uses an indirect method to help people discover the hypocrisy in themselves. The contrast between Jesus' direct teaching and indirect teaching appears throughout Matthew (see 13:1–23). While the two direct teachings in 6:1–8 and 7:1–5 helpfully point out the possibility of hypocrisy in us, some hearers might quickly

---

121. Via's interpretation of this passage is more convincing than that of other commentators who read Jesus' directions merely as a direct warning against false teachers: Nolland, *The Gospel of Matthew*; Turner, *Matthew*; Evans, *Matthew*; Hauerwas, *Matthew*; Hagner, *Matthew 1–13*; Blomberg, *Matthew*.

dismiss that it is actually the case with them. The indirect intervention in 7:15–20 allows such hearers more space to realize and acknowledge their own hypocrisy, assuming they take the time to consider it deeply enough.

Another difference to note is that all three interventions address distinct aspects or situations in a person's spiritual life: 6:1–18 addresses one's pious deeds, 7:1–5 addresses one's judgment of others' pious deeds (or lack thereof), and 7:15–20 indirectly addresses one's nature as being either a false or true disciple.

Finally, in these three interventions the subversive function of Jesus' teaching is especially apparent, as he directs disciples to examine themselves and root out the hypocrisy within them. Jesus' wise teaching undermines false self-understanding, and as a result his teaching paves the way for true self-understanding. Jesus' teaching in Matthew 6–7 is not in itself the gospel, which alone is the power of salvation and true self-understanding, but it is a gospel intervention. By exposing our hypocrisy, both directly and indirectly, Jesus' teaching turns us to gaze at our heart and acknowledge our need for help. As a wise subversive sage, Jesus undermines our pretense to self-righteousness, and by leading us to consent to our spiritual poverty, he makes it possible for us to receive his help and salvation.

Interventions in Paul: Self-Considering

Moving now to interventions in Paul, I will actually only focus on one intervention, one which Paul exhorts believers to again and again, and one which he personally demonstrates and models for us. I will call this intervention "self-considering." We will begin with his exhortations to believers about how they are to identify or "consider" themselves, and then look at his personal modeling.

Paul Exhorts Christians to Self-Considering

In Romans 6 Paul answers a question: "Since believers' sins are forgiven, and since God's grace increases where sin had increased, does this allow believers to continue in sin so that grace may increase?" (see Rom 5:20—6:1). He answers with a resounding "no," and he grounds it in Christian identity. Christians are those who have "died to sin," so of course they cannot continue to live in it (Rom 6:2). As those baptized into Christ Jesus, as those whose identity is defined by their identification with Christ, believers should by default consider themselves dead to sin; for, since Christ died to sin when he died on the cross, and since believers are those who identify with Christ, then believers too have died to sin.[122] Because they are united with Christ, Paul directs believers to consider themselves dead to sin. Dunn explains:

> the dying to sin here spoken of is not something independent of Christ, but is somehow a sharing in his death, a sharing in his transition from one era to the other. His readers therefore would very likely have heard Paul's opening response as, How can you who identified with Christ live as though Christ never died, as though sin and the law were still dominating factors for present life?[123]

With this explanation, Paul can exhort them to resist continuing in sin. As those dead to sin, believers can stop acting like slaves to sin and succumbing to its mastery over them (Rom 6:12–14). Their identity permits them to live differently.

Paul expresses the same idea in Ephesians where he contrasts the lives and identities of believers and unbelievers. Believers are living life as a process of maturation in Christ, growing up into Christ and becoming more like him (Eph 4:13, 15). Paul describes this process in terms of being built up in the knowledge of Christ (Eph 4:13a). This knowledge is not just cognitive but experiential and relational.[124] Growth in Christ stems from growing in one's personal identification with Christ. Unbelievers, however, live life out of a different identity devoid of this knowledge, "in the futility of their minds, being darkened in their understanding, excluded from the life of God because of the ignorance that is in them" (Eph 4:17b–18). The outcome of an identity formed apart from God is a life characterized by "sensuality," "impurity," and "greediness" (Eph 4:19). The lives of believers stand in contrast (at least in principle) because their identity is not defined by ignorance and futile thinking like unbelievers, as Paul says, "But you did not learn Christ in this way, if indeed you

---

122. By "identification with Christ" I refer to what Nygren and Schreiner have called "incorporation into Christ." Schreiner, *Romans*, 303–22; Nygren, *Commentary on Romans*; Bruce refers to this same idea by calling it "being united to Christ by faith." Bruce, *The Letter of Paul to the Romans*; Keener and Matera use more explicit "identification" language. Keener, *Romans*; Matera, *Romans*.

123. Dunn, *Romans. 1–8*, 327.

124. See Thielman, *Ephesians*, 281; Williamson and Healy, *Ephesians*, 121.

have heard him and have been taught in him, just as the truth is in Jesus, that in reference to your former manner of life, you lay aside the old self, which is being corrupted in accordance with the lusts of deceit" (Eph 4:20–22).[125] The foundational difference between believers and unbelievers is their identity: in the life of unbelief people define themselves apart from God and ground their identity in godlessness, but when people believe in Christ, they disown their godless identity.[126] In other words, since believers have died to sin, they have laid aside their "old self," or their former identity. Thus, when Paul writes in Romans 6 that the old self was "crucified with Christ," he means that through his death on the cross, Christ nullified the basis for an identity of unbelief (Rom 6:6).

When Paul exhorts believers to "put off the old self" (Eph 4:22) or to consider themselves "dead to sin" (Rom 6:11a), he is not primarily directing them to behave differently or to stop sinning but to stop understanding themselves apart from Christ.[127] The intervention employed here is not "stop sinning like you used to" but "stop identifying yourself like you used to." Now, both are inexorably connected, but by telling believers to see themselves differently Paul is giving them the basis for why they can stop letting sin reign in them (Rom 6:12–13). Nonetheless, self-understanding takes priority and not self-regulation or behavioral change, because the power to stop sinning is related to a change in identity.

In Paul's thinking, at the same time believers disown their former identity they also adopt a new one. On the heels of telling his readers to put off the old self, Paul also directs them to put on the new self, which is, he says, "created after the likeness of God in true righteousness and holiness" (Eph 4:24b). The main difference in the old self and new self concerns one's knowledge: the old self is an identity based on repressing one's knowledge of God, but the new self is based on consenting to that

125. See Williamson and Healy, *Ephesians*, 126–27; Fowl, *Ephesians*, 150; Best, *A Critical and Exegetical Commentary on Ephesians*, 426.

126. Fowl observes the connection between identity and moral conduct by noting that "a transformation of identity . . . enables and entails righteous, holy living." Fowl, *Ephesians*, 153. Unbelievers do not demonstrate a holy life because, as Best says, they are ignorant about both God and "their nature as people." Best, *A Critical and Exegetical Commentary on Ephesians*, 420.

127. Lincoln observes that the language of "putting off" and "putting on" refers to that of discarding and donning clothing, and that this change of clothing symbolizes an "exchange of identities." The old self and new self are individuals "identified either with the old or with the new order of existence." By using this language Paul is primarily concerned with identity, not one's behavior. Lincoln, *Ephesians*, 285.

knowledge, which is foundational to human existence. When believers put on the new self, they are identifying themselves as those who exist in relation to God and not apart from him. Believers are persons who consent to know God truly, just as they were created to do, and to know themselves in light of their relationship with him; they adopt the new self.

A question that arises here concerns whether to categorize the old self and new self as individual or corporate designations. The Greek word translated "self" (*anthropos*) can also be translated "man" or "human," denoting something beyond the individual.[128] Thus, Paul's concept of the old/new self or old/new human can be applied both to humankind corporately and to individuals.[129] In Ephesians 2:11–22, Paul uses "new self" corporately to refer to the new version of humanity inaugurated and created in Jesus Christ.[130] However, in Ephesians 4 and Colossians 3 "new self" has more of an individual sense, because Paul wants his readers to see themselves as having entered personally into this new kind of humanity, which Christ began.

How does the new self begin with Christ? By taking on human nature, dying in the body to sin, and being raised from the dead, Christ transformed human nature and established a new kind of human: a human defined not by ethnic identity (i.e., Jew), but as a member of the new creation: "For he himself is our peace, who has made us both one . . . that he might create in himself one new man in place of the two" (Eph 2:14, 15). Gentiles were those human beings without the law and thus outside the covenants of promise, so they did not have a relationship or reconciliation with God (Eph 2:12). Jews, on the other hand, were those humans who had received God's law, covenants, and promise of salvation. However, because the Jews failed to keep God's law even as the Gentiles had, they were just as in need of God's grace to be reconciled to him. Jesus Christ represents a new kind of human being, or "third race."[131] His human nature is new and different because, unlike the Gentiles, he was born under the law, and also, unlike the Jews, he kept God's law.

Believers also uphold God's law, according to Paul, because of their faith in Christ (Rom 3:31). When anyone identifies with Christ, whether Jew or Gentile, he or she becomes part of this new humanity and can

---

128. Danker, Bauer, and Arndt, *A Greek-English Lexicon of the New Testament and Other Early Christian Literature*, 81–82.

129. See Schreiner, *Romans*, 315.

130. Lincoln, *Ephesians*, 143.

131. Lincoln, *Ephesians*, 144.

claim its privileges.[132] The new humanity created in Christ is the ground of the Christian's identity and, thereby, his or her reconciliation. By identifying with that humanity, believers are counted members of it, and God grants them all the rights and privileges of membership; all the virtues and merits of Jesus' human nature are reckoned to those who place faith in him, and with his merits also comes his inheritance and sonship (Gal 4:5–7).[133] In union with Christ, "We receive a right status before God, since we are incorporated into the Son of God himself. All that he did is ours."[134] Believers' new identity through union with Christ means that they are reconciled to God as his beloved children, who can cry out, "Abba, Father" (Rom 8:15), and who may hear God reply, "Nothing will separate you from my love" (Rom 8:39).

One who has put on the identity of the new self personally experiences the gospel's power to save and reconcile people to God. Putting on the new self means I internalize the gospel and become conscious of my new spiritual life and restored relationship with God. Therefore, according to a Pauline perspective, the most important intervention for fostering the true self consists in putting off the old self and putting on the new, that is, "internalizing" the gospel.[135] If this intervention were to be summarized in a sentence, perhaps Paul's exhortation in Romans 6:11 would capture it best: "consider yourselves dead to sin and alive to God in Christ Jesus." This self-consideration entails consciously discarding an old identity constituted apart from God and simultaneously embracing a new identity centered on God in Jesus Christ. The most effective means of undermining the false self and building up the true self is to consciously

132. See Thielman, *Ephesians*, 164; Lincoln, *Ephesians*, 143–44; Fowl, *Ephesians*, 95; Williamson and Healy, *Ephesians*, 74.

133. This idea of Christians' spiritual union with Christ, through which they gain Christ's merits, has traditionally been referred to under a few synonymous headings: identification with Christ, incorporation into Christ, and union with Christ. Demarest outlines several benefits of union with Christ that the Christian obtains: death with Christ to the old order of existence; burial with Christ and thus freedom from sin's domination; spiritual life with Christ; resurrection with Christ and thus the putting on of the new self; and the guarantee of glorification with Christ and thus physical resurrection, eternal life, and participation in Christ's rule. See Demarest, *The Cross and Salvation*, 313–44.

134. Letham, *Union with Christ*, 83.

135. See a detailed explanation of internalization in Johnson, *Foundations for Soul Care*, 494–532.

consider oneself a new person who has died to one's old identity and now exists "in Christ."[136]

Paul Models Self-Considering

Paul models this "self-considering" in Philippians 3:1–12. His immediate purpose in the passage is to warn readers about false teachers who would try to persuade them to boast in their flesh, that is, to base their identity on their personal background and achievements, quite apart from faith in Christ.[137] To place one's confidence in the flesh like this corresponds exactly to living out of the old, sin-enslaved identity. Paul's model demonstrates how putting off the old self means disowning its particular features. Although these features are unique to Paul, they express the old way of identifying oneself apart from God that is common to all humans. Paul writes:

> If anyone else thinks he has reason for confidence in the flesh, I have more: circumcised on the eighth day, of the people of Israel, of the tribe of Benjamin, a Hebrew of Hebrews; as to the law, a Pharisee; as to zeal, a persecutor of the church; as to righteousness under the law, blameless. (Phil 3:4b–6)

Here Paul observes how he could understand himself in light of the old self if he chose to do so. He could boast in several laudable features of his life in the flesh: his heritage and upbringing as a *bona fide* Jew; his accomplishments as a student of the law, reaching the status of a Pharisee; his heart-felt passion in his accomplishments; and his status before others as a blameless and an ideal Jew. Evidently, Paul has put enough consideration into these things to be able to clearly articulate and disown them.

Paul exposes and discards all the ways he might boast in his flesh, saying that he counts them as rubbish and loss rather than gain (Phil 3:7–8). He recognizes that they are to be put off because of their ultimate worthlessness. One thing, however, has he chosen to put on and treasure for its ultimate value, as he says, "Indeed, I count everything as loss because of the surpassing worth of knowing Christ Jesus my Lord. For his

---

136. For a full treatment of how Paul uses "in Christ" language, see Campbell, *Paul and Union with Christ*.

137. Silva explains boasting and having confidence in one's flesh means that one depends upon "natural achievements" and "everything outside Christ" that one might employ to gain righteousness. Silva, *Philippians*, 149.

sake I have suffered the loss of all things and count them as rubbish, in order that I may gain Christ and be found in him" (Phil 3:8–9a).[138] Only by defining himself in Christ, Paul knows, can he gain what he formerly sought through his fleshly accolades, that is, not "a righteousness of my own that comes from the law, but that which comes through faith in Christ, the righteousness from God that depends on faith" (Phil 3:9b).

Therefore, just as Paul specifies the worthless confidences of his old self, he clearly articulates the desire he pursued through them: he wanted to gain righteousness. Indeed, he still does, and that is essential to note in order to recognize the goal of putting off and putting on. The key difference between the old self and new self is not the end goal—which is righteousness in either case—but the efficient cause that gets to the goal.[139] The efficient cause is to count as rubbish everything in our lives that we might boast in apart from Christ, and to count our relationship with Christ as being "surpassing worth" (Phil 3:8). Paul has seen that he cannot depend upon his flesh for righteousness but only on faith in Christ (Phil 3:9).

Placing faith in Christ, therefore, means boasting in him and identifying with all that we are in union with him. Just as Paul recognizes how his old identity found root and expression in his former way of life as a Pharisee and persecutor of the church, he also recognizes how his union with Christ comes to expression in his sufferings. Paul considers his suffering as a Christian to be a partaking in Christ's own sufferings.[140] Just as he understands his former identity in the flesh, he understands his new identity and the particular ways he personally partakes of union with Christ in his life and ministry.

Summary Thoughts on Paul's Intervention of Self-Considering

Let's summarize what we have collected from Paul's thinking about "self-considering."

---

138. Thus Silva remarks, "Paul recognizes the radical antithesis between his former way of life and the new hope offered to him; it was either one or the other." Silva, *Philippians*, 158.

139. Thus Silva distinguishes a worthless kind of righteousness gotten from the law and a true righteousness obtained by "abandoning one's own efforts and exercising faith." Silva, *Philippians*, 162.

140. Campbell, *Paul and Union with Christ*, 233–34.

First, Paul uses several different ways of expressing one overarching idea: considering oneself dead to sin but alive to God in Christ (Rom 6:11), putting off the old self and putting on the new (Eph 4:22–24; Col 3:9–10), counting everything as loss for the sake of Christ (Phil 3:1–11). In other texts beyond our study, Paul employs still more expressions of this idea: setting one's mind on things above and not on earthly things (Col 3:1–3), boasting in one's weaknesses (2 Cor 12:9–10), boasting in the cross (Gal 6:14), putting on the armor of God (Eph 6:10–17), and recognizing that Jesus Christ is in oneself (2 Cor 13:5). In all these cases Paul calls for believers to find their identity and understand themselves in relation to Christ and the gospel: as those united with Christ, believers are the recipients of the gospel promises and are beloved children who have been reconciled to God, counted righteous and freed from sin's mastery.

Second, when Paul models self-considering in Philippians 3, he demonstrates a certain level of specificity and clarity, and so he provides a model for how believers should go about recognizing and articulating the aspects of their old self that they must disown, the purpose and motivations for adopting a different identity, and the nature of that new identity as it is found in Christ.

Third, we must recognize that self-considering demands both objectivity and subjectivity. On the one hand, when Paul exhorts readers to put on the new self, he is directing people to identify and define themselves based on an objective criterion that exists independently, outside of them. That criterion is the new humanity inaugurated and created in Jesus Christ. Far from exhorting individuals to choose any new identity they might want out of their own imaginings and inclinations or those offered by other people, Paul argues that there is only one legitimate ground for their identity: their union with Christ. Thus, applying Paul's intervention of self-considering is a task in objectivity. On the other hand, it is also subjective, for it requires that believers consider themselves and recognize the unique forms and expressions that the old self takes in them, to disown this identity, and to internalize a new way of seeing themselves (e.g., their calling, ministry, suffering).

Conclusion

In this chapter we have been drawing out a Scriptural perspective on four questions: (1) Why do people reflect on themselves? (2) Why do they understand themselves wrongly? (i.e., constructing a false self) (3) What does true self-understanding entail? And (4) What interventions can foster true self-understanding? Beginning with (1), let's look at what we've found.

First, the Bible portrays self-understanding as spiritually and ethically useful. Knowing oneself helps a person to partake in loving communion with God and others. Self-understanding also helps people to fulfill God's greatest commands to love him and other people.

Second, we have seen that foolishness, hypocrisy, and the flesh all contribute to false self-understanding. Because we are fallen, we have a severely distorted ethicospiritual vision, leading us away from the Source of life and truth. Furthermore, we cannot solve this problem on our own; we are enslaved to sin.

Third, we have seen that, according to Scripture, true self-understanding means increasing in wisdom, aligning ourselves with the wisdom of the universe—the wisdom of Yahweh—and not walking in self-delusion like the fool. When we "trust in the Lord" and "lean not on our own understanding," we are open to seeing ourselves as we truly are. We see both the outward deeds and the inward thoughts and intentions of the heart, and, as a result, we see our lack of wholeness, realizing the discrepancy between what we appear to be and what we truly are. Recognizing our lack of wholeness, we can then consent to receive the wholeness and salvation God offers in Christ. Having debunked the cover stories, we perceive and consent to the hidden real story: we are created by God for sonship, we are fallen from that glorious calling, we are loved graciously by God in Christ, and we are bodily, ethically, and spiritually incomplete.

Finally, according to a biblical perspective, the efficient cause of true self-understanding is the gospel. When one understands oneself in light of the gospel, he or she becomes a more integrated and whole person in heart and deed. Freed from sin's deception, believers see their true moral and spiritual condition, and through this new understanding they are empowered to experience salvation and become more whole, until their salvation is complete. Since the gospel of Jesus Christ is the efficient cause of true self-understanding, interventions that promote true self-understanding must be interventions based in this gospel. To rely on interventions based in human wisdom is foolish, as Proverbs teaches. Folly, or doing what seems right "in one's own eyes," leads to self-delusion, but wisdom leads to self-knowledge, and as people seek the wisdom of

Yahweh they will expand in light and true self-understanding. Although Proverbs does not reveal the Gospel of Christ, coming as it did many centuries later, it does invite readers to put their trust in the God whom the incarnate Christ would later reveal, calling them to a humble child-like trust in God and to a mature adult-like responsibility for choosing the path of wisdom. Likewise, Matthew, aware of people's resistance to trust in God and in his son Jesus Christ, subversively exposes and undermines readers' foolishness and hypocrisy through the three interventions we saw in Jesus' teaching (i.e., practicing piety in secret, judging oneself when inclined to judge another, and judging others by their fruit), making it possible for people to consent to their spiritual emptiness and to receive Christ's salvation. Finally, Paul's gospel-intervention of self-considering models a personal exchange of identity, in which believers consciously repudiate confidence in the flesh and all that they might boast in for salvation outside of Christ, and in which they internalize the gospel and depend upon their union with Christ for salvation.

I do not presume that the Scriptural perspective proposed in this chapter is *the* Scriptural perspective on the false self and true self. Due to my limitations, many insights from the Bible that bear on this study's questions have been omitted, and many that have been included could have been stated better. However, in the next chapter, what I have offered here will hopefully be confirmed and supplemented by others in the Church's tradition, whose writings elucidate and draw from Scripture's teaching.

3

Christian Perspectives

This chapter is, somewhat, a practice in imagination. I want to imagine how other Christians besides myself—Christians who have both understood and practiced Christianity better than me—might answer the four questions of this book: (1) Why do people reflect on themselves? (2) Why do they understand themselves wrongly? (i.e., constructing a false self)? (3) What does true self-understanding entail? And (4) What interventions can foster true self-understanding?

The writers I've chosen to "interview" are Augustine of Hippo (354–430), Martin Luther (1483–1546), Søren Kierkegaard (1813–1855), and Thomas Merton (1915–1968). Besides the fact that they were devoted students of Scripture, followers of Christ, and writers whose works have stood the test of time, I chose these four representatives based on two criteria. The first criterion was relevance, or how directly they addressed the self, false self, and true self in their writings. In relating the ideas of certain Christian figures to the questions of this study, I want to avoid too much extrapolation and instead be able to show as parsimoniously as possible how their works address the questions of our study. The second criterion was influence, or how greatly the person's thinking about the subject is generally considered to have shaped the Christian tradition. Due to the limitation of space, this chapter is just an introductory attempt to recollect the history of Christian thought on the subject. Many important thinkers, pre-modern and modern, had to be left out, e.g., Thomas Aquinas, Theresa of Avila, John Calvin, Karl Barth, C. S. Lewis, Elenore Stump, Richard Rohr, David Benner, and Brené Brown, to name a few.

Augustine of Hippo

Augustine (354–430) is the earliest representative of Christian perspectives in our study. He brings a particularly philosophical and mystical approach to the subject of the self, and his thinking has influenced the course of thought on the subject for generations.[1]

Augustine on the Self

Turning Inward to See the Self

Augustine was influenced by the Neo-Platonist philosopher Plotinus, who elaborated Plato's antithesis between spirit versus matter and eternal versus temporal. Augustine described these oppositions with the language of "inner" and "outer." He writes:

> Come now, and let us see where lies, as it were, the boundary line between the outer and inner man. For whatever we have in the mind common with the beasts, thus much is rightly said to belong to the outer man. For the outer man is not to be considered to be the body only, but with the addition also of a certain peculiar life of the body, whence the structure of the body derives its vigor, and all the senses with which he is equipped for the perception of outward things; and when the images of these outward things already perceived, that have been fixed in the memory, are seen again by recollection, it is still a matter pertaining to the outer man.[2]

The outer man is our body, bodily energy, and bodily senses. But it is also "whatever we have in the mind common with the beasts," that is, mental images and memories of outer things. Just as a dog can remember his master's voice and where he buried his bone, our minds can hold memories of outer things.

The inner man is, then, more than just our mind, since we share many mental abilities with animals. It is, rather, any mental abilities we have that exceed those of other animals. The first of these abilities is reason: "there where something first meets us which is not common to ourselves with the beasts reason begins, so that here the inner man can

1. Taylor, *Sources of the Self*, 127–42.
2. Augustine, *The Trinity*, 12.1.1.

now be recognized."[3] Unlike the beasts, our reasoning ability allows us to judge outer things according to unchangeable eternal standards that are only grasped by the intellect. These standards cannot be perceived by bodily senses. They are not sensible but intelligible, i.e., understood through reason. Reason equips us to discern these standards and to use them. The Pythagorean theorem is an example: there exists an unchangeable intelligible rule about triangles, and through reason, humans have grasped this rule and expressed it in a formula, $a^2 + b^2 = c^2$. Reason is used in mathematics, grammar, and every other human skill whereby we apply knowledge of the world and outer things. Yet, reason's higher functions deal with inner realities. The first is the inner self.

The inner self is "an inner space proper to the soul."[4] Like the Pythagorean theorem, the inner self is intelligible, not sensible. We cannot perceive it with the senses. It is perceived by the mind. But what is it? Philip Cary notes that Augustine's "inner self" is distinct from the "inner man" discussed above.[5] The difference between the inner self and inner man is similar to that of the Me-self and the I-self: the inner self corresponds to the Me-self as something that is observed, and the inner man corresponds to the I-self as something that observes. The inner man is the capacity a person has for reasoning. It is our inner man that allows us to perceive our inner self. In other words, to speak of the inner man observing the inner self is just to say that we can turn "inward" and observe our own reasoning. The inner self is what we see when we turn inward.

Turning Inward and Upward to See God

Augustine's concern in these matters goes beyond philosophical distinctions. The inward turn to the inner self is one stage in a series of crucial turnings or "conversions" in a person's understanding. In Book 7 of *Confessions*, Augustine expresses how the purpose of turning *inward* is to turn *upward* to God:

> Being admonished by all this to return to myself, I entered into my own depths, with You as guide; and I was able to do it because You were my helper. I entered, and with the eye of my

---

3. Augustine, *The Trinity*, 12.8.13.

4. Cary, *Augustine's Invention of the Inner Self*, 39.

5. Cary, *Augustine's Invention of the Inner Self*, 48–49.

soul, such as it was, I saw Your Unchangeable Light shining over that same eye of my soul, over my mind.[6]

Augustine here describes how turning to consider his inner self led his thoughts upward. By considering his mind, he was drawn beyond his mind to "the Unchangeable Light," who is God.

Earlier in Book 7, Augustine explains more fully the reasoning that led to apprehending God through inward reflection. This process began by turning away from considering outward things to looking into the soul.[7] First, a person turns from bodily senses to consider the processes of the cognitive faculty that receives bodily sensations, which is a faculty humans hold in common with other animals; but higher than this is one's reason, or the cognitive faculty that judges the data received from bodily sensations. By considering the faculty of reason a person may recognize that it is changeable, and thus not a perfect guide for judging truth from falsehood. Finally, this recognition reveals a standard that exists above and beyond one's reason and by which one's reason is judged, and by discerning this standard one discerns the intelligible things that are intrinsic to God's nature and to which sensible creation points.[8] In other words, by exploring my cognitive and reasoning powers of judgment to search out their end, I discover that they must be grounded in a being higher than myself, since they are designed to meet a standard, which is of the same kind (i.e., intelligible) but of a wholly different degree (i.e., divine perfection).[9]

The Power That Turns Us

The efficient cause of this reflection is God's power or grace that turns a person to faith. In the quote above, Augustine observes that he was warned, led, and helped to turn inward. The power behind the inward turn is God, who calls people to consider their soul and what exists above it, rather than to fixate on outward things. Augustine calls this action of God "prevenient grace." The beginning of a person's turn to the inner self consists of God graciously drawing one to faith.[10] God speaks to humans

---

6. Augustine, *Confessions*, 7.17.23.

7. See Augustine, *Confessions*, 7.23.132–33.

8. Cary, *Augustine's Invention of the Inner Self*, 65–66.

9. Taylor, *Sources of the Self*, 132–36.

10. Cary, *Inner Grace*, 101–5. Augustine's understanding of prevenient grace is not

through many signs, but the one true efficacious cause of turning inward and finding God is the fact that the human mind and God's mind are intrinsically connected; within and above the soul is God himself, and people are drawn toward God as they are drawn toward the good of their own soul. The only reason people would not follow this leading would be their choice to fixate on outward things. The human will is made to draw inward to God, but people may choose to look outward instead, and this is more fully explained in Augustine's doctrine of sin.

Summary of Augustine on the Self

To summarize, Augustine believed human beings are created with the capacity to see intelligible realities, and this capacity he called the soul, mind, or inner man. Humans may use this capacity upon themselves to observe it at work; that is, they may use the mind to think about the mind, to think metacognitively. The purpose of such reflection is, according to Augustine, to go beyond knowing their own mind in order to know the Mind above all minds. But not only is God the goal of exploring the inner self, he is the cause. God dwells within the soul, and if people are ultimately drawn to God, it is because God exists at the core of their being. No outward sign is efficacious in itself, for only by considering intelligible realities within our soul can we apprehend and come to know God.

Augustine on the False Self

Turning Inward but Not Upward

In the beginning, God made humans with souls naturally attuned to and desirous of God's will, and his instruction to the first human was "very light" and easily obeyed: "in order to make a wholesome obedience easy to him, [God] had given him a single very brief and very light precept by which He reminded that creature *whose service was to be free* that He

---

as straightforward as presented here. Augustine seems to have never decided whether prevenient grace consists in the external call of God or in the connection he thought that man has to God by virtue of the inner self. I have focused on the latter because it is more compatible with his commitment to the Platonic antithesis between the sensible and intelligible.

was Lord."[11] Human souls are meant to willingly consent to God's will, to gravitate towards life in him, rather than living in sin.

People, however, have subverted their freedom from willing good for themselves through obedience to God, to willing good for themselves through sin, which is futile:

> For what else is man's misery but his own disobedience to himself, so that in consequence of his not being willing to do what he could do, he now wills to do what he cannot? For though he could not do all things in Paradise before he sinned, yet he wished to do only what he could do, and therefore he could do all things he wished.[12]

The turn away from God towards sin was paradoxically against humanity's nature and wellbeing. Augustine connects the moral depravity of this sinful turn with ontological diminishment:

> being turned towards himself, his being became more contracted than it was when he clave to Him who supremely is. Accordingly, to exist in himself, that is, to be his own satisfaction after abandoning God, is not quite to become a nonentity, but to approximate to that.[13]

Fallen human nature is ontologically lessened or "contracted." Although sinners continue to exist, they "approximate" non-existence, because they have "turned towards" themselves. In other words, since the hearts of fallen human beings seek "satisfaction" in themselves rather than God, they have moved closer to non-being. In a futile attempt to find life apart from God, human beings begin to slip into dissolution, and, as Augustine puts it, they become "contracted" and turned in on themselves, so that they are cut off from their source of life and of truth.[14]

---

11. Augustine, *The City of God* (1950), 14.15.462, my italics.

12. Augustine, *The City of God* (1950), 14.15.463.

13. Augustine, *The City of God* (1950), 14.13.460.

14. I am indebted to Jenson, who shows how Augustine connected human beings' ontological break-down with their fall into delusion, "The inclination towards self is an ontologically downward movement. . . . In turning my back on truth and living a lie, I actually become less of a creature. . . . Augustine's metaphysical framework, with its sense of an actual sliding towards nothingness, allows us to sense this more acutely than contemporary society's more existential language which can speak of not being real in a way that evokes a sense of personal hypocrisy and maybe dis-integration, but not an actual diminishing." Jenson, *The Gravity of Sin*, 23–24.

A Half Turn is a Whole Lie

The soul naturally needs and desires God, because it is made to thrive on reality, not unreality.[15] But when people turn in on themselves, they lose touch with the truth, and their needs are thwarted.

Here an apparent contradiction surfaces: if turning inward leads to falsehood, then why would Augustine tout the "inward turn," as I described in the previous section? According to Augustine, crucial to the inward turn is the subsequent upward movement by which the soul encounters God; without it, the soul can become ingrown.

Thus, there are two ways humans may turn toward themselves: either in pursuit of God as the source of life and truth, or in pursuit of life and truth in oneself. Augustine calls the latter "living according to man" and the former "living according to God":

> When, then, a man lives according to himself—that is, according to man, not according to God—assuredly he lives according to a lie; not that man himself is a lie, for God is his author and creator, who is certainly not the author and creator of a lie, but because man was made upright, that he might not live according to himself, but according to Him that made him—in other words, that he might do His will and not his own; and not to live as he was made to live, that is a lie.[16]

By refusing to align with God's will (i.e., living "upright"), humans live a lie, and their falsity is demonstrated, says Augustine, precisely in the fact that they still desire good for themselves even while they seek to live in a way that foils their desire:

> Man obviously wills to be happy, even when he is not living in a way that makes it possible for him to attain happiness. And what could be more false than such a will? It is no mere empty words, then, to say that every sin is a falsehood. For sin only takes place due to our willing either that things should go well for us or that they should go badly for us. Thus the falsehood is this: we sin so that things may go better for us, and instead the result is that they get worse. What is the reason for this except that a man's wellbeing can only come from God, not from himself?[17]

---

15. Cary, *Outward Signs*.

16. Augustine, *The City of God* (1950), 14.4.

17. Augustine, *The City of God* (2013), 14.4.

Here Augustine describes how those who seek good for themselves by living "according to man" are deceived at once about their moral, ontological, and epistemological orientation.[18]

Stuck on Sensible Things

Significantly, Augustine linked the movement towards sin/non-being/falsehood with a fixation on outward sensible things and experiences (e.g., food, sex, the flesh/human nature of Christ) that are substantially lesser than intelligible truths (e.g., the Pythagorean theorem, the inner self, the deity of Christ).[19]

Sin occurs when a soul gravitates towards lower, outward things instead of towards God who is supreme:

> And I inquired what iniquity was, and ascertained it not to be a substance, but a perversion of the will, bent aside from Thee, O God, the Supreme Substance, towards these lower things, and casting out its bowels, and swelling outwardly.[20]

Humans should move towards God, who exists within and above the soul, but instead people veer their wills towards things that are lower than God and external to the soul. The sinful corrupt soul establishes loving attachments with external (or "fleshly") things that draw it away from God.[21] The significance of this strain in Augustine's thinking comes to the fore in his understanding of salvation in Christ.

Augustine on the True Self

Using All Things as Signs to God

For Augustine, to be saved means to see God clearly and to understand all external things as signs of him, through Christ's mediation. Salvation involves recognizing that all created things point to their Creator, as if in response to a person who sought God among them the created things

18. Morally, in the sense that they falsely think "living according to man" is right. Ontologically, because they think it promotes wellbeing. Epistemologically, because they think they are the most certain ground of knowledge, or truth.

19. See Cary, *Outward Signs*.

20. Augustine, *The City of God* (2013), 14.15.

21. Cary, *Outward Signs*, 7.

said, "We are not God, but He made us."[22] People who see God realize the truth that God is not to be found or known in the same way as external things are, with our body; rather, God is discerned with the soul, or mind.[23] Thus, people who have been saved from the sinful attachment to external things understand that these visible, bodily, and sensible things signify the invisible, incorporeal, and intelligible God. These people realize that God cannot be perceived with bodily senses, as if God could be seen with the eye, or felt, or heard. Rather, people whose love has been redirected to God seek and know God through the soul with the sight of the mind.

People who apprehend God with the mind do so because they have stopped idolizing things they perceive with their body. Whatever people love or worship most becomes the terminus of their understanding. If their love settles merely on external things, they will not apprehend God. We can see God reflected in created things if we love those things as a substitute for God. Lovers cannot see past the object of their love, and if the object of their love is an external thing meant to signify something higher than it—e.g., the Creator—they will not be able to recognize this truth. The object of love is all that is seen, and when external things are all that is seen, then God is not seen through them. Sin consists in the soul loving external things as a substitute for God, leading to the inability to see past those things to God. Salvation, however, consists in the soul turning its gaze away from sinful attachments and directing our love towards God, so that God may be truly known.[24] Loving God allows us to pass beyond the things that he made and to recognize them as bodily, created signs that signify the incorporeal, uncreated God.

Augustine believed the most direct sign to God is the inner self. For this reason, in Augustine's system the self-concept closest to the contemporary notion of the true self is the inner self. Perhaps we could even say that the inner self is "more true" in Augustine's thinking than the outer self, because it leads to God. Moreover, the reason it leads to God is because God's grace works directly upon it: God's prevenient grace moves the soul to turn to him.[25] When God frees the soul to love him, a person

22. Augustine, *Confessions* (2014), 10.6.9.

23. Augustine, *Confessions* (2014), 10.6–7.

24. Cary, *Outward Signs*.

25. See Cary, *Inner Grace*, 113–15.

may then use external signs rightly and follow them to internal, intelligible truths that the inner self grasps with faith.

Using God Incarnate as a Sign to God

Where does Christ fit into salvation according to Augustine? As the God-man, Jesus Christ is the sole mediator between God and humans.[26] As mediator, Christ serves as the way for human beings to reach God, teaching them to look past externals to inward things.

While Augustine affirms Christ's incarnation in a Nicene fashion, he does not believe Christ became human so that people would fixate on his flesh, but that they would look beyond his human nature to his unseen divinity. Cary explains Augustine's view:

> From the orthodox conclusion that Christ is mediator in his humanity, Augustine draws the conclusion that Christ's humanity is means not end, a Way by which we travel but not the destination at which we arrive. Our hearts are purified by faith not to gaze at the glory of God in the human face of Jesus Christ, as in the Eastern Orthodox theology of transfiguration, but to contemplate the eternal Truth prior to all creation and present even apart from the incarnation to every pure mind. . . . Christ comes in the flesh to direct us away from fleshly things, not to get us clinging to his body—even his body fixed on the cross or freed from the grave.[27]

Therefore, people are saved through Christ, who mediates between God and humans by being the bridge (i.e., God-man) from the external realm (i.e., through his humanity) to the inner realm (i.e., through his divinity).

According to Cary and Jenson, Augustine's de-emphasis on Christ's flesh (and on sensible things in general) renders a significant chink in his account of the "inward, upward turn" through which salvation happens. Christ incarnate is the "way to God" primarily in a Platonic sense: Jesus' human nature is "ultimately instrumental and of only temporary

---

26. Augustine, *The City of God* (1950), 11.2. Jowers lists four reasons that Augustine said Christ became man: "1) to be assured of God's love and thus rescued from despair; 2) to be humbled that we may seek salvation from Him and not ourselves; 3) to be shown an exemplar of how we must live in order to attain eternal salvation; and 4) a sacrifice of one who is both God and man to atone for our sins." Jowers, "Divine Unity and the Economy of Salvation," 77.

27. Cary, *Outward Signs*, 133–34.

importance."[28] Jenson continues, "It offers a 'short cut to participation in his own divine nature', but our hope is in the day when his office of mediator will cease and we will participate in the divine life directly."[29]

Augustine considers the inward turn, therefore, not as a gaze upon the image of the incarnate Christ or upon any image of sensible things, but upon the intelligible soul, which is the image of God. By gazing upon themselves, people are humbled to find that they are not self-sufficient, but that "there is someone who is at once more deeply foundational and far above us in grandeur."[30] Christ mediates this realization by his example; he humbled himself by becoming a man, and because of his humility he was exalted. Christ shows people that they need to lower their proud eyes from themselves, so that they can raise them up to God. Yet, even though looking upon Christ's humility (i.e., his becoming a man) points the way to God (i.e., being humbled), it is not the same as looking upon God. For, it is not Christ's human nature that is to be dwelt upon, but his divinity: "Our hearts are purified by faith not to gaze at the glory of God in the human face of Jesus Christ . . . but to contemplate the eternal Truth prior to all creation and present even apart from the incarnation to every pure mind."[31]

In this respect, Augustine's Platonic perspective puts him at odds with Scripture, in which salvation consists in looking at the whole Christ, not just at his divinity (2 Cor 3:18; 4:6). Consequently, Augustine's conception of the inward turn is inadequate insofar as it consists of seeing "through" the human image of Christ rather than focusing there: "He looks for the *imago Dei* in himself without sufficient attention paid to Christ, who is himself the *imago Dei*. . . . Where he fails is in neglecting to look to *Christ* to see God."[32]

Augustine on Interventions

As we have seen, Augustine framed his discussion of sin in terms of the outer self versus the inner self, or of body versus soul/mind. Such a framing of humanity's problem also frames the solution: to be restored to

28. Jenson, *The Gravity of Sin*, 35.

29. Jenson, *The Gravity of Sin*, 35. See Augustine, *The Trinity*, 1.3.20.

30. Jenson, *The Gravity of Sin*, 41.

31. Cary, *Outward Signs*, 123.

32. Jenson, *The Gravity of Sin*, 43.

wholeness as a human being—that is, to be saved—involves a conversion, or a turning away from seeking God in external things to seeking him through the inner self. Interventions fostering this conversion would, therefore, interrupt people's fixation and love of sensible things and direct them to consider intelligible realities, ultimately ending in the intellectual vision of God. What form would such interventions take?

Only Intelligible Things Have Power to Convert

It seems that Augustine was conflicted about the answer, for although he upheld the importance of external signs, such as the sacraments, he believed the real work of conversion happens in the mind, in the realm of ideas. That being the case, whatever is external to the mind, or whatever is sensible rather than intelligible, has no power to convert.[33] In other words, according to Augustine, the only efficacious interventions for conversion are those within the mind itself.

Conversion is fostered by thought, reflection, and reason. The problem we must overcome is the impurity of our minds and sinful attachment to earthly things; our minds can reach up to God, but in order to do this we need to take our attention away from external things. Once we replace our desire for sensible things with a right desire for God, our minds will be purified so that we can know God: "Purity of heart, interpreted Platonistically as a mind cleansed of desire for sensible things, is evidently all we need to see God."[34]

Only Christ Can Show Us the Way

At the same time, Augustine was no mere Platonist. He did not believe that people can purify themselves through reason alone. Rather, Augustine believed sinners are saved through Christ.

Although the inward turn has its dangers due to its lack of focus on Jesus' humanity, Augustine avoided the error and pride of the Neoplatonists who thought humans could find God simply by looking inside themselves. Such pride brought about humanity's fall: "man, who had become pleased with himself due to his pride, was now given over to himself. . . . He had forsaken eternal life, and, unless delivered by grace,

33. Cary, *Outward Signs*.
34. Cary, *Augustine's Invention of the Inner Self*, 74.

he was condemned to eternal death."[35] Since in pride humans fell into themselves, their salvation consists in more than an inward turn, which just tends to induce pride.

The way back to God is the path of self-abasement and humility.[36] Augustine writes, "there is in humility something that lifts up the heart, and there is in exaltation something that brings it down."[37] That "something" is the direction taken: either *toward self* (pride) or *toward God* (humility). Humbled people move toward God. That is why humility is a virtue, leading to God, whereas pride is a vice: "in one the love of God comes before all else and in the other love of self."[38] The reorientation of humility stops people from "being pleased" with themselves, so that they "who were pleased with themselves when they were seeking their own name might be pleased with [God] when they seek [his] name."[39] Humility is the true way to goodness and happiness, because it ends with pleasure in God, which is exactly what makes people most satisfied.

But how do sinners come to see humility in this light? While humility is not valued in the "city of man," Augustine says, it is "especially commended in the city of God . . . and humility is especially proclaimed in its king, who is Christ."[40] In Christ, humanity's pride is put to shame and cast down; yet, in this humbling, humanity is also raised up. While in one sense Jesus' crucifixion demonstrates the futility of pride that leads to death, it also displays the process of humbling that results in exaltation. By dying the death humanity deserved, Jesus showed that death is the just outcome of the race that fell to pride. Yet, paradoxically and wonderfully, Christ's willing embrace of death also showed that death—when accepted humbly as the end and death of sin—can be the path to life. Augustine explains:

> For death is undoubtedly the punishment of all who are born in unbroken succession from the first man. But, if it is undergone for the sake of godliness and righteousness, it becomes the glory of those who are born again; and so, even though death is the

35. Augustine, *The City of God* (2013), 14.15.122.
36. Jenson, *The Gravity of Sin*, 33.
37. Augustine, *The City of God* (2013), 14.14.121.
38. Augustine, *The City of God* (2013), 14.14.120.
39. Augustine, *The City of God* (2013), 14.14.121.
40. Augustine, *The City of God* (2013), 14.14.120.

retribution for sin, it sometimes ensures that there is no retribution for sin.[41]

Augustine believed that because of the "wondrous grace of the savior the punishment of sin has itself been turned to the service of righteousness."[42] Sinners are saved from the descent of their pride by trusting that, by accepting death like Christ did (as the just end of their sin), they will receive life as he did (as the just reward of his righteousness). For Christians, "It is not that death, which was previously an evil, has now become good; it is rather that God has bestowed such wondrous grace on faith that death—which everyone agrees is the opposite of life—has become the means of passing into life."[43] Death, the most extreme form of human humbling, is transformed into the greatest exaltation for humans because of Christ.

Progressing Gradually toward Seeing God

Despite holding the mediation of God's grace through Christ as essential to salvation, Augustine seems to have considered just as important the primacy of intelligible things over sensible things. Augustine commends rational and reflective kinds of interventions because he believes they alone can effectively draw people's intellectual attention—and thus their love—away from lower things to God.

This movement, however, must be gradual in order to be effective, for otherwise it would repulse the mind that has not grown strong enough to receive the vision of God. Just as a person who through long days in darkness can't bear much light, and most of all a direct vision of the sun, so the mind that through many years has loved created things and become too weak to look on God's brightness withdraws from seeing God, turning away in pain and fear.[44] The most effective way to build up strength of vision is to gradually direct one's loves to brighter and brighter things; a classic liberal arts education, for example, would serve to turn one's mind away from lesser goods to greater goods, and ultimately to the Supreme Good.[45]

41. Augustine, *The City of God* (2013), 13.6.73.
42. Augustine, *The City of God* (2013), 13.4.72.
43. Augustine, *The City of God* (1950), 13.4.72.
44. Augustine, "Soliloquies," 1.23.
45. Cary, *Augustine's Invention of the Inner Self*, 73–76.

Augustine believed in a Christian vision of God, and so the movement towards God involved placing faith in explicitly Christian signs that pointed away from themselves to God. Because of the mind's impurity and inability to grasp the beatific vision, it must be made purer and stronger through faith:

> But because the mind itself, by nature the seat of reason and intelligence, is enfeebled by dark and inveterate faults and is unable not only to cling to and enjoy but even to endure God's immutable light, until it has been renewed from day to day, and healed, and made capable of such happiness, it had first to be trained and cleansed by faith.[46]

Thus, faith in the fleshly mediation of Christ, the testimony of Scripture, and external signs like the sacraments are necessary to train the mind to turn towards the pure vision of God.[47] However, while he valued the utility of these external signs, he thought they must be transcended in order to reach the truth, which is only received internally by the mind.

Summary of Augustine's Contribution

Augustine's overemphasis on the (Neoplatonic) turn towards the inner self stifles the role of faith in Christ. As I argued earlier, the problem of sin, deception, and pride requires gazing at Jesus, not just using him as a way to clear our intellectual vision and ascend to higher thoughts. While the inward turn may indeed lead people upward to God, this can only happen if God is seen in the face of Christ.

Nevertheless, Augustine's view bears great relevance for forming a Christian perspective on the true self and the false self. Human beings were created to thrive in their participation in the divine life. The turn away from God towards falsehood (sin, ontological dissolution) goes against human nature and wellbeing. By implication, then, whereas true self-understanding fits with wellbeing, false self-understanding comports with the downward spiral of sin towards death.

Likewise, whereas the true self results from living "according to God," the false self results from people living as if the ground of morality, ontology, and epistemology were to be found in themselves. Living according to themselves, people fixate on sensible things and experiences,

---

46. Augustine, *The City of God* (2013), 11.2.3.

47. Augustine, *The City of God* (2013), 11.2–3.3.

rather than following them as signs to God. To be saved means to see God clearly and to understand all external things as signs of him, through Christ's mediation. Of utmost need is an "inward upward turn" away from the merely sensible world, leading to the humble reflection that the ground of our knowledge and being is not ourselves but God. Getting stuck in either outward sense experiences or an inner turn that never moved "upward" correlates with false self-understanding. On the other hand, an inwardness that leads to a humble ascent to God correlates with true self-understanding.

The humility required to reorient to God comes from looking to Christ's humbling as a man, who died the death belonging to sinful humanity. Sinners mired in pride and deceit are humbled and enlightened by looking to Jesus and following his example of dying and ascending. Faith in Christ's incarnate mediation, therefore, is bound up with recognizing the truth about oneself.

Seeing the truth, however, does not come all at once. Augustine emphasizes that understanding the truth can only occur gradually. We start out in darkness, and we can handle illumination only by degrees. We require training, as students moving through a course of instruction, developing and strengthening our ability to grasp and love what is true.

Martin Luther

Martin Luther provides a psychological perspective on the self that is deeply grounded in theology. Knowledge of the self, in his view, is meant to lead to self-conscious grounding in God.

Luther on the Self

God Creates Individuals

Luther's theology of creation provides the necessary context for understanding his view of the self. God creates both the human race and the individual human. God's act of creation in the beginning was profoundly personal.[48] Rather than merely initiating creation and setting it up to run its course, God formed every single creature through his word. Luther writes:

48. Schwanke, "Luther's Theology of Creation," 201–2.

> If you look at my person, I am something new, because sixty years ago I was nothing. Such is the judgement of the world. But God's judgement is different; for in God's sight I was begotten and multiplied immediately when the world began, because God's words "Let Us make man" created me too.[49]

God created humanity and also individual humans. Luther's theology of creation highlights the importance of human individuality and the personal, one-on-one relationship that God has with every man. Luther does not want us to miss the fact that every person is one whom God creates, addresses, and waits upon to respond.

Self-Conscious Grounding in God

Human existence is grounded in God. Luther believed that God's dialogue with human beings is what creates and sustains them; humans exist as dialogical creatures.[50] But further, humans are constituted by a self-conscious grounding in God, as Slenczha explains:

> To be precise: every doctrine of creation, also those of the pre-Reformation period, holds that human creatures are externally constituted and grounded inescapably in someone outside themselves. But, according to Luther, this does not simply describe an objective view of the human life as being constituted by another person or by God, but is a manner of self-awareness—not simply being constituted but being aware of being constituted.[51]

To become whole human beings requires a conscious relationship with God, in which we consent to receive our identity from God within that relationship.

Luther on the False Self

Self-Deceived Grounding in Oneself

Like Augustine, Luther associated sin with attraction to the world and a carnal orientation toward life rather than a spiritual orientation. However, Luther's understanding of flesh and spirit and of the outer and inner

---

49. As quoted in Schwanke, "Luther's Theology of Creation," 202.
50. Schwanke, "Luther's Theology of Creation," 205.
51. Slenczka, "Luther's Anthropology," 217.

person was markedly different. Whereas Augustine focused on these categories as two ontological parts of human beings (i.e., body-soul), Luther understood them to describe two different orientations that humans can take. According to Luther, the flesh and the outer man do not refer to the lower part of human nature (i.e., the body), and neither do the spirit and inner man refer to the human soul; rather, they describe two opposing ways that humans relate to God: the fleshly human opposes God, while the spiritual human clings to him through faith.[52]

Luther understood the Pauline contrast between spirit and flesh in a different way than Augustine: the purpose of the contrast is not to pit intelligible reality (spirit) against sensible (flesh), following Greek philosophers like Plotinus, but to draw out the antithesis between confidence in the flesh (i.e., one's own abilities) and confidence in one's relationship with God. For Luther, this antithesis between flesh and spirit is just another way of stating the difference between sin and faith.

According to Luther, sin is the opposite of faith; sin is unbelief.[53] But to comprehend Luther's view, we must ask about the content of faith and unbelief: What does faith grasp that the sinner refuses to believe? For the believer, the answer is that "God's goodness reaches me." Whereas sin consists fundamentally in doubting and despairing of God's love, faith consists in trusting that God's goodness reaches me: "it is faith understood as trust which ascribes to God all positive predicates, in that it expects all things from him."[54]

Just as Luther understood humanity's constitution to be profoundly personal and spiritual, he understood humanity's dissolution in sin to be the same. People receive their true humanity and wellbeing by knowing and experiencing themselves to be grounded in God. By refusing to know themselves in this way, they have lost a core feature of human existence. According to Slenczka, for Luther the aim and result of sin is to ground one's existence in oneself, cut off from relationship with God.[55] Sin is both the refusal to trust in God and the confidence people have to save themselves, to attain wellbeing alone.

However, since by definition we are only truly ourselves when we consent to our grounding in God, by presuming to ground ourselves

---

52. Slenczka, "Luther's Anthropology," 216.

53. Batka, "Luther's Teaching on Sin and Evil," 241–42.

54. Slenczka, "Luther's Anthropology," 216.

55. Slenczka, "Luther's Anthropology," 222.

outside of God we forfeit a humanity that is genuine and authentic. Because people do not understand themselves in relation to God as the creator and sustainer of their existence, their lives become corrupt and their humanity vitiated. False self-understanding, then, lies at the core of humanity's fallen condition:

> Luther asserted that the sinner's inability to recognize sinfulness in himself is not an incidental element in this sinfulness, as if the question of what is actually sin in the human essence can be answered quite apart from this assertion. Rather, it is this inability to know oneself correctly that is the determining factor in sin itself.[56]

In sin, I know myself wrongly. Rather than knowing myself as dependent being who is constituted by God, as a sinner I conceive myself as independent and self-sufficient, not needing redemption.

Luther believed that sin exerts its power over the individual through self-deception. Every capacity of humans, including reason, is under sin's power, so people use reason to deceive themselves into believing they are self-sufficient and autonomous. It is the failure to understand oneself accurately that empowers sin. Sin does not necessitate a total lack of self-understanding, and people can recognize certain features of themselves apart from faith, such as the material nature they share with other animals, as well as the capacity for rational thought that sets them apart.[57] Nonetheless, in sin humans cannot conceive of their fundamental dependence on God or of their created purpose to be in relationship with God. Sinners choose to trust in themselves rather than God. Sinners remain deceived in sin by believing a lie about themselves: that by their own abilities, especially their power of reason, they can achieve true humanity, salvation, wholeness, the good life, and so on.

Leaning on Our Own Understanding

Through reason and conscience, we can apprehend the demands of God's law on us, but by relying on reason, we presume that we can fulfill these demands. Slenczka explains the three postures Luther said people take to the voice of the law:

---

56. Slenczka, "Luther's Anthropology," 222.
57. Slenczka, "Luther's Anthropology," 217–18.

The posture of ignorance suppresses it or does not listen to it. In the posture of '*superbia*' (pride) people regard the law as something they can fulfill and deal with it on the basis of this presumption; this is a condition in which they deceive themselves and become obdurate. It slips into '*desparatio*' (despair) when they realize that the demand to give account of oneself does not expect only the fulfilling of the law in external actions but the harmony of the human will with God's will in this demand.[58]

Sometimes our response is to avoid the law, sometimes to pursue its fulfillment, and sometimes to face it but despair of its fulfillment. In all three forms of response sinners presume it is up to them to keep the law and that it is in their power. The basis for this presumption is the power of reason: "Sinners see reason, which distinguishes them from other forms of life, as the foundation for complying with the demand within themselves."[59] By placing such confidence in their power to reason, people lock themselves into sin and self-deception.

Luther on the True Self

Receiving Love to Become Loving

Salvation, according to Luther, centers on justification. The gospel's declaration of forgiveness means that anyone who receives it is forgiven and made new.[60] The word of the gospel effects a new status and life for the sinner who believes, just as God's word of creation effects something out of nothing: "Justification by faith alone, in which God creates new creatures out of the nothingness of sin, parallels Luther's doctrine of creation, in which God creates and preserves all things out of nothingness."[61]

According to Luther, when someone receives forgiveness and believes, he or she is enabled to cooperate with God in sanctification. Good works certainly must come in the Christian's life, like a tree naturally produces fruit. Further, a Christian should approach life in the world as

---

58. Slenczka, "Luther's Anthropology," 224.

59. Slenczka, "Luther's Anthropology," 224.

60. Scholars have disagreed on Luther's view of justification, particularly concerning its qualifications as forensic and effective. I will assume the traditional view against the "Finnish" school led by Mannermaa. For both perspectives, see Mattes, "Luther on Justification," 264–73; Mannermaa, *Christ Present in Faith*.

61. Mattes, "Luther on Justification," 265.

a servant who loves his neighbor, unceasingly seeking the good of others in faithful action.

The life of the Christian *coram mundo* (before the world), however, must be distinguished from life *coram Deo* (before God), and the former must be fueled by the latter. Salvation means that believers continually receive the Spirit and by the *vita passiva* of faith allow God to work within and through them.[62] Faith forms and orients love, and love is the outward expression of those who live a receptive life of faith.[63]

Moreover, Christians' progress in sanctification cannot be measured by the amount or weightiness of good works, as many opponents of Luther held.[64] Rather, progress in such terms is largely hidden, and what marks sanctification is not outward piety or the absence of sin but the fuller awareness of sin and God's grace.[65]

Boldly Believing in the True Self

The believer's salvation in this life is chiefly characterized by faith in the gospel, which is the fight to believe the truth about oneself. Luther maintained that—in contrast to the monastic vision of holiness and piety touted by Catholicism in his day—the real challenge for Christians is to boldly believe what the gospel declares about them as sinners and saints.[66] This is the most important and formidable task of Christian living, because it directly confronts the fleshly condition that defined humanity's old existence in slavery to sin, death, and the devil. Salvation entails redemption and liberation from bondage to these evil powers.[67] Under them, people are held captive to falsehood and self-deception, so that they cannot know who they truly are, but through receiving the gospel they take hold of the truth about themselves: that they are simultaneously a saint and a sinner, *simul justus et peccator*.[68] To receive this identity means consenting to the plight of our sinful condition, which remains throughout our earthly life. Salvation in this life means neither

---

62. Mattes, "Luther on Justification," 265.

63. Wannenwetsch, "Luther's Moral Theology," 128–29, 133–34.

64. Arnold, "Luther on Christ's Person and Work," 278.

65. Silcock, "Luther on the Holy Spirit and His Use of God's Word," 305.

66. Strohl, "Luther's Spiritual Journey," 155–58.

67. Arnold, "Luther on Christ's Person and Work," 284.

68. Althaus, *The Theology of Martin Luther*, 242–45.

instantaneous nor gradual sinlessness. Rather, it means owning my sin and believing it goes so deep that I cannot plumb its depths. On the other hand, salvation also means I believe my sin has been imputed to Christ and expiated in his death. In a "happy exchange," my sin is transferred to Christ and Christ's righteousness is imputed to me.[69] The identity believers' receive in union with Christ is that of another person, the crucified and risen Christ.[70] As one who is crucified, I trust that I am a sinner who must die, but as one who is risen, I also trust that I am counted righteous and will live.[71]

Luther on Interventions

Four Gospel-Imaging Interventions

Luther believed that the primary intervention for fostering this new identity is the gospel. Salvation means we discard a theology of glory, in which we presumed to save ourselves, and instead live by a theology of the cross, in which, as both helpless sinners and righteous sons and daughters, we receive God's love and grace. Kolb captures Luther's understanding in a few sentences,

> until sinners recognize their failure to trust in the true God, revealed in Jesus Christ, they are blind to the depth and the root cause of their troubles in this world. The law crushes sinful pretensions to lordship over life in many ways, but only by driving people to the cross can it focus their understanding clearly enough to see that the original, root, fundamental sin that perverts and corrupts life lies in this lack of trust. When his human creatures do apprehend who God is, in the fullness of his love, they then see themselves as his beloved children. This perception of ourselves as the heirs of Christ and members of the Father's family liberates us from the bondage of caring for ourselves and presiding over our own destinies.[72]

According to Luther, sin is fundamentally about doubting, mistrusting, or disbelieving who God is for us, so that we rely on ourselves. Salvation is, therefore, about trusting that God loves us as his own children, so

---

69. Bayer, *Martin Luther's Theology*, 225–30.

70. Slenczka, "Luther's Anthropology," 220–22.

71. Kolb, "Luther on the Theology of the Cross," 51–56.

72. Kolb, "Luther on the Theology of the Cross," 52.

that we rely on him. Further, whereas mistrust of God is always accompanied by a false perception of oneself, trust in God is accompanied by a right perception. Mistrust breeds an identity of self-reliance and idolatry, which results in despair. When people mistrust God, they make themselves out to be self-sufficient, as if they were God, and the weight of this false identity will eventually crush them. But if they trust in God, they will receive the gospel, which is the truth about themselves as dependent children of God, and this identity brings hope and joy.

In the following passage, Luther asserts that God has ordained the use of four particular "images" that effectively communicate his Word and gospel:

> In the New Testament we have Baptism, the Lord's Supper, absolution, and the ministry of the Word. . . . These are the divine images and "the will of the sign." Through them God deals with us within the range of our comprehension. Therefore these alone must engage our attention.[73]

Let us begin with "the ministry of the Word," or preaching.[74]

Preaching

Luther maintained that when the gospel is preached, God himself is speaking.[75] Effective preaching is not information about God but *Deus loquens*, God speaking. Wingren explains the difference between sermons about God and sermons that communicate God's voice:

> The Lutheran assertion that . . . preaching, in so far as it is Biblical preaching, is God's own speech to men, is very difficult to maintain in practice. Instead it is very easy to slip into the idea that preaching is only speech about God. Such a slip, once made, gradually alters the picture of God, so that he becomes the far-off deistic God who is remote from the preached word and is only spoken about as we speak about someone who is absent.[76]

---

73. Luther, *Luther's Works*, 2:47.

74. While Luther maintained the importance of the written word, he considered preaching more important than writing. For that reason, observations are limited to his thoughts on preaching. See Ferry, "Martin Luther on Preaching," 271; Silcock, "Luther on the Holy Spirit and His Use of God's Word," 300–302.

75. Wilson, "Luther on Preaching as God Speaking," 63–76.

76. Wingren, *The Living Word*, 19.

While the human preacher communicates God's speaking through his own personality, it is still God's word that is preached.[77] Preaching allows people to hear the gospel as God's word to them. Preaching is a vocalized word that reaches people through the human voice, thus coming to people in a familiar and personal way. In this regard, preaching the gospel has an advantage over other forms of conveying the gospel. As God's speaking, preaching initiates a conversation with the individual hearer. By speaking to people in preaching, God calls for personal responses from them.[78]

Baptism and the Lord's Supper

Luther thought the sacraments of baptism and the Lord's Supper communicated the gospel. A sacrament is a sign combined with a divine word of promise. Luther says, "For to constitute a sacrament there must be above all things else a word of divine promise, by which faith may be exercised."[79] Thus, one may say that the word of the gospel "interprets the sacraments, and the sacraments enact the gospel."[80] God has instituted two such sacraments in Scripture: baptism and the Lord's Supper.[81] The promise attached to these signs is forgiveness of sins, life, and salvation. The individual's conscience, which is easily dissuaded of God's love, needs baptism and communion as an experiential expression of God's salvation in Christ: "The Supper is not a general announcement about the how of human salvation; it is the experience of one's personal salvation through the body . . . in the here and now."[82]

Baptism and the Lord's Supper both convey the same word of promise, the gospel, but in different ways. Baptism is the act of being immersed

77. Wilson, "Luther on Preaching as God Speaking," 67.

78. Wilson, "Luther on Preaching as God Speaking," 71.

79. Quoted in Althaus, *The Theology of Martin Luther*, 345.

80. Silcock, "Luther on the Holy Spirit and His Use of God's Word," 300.

81. Althaus explains why other practices and institutions, such as marriage, are not sacraments: "Sacramental character ultimately depends on the presence of a divine word of promise. Where this is missing, as in marriage or confirmation, one cannot speak of a sacrament. On the other hand, however, there are realities and deeds in the Christian life such as prayer, hearing and meditating on the word, and the cross, to which God has attached a promise. But they lack the characteristic of a sign or a symbol. This is the case, for example, in the so-called sacrament of penance." Althaus, *The Theology of Martin Luther*, 345–46.

82. Strohl, "Luther's Spiritual Journey," 159.

in water and brought back up, and this act signifies that the sinful, old life of a person is put to death and that he is raised to new life.[83] Although its enactment is a one-time event, Luther taught that believers should cling to baptism as a daily practice. Since their baptism is a symbol of their death to sin and of their resurrection, it applies to the rest of their lives as a believer.[84] They must daily remember that they have died and been raised:

> It signifies that the old creature in us with all sins and evil desires is to be drowned and die through daily contrition and repentance, and on the other hand that daily a new person is to come forth and rise up to live before God in righteousness and purity forever.[85]

In baptism, Christians consent to and participate in God's killing of the sinful, Adamic existence (i.e., the old man). Baptism is, ultimately, a reminder of our justification: "In baptism we are immediately given complete forgiveness of sins and purity in God's judgment."[86]

As in baptism, the effect of the Lord's Supper is to strengthen the individual's faith in God's gift of forgiveness, life, and salvation for him.[87] The Lord's Supper strengthens one's faith by depicting the New Covenant (or Testament), which consists of Christ's body and blood, symbolized in bread and wine. Luther says, "The body and blood contain the New Testament; the New Testament conveys the forgiveness of sins; the forgiveness of sins brings eternal life and salvation."[88] The body and blood are Christ's who died on the cross, and so in receiving this sacrament, believers trust that Christ's work on the cross to forgive sins applies to them. Luther taught that Christ instituted the Lord's Supper as a last will and testament for his disciples and all believers.[89] As such, the Lord's Supper conveys the legacy that Christ's heirs receive after his death: forgiveness, life, and salvation. Luther opposed the Catholic view of the Mass as a sacrifice that confers forgiveness *ex opera operatum*, instead holding that it calls us to remember, strengthens our faith, and comforts

83. Althaus, *The Theology of Martin Luther*, 354.

84. Althaus, *The Theology of Martin Luther*, 354–55.

85. Kolb et al., *The Book of Concord*, 360.

86. Althaus, *The Theology of Martin Luther*, 356.

87. Althaus, *The Theology of Martin Luther*, 401–3.

88. Althaus, *The Theology of Martin Luther*, 401.

89. Schwarz, "The Last Supper," 198–210.

us when we despair because of a troubled conscience.[90] Those who feel their unworthiness are reminded by the Lord's Supper that forgiveness is given to them to believe and not doubt.

Absolution through Confession

Finally, Luther pointed to a fourth gospel intervention: absolution through confession.[91] He said, "We must have much absolution so that we may strengthen our fearful consciences and despondent hearts against the devil. Therefore no one should forbid confession."[92]

Rittgers identifies the following parts of confession as it was practiced by Luther and other evangelical reformers: "an examination of faith (that is, knowledge of the catechism) and outward moral conduct, an acknowledgement of one's depravity, and a voluntary confession of private sins followed by pastoral counsel and absolution."[93] Believers may receive absolution through general or private confession, but Luther stressed the importance of private confession, because it demonstrated that the gospel is God speaking to the individual.[94] Luther did not consider absolution to be a sacrament, yet, when received in faith it cleansed the conscience.[95]

The power of absolution resides in the Word of God and not in any other person or authority, and for this reason any Christian can administer absolution.[96] In fact, a person strong enough in faith can confess and receive forgiveness without the aid of another, but through simply hearing and responding to the preached Word.[97]

The power of confession and absolution comes from the fact that the word of absolution (e.g., "You are forgiven") is God's Word of absolution: "For Christ did not intend to base our comfort, our salvation, our confidence on human words or deeds, but only upon himself, upon

90. Strohl, "Luther's Spiritual Journey," 162–63.

91. Luther strongly opposed the Catholic sacrament of penance, which he distinguished from confession. See Rittgers, "Luther on Private Confession," 312–31.

92. Luther, *Luther's Works*, 51:99.

93. Rittgers, "Luther on Private Confession," 313.

94. Rittgers, "Luther on Private Confession," 314–16.

95. Rittgers, "Luther on Private Confession."

96. Rittgers, "Luther on Private Confession," 313.

97. Rittgers, "Luther on Private Confession," 313, 315.

his words and deeds."[98] Like preaching, baptism, and the Lord's Supper, absolution is simply a form of the gospel. The word of absolution is particularly akin to preaching in that it is God speaking the gospel: "For it is not the voice or the word of the person speaking it, but it is the Word of God, who forgives sin."[99]

In summary, what we have labeled as interventions Luther called "images" or "masks," referring to his belief that God was hidden behind them. These interventions serve as external signs of God, communicating God's Word of promise, the gospel. Their efficacy lies in this fact. Furthermore, while we must receive these images of the gospel in faith, our faith is not sufficient in itself; what helps us is not our faith but the object of our faith. Luther made this distinction in order to preserve faith from becoming, as Trigg says, "one more exercise in human spirituality to add to all the others," and to place "the weight entirely on the promise of God."[100] Faith must be *in God's Word*, however it is spoken, whether in preaching, baptism, the Lord's supper, absolution, or another form.

Søren Kierkegaard

Moving now to Søren Kierkegaard, we find a spiritual heir of Luther, whose insights arose from his faith in God's Word. Kierkegaard held that humans are only truly fulfilling their natural design when they relate themselves to God.

Kierkegaard on the Self

Relating as Spirit

Lying at the core of what it means to be human, says Kierkegaard, is the capacity for self-consciousness. The power to be conscious of oneself and to relate to oneself as the object of one's consciousness makes human beings unique among God's creatures. Kierkegaard said that God created humanity with this power so that humans could relate to him in a special way: as spirit. While all creatures stand in relation to God by virtue of their dependence upon him as the one who created and sustains them,

---

98. Luther, *Luther's Works*, 35:10; see Trigg, "Luther on Baptism and Penance," 318.
99. The Augsburg Confession, Article 25.1 in Kolb et al., *The Book of Concord*, 72.
100. Trigg, "Luther on Baptism and Penance," 317.

only human beings are "spirit." To be spirit means that humans relate to God (and others) self-consciously.

Here are a few passages that summarize Kierkegaard's understanding of human beings:

> A human being is spirit. But what is spirit? Spirit is the self. But what is self? The self is a relation that relates itself to itself. . . . A human being is a synthesis of the infinite and the finite, of the temporal and the eternal, of freedom and necessity, in short, a synthesis.[101]

> The human self is such a derived, established relation, a relation that relates itself to itself and in relating itself to itself relates itself to another.[102]

> man's superiority over the animal . . . distinguishes him in quite another way than does his erect walk, for it indicates infinite erectness or sublimity, that he is spirit.[103]

As Kierkegaard says, being spirit relates to two other defining characteristics of humanity: being a *self* and a *synthesis*.

First, a spirit is a self which is "a relation that relates itself to itself." Human beings, therefore, are defined as being essentially reflexive, that is, they can relate to themselves. Furthermore, because they are such a self-conscious/reflexive being, they can relate to "another," that is, God. The reason for this is that the capacity for consciousness can be directed to anything. As a result, consciousness of self is intimately tied to consciousness of God: the human self is "a derived, established relation" that senses and understands itself out of its relation to another person, especially God, who made humans to relate primarily to him. The highest form of spirit is relating self-consciously to God; however, there are other forms of spirit and other persons to whom one might relate.[104] Although the God-relationship is the most important one—the one intended to make people really human in the fullest sense—other relationships can

---

101. Kierkegaard, *The Sickness unto Death*, 13. To be clear, Kierkegaard's usage of "self" refers to the self-as-subject or the I-self.

102. Kierkegaard, *The Sickness unto Death*, 13–14.

103. Kierkegaard, *The Sickness unto Death*, 15.

104. As Evans says, "spirituality can take many forms and can have various qualities. If my being as spirit is constituted by relationships, then the nature of those relationships will determine the nature of my being. What I relate to and the character of those relations shape my identity." Evans, *Søren Kierkegaard's Christian Psychology*, 47.

shape people and determine who and what they are and try to become. A self's relationships, whether with God or others, provide a "criterion" or ideal to which the self stretches and strives to attain.[105] To the degree that people relate to God, they are more or less conscious of their highest criterion and who and what they truly are and are meant to become. Thus, Kierkegaard says:

> A cattleman who (if this were possible) is a self directly before his cattle is a very low self, and, similarly, a master who is a self directly before his slaves is actually no self—for in both cases a criterion is lacking. The child who previously has had only his parents as a criterion becomes a self as an adult by getting the state as a criterion, but what an infinite accent falls on the self by having God as the criterion![106]

The nature of humans as spirit means that people judge themselves according to a relationship with another (i.e., an outside criterion), whether it be God, another person, or even a lesser creature (e.g., cattle). And, furthermore, the power that enables humans to do this is self-consciousness; people are able to judge themselves against an outside criterion because they can be conscious of themselves.

Living as a Synthesis of Finitude and Freedom

Kierkegaard also wrote that humans are "a synthesis of the infinite and the finite, of the temporal and the eternal, of freedom and necessity, in short, a synthesis."[107] Although humans have much in common with other animals, the power of self-consciousness sets them apart. While God created other creatures to exist and be what they are automatically, with no self-consciousness or choice, God created humans with the power and freedom to willfully choose whether or not to be themselves. Humans are superior to other animals because they are spirit or self, and because in their self-consciousness they have some sense of God's infinity, eternality, and freedom. However, this sense is very limited, because humans will never fully possess these divine attributes due to

---

105. Kierkegaard, *The Sickness unto Death*, 79.

106. Kierkegaard, *The Sickness unto Death*, 79.

107. Kierkegaard, *The Sickness unto Death*, 13.

their finitude, temporality, and necessity.[108] We live in the middle of these two dimensions of our being.

In essence, what Kierkegaard means in saying that humans are a synthesis is that humans yearn to be like God while being very much unlike God. On the one hand, we are unlike God because we are physical creatures restricted by our bodily nature, temporal existence, and dependence on things outside of us. On the other hand, we are spiritual/self-conscious beings who are free to choose whether to be what God intends us to be or to refuse. The spiritual (i.e., infinite, free, eternal) side of the synthesis constitutes humanity's superiority and "infinite erectness or sublimity"; this is what it means for humans to be made in the image of God. In this regard, Kierkegaard understood the power of self-consciousness to be a great gift and advantage, for it means that when God calls us to be ourselves, he calls us to be like him in freely embracing our nature and existence.

Kierkegaard on the False Self

Choosing Despair

Although Kierkegaard considered humanity's self-consciousness to be characterized by synthesis, he also saw that capacity contributing to humanity's worst misfortune and misery, which he called *despair*.[109] Because God gives us the freedom to choose whether or not we will relate ourselves to him (i.e., with him as our criterion), it is possible to refuse to do so, and thereby to forfeit what God intends for us. To forfeit our spiritual nature is to live in despair. Again, the condition that leads to despair is our freedom to self-consciously relate ourselves to God or not:

---

108. Evans elaborates more fully, saying, "Infinity, eternity, and freedom focus on what we might call the expansive poll of the synthesis. Fundamentally, it is the power of consciousness that underlies this aspect of the self. Consciousness gives us the power to imagine what does not exist. . . . This expansive, infinitizing pole is hardly the whole story, however. The limiting, finite side of the self comes clearly into view when I reflect on my bodily character. Because I am a physical being, I have only a limited number and range of experiences. The body informs me that I have not chosen to be born at all and that I did not choose to be born to my particular parents at a particular place. My bodily character highlights the precariousness of my being, my constant dependence on conditions that I try to control with varying degrees of success." Evans, *Søren Kierkegaard's Christian Psychology*, 51.

109. Kierkegaard, *The Sickness unto Death*, 15.

> Where then, does the despair come from? From the relation
> in which the synthesis relates itself to itself, inasmuch as God,
> who constituted man a relation, releases it from his hand, as
> it were—that is, inasmuch as the relation relates itself to itself.
> And because the relation is spirit, is the self, upon it rests the
> responsibility for all despair at every moment of its existence.[110]

Humanity's worst misery, despair, emerges out of two realities: first, God makes despair possible since he allows humans to understand and choose their existence as they wish; and second, humans bring it about by wrongly construing and choosing their existence. Thus, the responsibility for despair rests on the way a person chooses to act as spirit or self, in "relating itself to itself."

In actuality, as sinners all human beings choose despair, according to Kierkegaard. Rather than choose to be what God calls them to be, people reject that way of life and live in despair. Using the analogy of physical health and sickness, Kierkegaard explains:

> Just as a physician might say that there very likely is not one
> single living human being who is completely healthy, so anyone
> who really knows mankind might say that there is not one single
> living human being who does not despair a little, who does not
> secretly harbor an unrest, an inner strife, a disharmony, an
> anxiety about an unknown something or a something he does
> not even dare to try to know, an anxiety about some possibil-
> ity in existence or an anxiety about himself, so that, just as the
> physician speaks of going around with an illness in the body, he
> walks around with a sickness, carries around a sickness of the
> spirit that signals its presence at rare intervals in and through an
> anxiety he cannot explain.[111]

As we have seen, being spirit means that we can relate to God self-con-sciously. However, when this advantage is forfeited, we become sick in spirit. This sickness is despair, or the failure to be the spirit or self we were created to be. Every person chooses through their freedom to deny their self-conscious relationship with God. Whether knowingly or not (and usually they do not know), all people live in some degree of despair as a result of this choice, although they mostly experience it as a secret sense of anxiety—a nagging worry that seems little, but which is in fact

110. Kierkegaard, *The Sickness unto Death*, 16.

111. Kierkegaard, *The Sickness unto Death*, 22.

an anxiety about their very existence, which is doomed to eternal despair due to their own choice.

Why do humans use their freedom to choose despair? The reason is ultimately inexplicable, and Kierkegaard says it is foolish to try, eschewing any "scientific" or objective explanation of why humans live in despair.[112] However, he does think we can know when despair first entered human existence: through the sin of Adam and Eve. Their fall was a descent into despair.[113] Thus, Kierkegaard defines sin as despair, saying, "Sin is: before God in despair not to will to be oneself, or before God in despair to will to be oneself."[114] Nonetheless, human sinfulness or despair is universal, and every person in his or her own way "carries around" this sickness by choosing either "not to will to be oneself" or to "will to be oneself."

Despairing Unconsciously

When people usually think of despair they assume it is a feeling of despair, but this is only a superficial and misleading understanding, according to Kierkegaard.[115] Furthermore, people assume that despair is over something lost, like a career or a lover.[116] Actual despair, however, is always despair over oneself, as Evans explains: "Despair is basically a failure to be my self, a failure to be a self at all. Being aware of this failure constitutes the feeling of despair. It is a feeling of one's own nothingness and worthlessness."[117] As a result, humans despair over their existence, and because their spiritual condition is so despairing, they hide it from themselves. This explains why most of the time real despair goes unnoticed: people want to avoid it, and so they stifle any sense of self-consciousness as a spiritual being before God. Despite their unconsciousness of despair, however, people are no less despairing, as Kierkegaard says, "to be unaware of being defined as spirit is precisely what despair is."[118]

---

112. Although the cause of sin in general cannot be discovered, Kierkegaard says one may know how sin began in oneself. See his discussion in Kierkegaard, *The Concept of Anxiety*, 50–51.

113. Evans, *Søren Kierkegaard's Christian Psychology*, 61–64.

114. Kierkegaard, *The Sickness unto Death*, 81.

115. Kierkegaard, *The Sickness unto Death*, 23.

116. Kierkegaard, *The Sickness unto Death*, 19–20.

117. Evans, *Søren Kierkegaard's Christian Psychology*, 65.

118. Kierkegaard, *The Sickness unto Death*.

How do people hide their despair? By deceiving themselves. The unconsciousness of despair is self-willed, because everyone begins with some kind of awareness of God, and in order to avoid despair each person must repress his or her spiritual consciousness. This repression can take many forms.[119] We can "delay" by neglecting to respond to our spiritual consciousness until we have naturally forgotten about it. One can distract oneself from despair, as Kierkegaard says, "through work and busyness as diversionary means, yet in such a way that he does not entirely realize why he is doing it, that it is to keep himself in the dark."[120] Gradually, through self-deception, people become unconscious of their spiritual nature and their despair, and thus they succeed in "not willing to be oneself," or the person God calls them to be. While God allows for this deluded condition, the fault lies with humans: "Is it something that happens to a person? No it is his own fault. No one is born devoid of spirit, and no matter how many go to their death with this spiritlessness as the one and only outcome of their lives, it is not the fault of life."[121]

Kierkegaard regarded the unconsciousness of despair as a great tragedy and misery. The fact that most people live in despair due to false self-understanding is so wretched that Kierkegaard thought he could weep for eternity.[122] The only life that really counts as a wasted life, worth shedding such tears, is one lived without having known one's true self before God. Kierkegaard says,

> there is so much talk about wasting a life, but only that person's life was wasted who went on living so deceived by life's joys or its sorrows that he never became decisively and eternally conscious of spirit, as self, or, what amounts to the same thing, never became aware and in the deepest sense never gained the impression that there is a God and that "he," he himself, his self, exists before this God.[123]

119. Evans, *Søren Kierkegaard's Christian Psychology*, 86–88.

120. Kierkegaard, *The Sickness unto Death*, 48.

121. Kierkegaard, *The Sickness unto Death*, 102.

122. Kierkegaard, *The Sickness unto Death*, 27.

123. Kierkegaard, *The Sickness unto Death*, 26–27.

Kierkegaard on the True Self

Choosing Oneself and Resting Transparently in God

A life not wasted, according to Kierkegaard, means living self-consciously before God. When people are healed from the sickness of despair, they consent to their spiritual self, that is, their relationship to God and his calling upon them. Kierkegaard describes such spiritual health in these words: "The formula that describes the state of self when despair is completely rooted out is this: in relating itself to itself and in willing to be itself, the self rests transparently in the power that established it."[124] Therefore, as opposed to the condition of despair, spiritual health means that people choose to respond willingly to God and to "rest transparently" in relationship with him. Kierkegaard equates this condition with faith: "Faith is: that the self in being itself and in willing to be itself rests transparently in God."[125]

What does it mean for a self, to "be itself" and to "will to be itself"? It means that people accept who they truly are, and that they also consent to become all that God has made them to be. By faith people relent from their sinfulness and despair, in which they denied their true self and rejected the ideal God set before them. "Faith is the cure that enables a person to accept the concrete being he is, warts and all, and to move toward becoming the ideal person God has created him to be, since for God all things are possible."[126] Thus, for the self to "be itself" means that a person consents to his or her true self, and for the self to "will to be itself" means a person consents to conform to the ideal self to which God calls him or her.

What does it mean to "rest transparently in God"? It means that when people consent to the true self they are and the ideal self they must become they do so openly before God. Rather than, in despair, using their freedom to deny their self-conscious relationship with God, they embrace or "rest in" this relationship. Thus, Kierkegaard understood salvation and the real Christian life to consist of what he called "earnestness," or recognizing that God pays attention to oneself.[127] Furthermore, rather than avoiding God's gaze, a person who is "transparent" before God consents to God's full and complete knowledge of him or her.[128]

124. Kierkegaard, *The Sickness unto Death*, 14.

125. Kierkegaard, *The Sickness unto Death*, 82.

126. Evans, *Søren Kierkegaard's Christian Psychology*, 120.

127. Kierkegaard, *The Sickness unto Death*, 68–69.

128. In Evans' words, Kierkegaard's idea of transparency means "to be totally open

Therefore, on the one hand, for people to be totally open before God requires they be open to themselves, having true self-understanding. The more people are honest with themselves about who they are, the more they can be honest with God, since what is not known about oneself cannot be divulged to another. True self-understanding is—at least to a certain extent—necessary for salvation.

Accepting an Absurd Invitation

On the other hand, for people to be honest with themselves and God requires something more than self-examination or "inwardness." Salvation, the cure for despair, and true self-understanding come from outside through an encounter with God in Jesus Christ that either results in faith or offense. Kierkegaard thought that only a Christian can recognize or accept healing from despair: "to be aware of this sickness is the Christian's superiority over the natural man; to be cured of this sickness is the Christian's blessedness."[129] What does a Christian have that the natural man does not? The teaching of Christianity, or the gospel, as Kierkegaard describes it here:

> Christianity teaches that this individual human being—and thus every single individual human being . . . exists *before God*, this individual human being who perhaps would be proud of having spoken with the king once in his life, this human being who does not have the slightest illusion of being on intimate terms with this one or that one, this human being exists before God, may speak with God any time he wants to, assured of being heard by him—in short, this person is invited to live on the most intimate terms with God! Furthermore, for this person's sake, also for this very person's sake, God comes to the world, allows himself to be born, to suffer, to die, and this suffering God—he almost implores him and beseeches this person to accept the help that is offered to him![130]

---

and honest with God and with oneself. To be transparent is to have nothing to hide. Of course, I cannot really hide anything from an omniscient God, so Kierkegaard's meaning here must be that I willingly reveal everything and anything to God." Evans, *Søren Kierkegaard's Christian Psychology*, 58–59.

129. Kierkegaard, *The Sickness unto Death*, 15.

130. Kierkegaard, *The Sickness unto Death*, 85.

This message challenges human reason to the point of offense. True Christian belief, as opposed to what Kierkegaard called "Christendom," is founded on real historical facts that exist outside of people's imagination of it (e.g., that God became human) and that demonstrate such outrageous, gratuitous beneficence so as to seem scandalous and absurd (e.g., that God died for oneself and pays attention to the details of one's life). Kierkegaard likened the way the gospel comes to a person to the way a poor day laborer might receive the news that the mightiest emperor who ever lived had sent for him and said he wanted the day laborer to become his son-in-law; this person would find the message so strange and extraordinary so as to be incredible, and he would be tempted to disbelieve it and be offended, thinking it must be a joke or a ploy to make a fool out of him.[131] To believe such a message, says Kierkegaard, would require a "humble courage."[132] In the same way, those who are saved must make a leap beyond what shrewd reason tells them and receive God's encounter by faith, or else balk at the offer.[133]

Kierkegaard on Interventions

Calling People to Spiritual Self-Consciousness

The therapeutic goal in Kierkegaard's writings was to help people understand their spiritual condition, or to promote true self self-understanding, and to undermine their despair, that is, their lack of proper self-understanding. This goal directly depends on encountering God through Jesus Christ. As creatures of God, humans are meant to live in a special, intimate relationship with him. But this knowledge has been repressed. Therefore, Kierkegaard's goal was to help people gain more spiritual self-consciousness, which consists in being and knowing oneself, and in knowing God ever more fully.[134]

131. Kierkegaard, *The Sickness unto Death*, 84.

132. Kierkegaard, *The Sickness unto Death*, 85.

133. Kierkegaard distinguished between a pseudo-faith called "religiousness A" and real Christian faith called "religiousness B." The former tries to approach God with reason, but this approach fails because it prioritizes one's understanding, self-sufficiency, and self-determination over one's trust in God. See Evans, *Søren Kierkegaard's Christian Psychology*, 111.

134. Becoming more of a self and more conscious of oneself are inextricably tied to becoming more conscious of God and vice versa: "The more conception of God, the more self; the more self, the more conception of God." Kierkegaard, *The Sickness unto Death*, 129.

This goal was a humble one, for Kierkegaard did not presume to save people from despair but to point them to salvation. Since he believed that human beings are free to choose whether or not to be in relation with God, Kierkegaard did not think any technique or method could be guaranteed to move a person to faith.[135] Rather than convince people through reason (or deception) or coerce them with shame or fear, he called them to consider themselves as individuals—and especially as those who exist before God.[136]

Compelling Awareness by Communicating Indirectly

Kierkegaard's method for accomplishing this goal was a form of indirect communication modeled off of Socrates.[137] Like Socrates, Kierkegaard believed his countrymen were blind to the truth, and so he tried to become a stinging gadfly and arouse them out of self-deception.[138] He also believed that a direct approach to the problem (i.e., telling people who claimed to be Christians that they were deluded) would fail because a direct approach "presupposes that the recipient's ability to receive it is entirely in order, but here that is simply not the case—indeed, here a delusion is an obstacle.[139]

---

135. Evans, *Søren Kierkegaard's Christian Psychology*, 118–19.

136. Kierkegaard hoped that (at least a few) readers might read his works conscious of themselves not as one among the crowd but as "single individuals": "there is in a religious sense no public but only individuals, because the religious is earnestness, and earnestness is: the single individual. . . . And this is my faith, that however much confusion and evil and contemptibleness there can be in human beings as soon as they become the irresponsible and unrepentant "public," "crowd," etc.—there is just as much truth and goodness and lovableness in them when one can get them as single individuals. Oh, to what degree human beings would become—human and lovable beings—if they would become single individuals before God!" Kierkegaard, *The Essential Kierkegaard*, 135.

137. Evans, *Søren Kierkegaard's Christian Psychology*, 117.

138. Kierkegaard believed Socrates had called himself a gadfly because he tried, like Kierkegaard, to "sting" his contemporaries: "Why is it that no contemporary age can get along with witnesses to the truth. . . . This happens because his contemporaries . . . feel the sting of his existence; he forces them to a more strenuous decision. . . . I wonder why Socrates compared himself to a gadfly if it was not because he understood that his life among his contemporaries was a sting." Kierkegaard, *The Essential Kierkegaard*, 412.

139. Kierkegaard, *The Essential Kierkegaard*, 467.

In order to remove the obstacle of self-delusion, Kierkegaard's writings obliquely attempt to cast readers' reflections back to them, as in a mirror, and to make them more self-aware.[140] Writing under pseudonyms (e.g., Victor Eremita, Johannes de Silentio, Anti-Climacus), Kierkegaard produced works that presented different viewpoints on life held among his readers and gave them various personae with which they could relate and possibly catch a glimpse of themselves:

> He hoped his readers' encounter with these literary personae—aesthetes, ethical persons, and religious persons—would be like looking in a mirror. He hoped they would experience a shock of self-recognition that would startle them into moving on to the next stage.[141]

Thus, readers in the aesthetic stage (i.e., living by impulse and desire, without an external ethical commitment) might see themselves in the impulsive, aesthetic life of "Don Juan," who seduces hundreds of women, or in the more sophisticated aesthetic life of "A," who gratifies his desires for pleasure by listening to Mozart or watching a play. The aesthetic stage, as Kierkegaard calls it, is contrasted with the ethical stage in *Either/Or*, a pseudonymous work that pits the papers of the aesthete "A" with the letters of an ethical man named Judge William, also known as "B." Readers of *Either/Or* are confronted with the contrast between these two personae in order to force a choice of living either in the aesthetic stage of life or to ascend to the ethical stage. Readers who found themselves truly caught in this choice would be led to "inwardness" and "earnestness," that is, they would be forced to question whether they would continue living in immediacy and hedonism or if they would commit themselves to a higher set of values, given by God.

This is, however, just the beginning of Kierkegaard's artifice. For in actuality, the crucial issue is not that of choosing between the aesthetic and ethical, but of rising above both into the religious. The ethical life is not sufficient in itself, because it is not enough for people to take responsibility for themselves or to commit to a moral life; for, just as the purely aesthetic life is cut off from anything higher than itself, an ethical life based on moral striving is cut off from God. In opposition to living in this ethical autonomy, to live "religiously" means resigning oneself to utter dependence on God, because one acknowledges the impossibility

---

140. See Kierkegaard, *The Essential Kierkegaard*, 451.
141. Evans, *Søren Kierkegaard's Christian Psychology*, 96–97.

of upholding an ethical life. Although the truly religious person gives up on self-righteousness and realizes the necessity of grace, he or she does not take God's forgiveness and help for granted, as if it were applied to everyone regardless of their faith.[142] The religious person has become a Christian by receiving God's help through faith in Jesus Christ.

In order to lead readers to the realization that they are not living this way, as true Christians, Kierkegaard portrayed the religious viewpoint in other works (both under pseudonyms and his proper name), and in writing these he set up a contrast between the religious life and the others, the aesthetic and ethical. By interlacing all these works, that is, by moving from an aesthetic work to a religious (and vice versa), and by writing under a pseudonym in one place and his proper name in another, he provoked his readers to ask, first, which kind of life were they now living, and second, which kind of life Kierkegaard was promoting.

The goal of his authorship and its artifice was to help readers recognize their true selves and choose to move toward becoming true Christians (i.e., their ideal selves), but the method for leading them to the truth was, ironically, deceptive![143]

Kierkegaard attempted to clarify the nature of his works and, in particular, his reasons for using artifice and deception in his pseudonymous authorship.[144] The equivocality and "duplexity" that characterized his writings was intentional, not the result of changes in his thinking. No, he had always meant to employ the multiple contradictory perspectives of

---

142. The "humorist" represents people who, after working through the ethical stage, resign themselves to the fact that they cannot achieve its demands, and thus come to a relaxed attitude of "humor." The humorist, Evans explains, "has seen the problem of guilt, the humoristic contradiction between the ideals we humans recognize and our feeble progress toward those ideals. The humorist thinks we can smile at that contradiction because he believes that at bottom we are all saved." Evans, *Søren Kierkegaard's Christian Psychology*, 111.

143. In describing his writings as deceptive, Kierkegaard maintains that his goal was still to lead to the truth. His pseudonymous aesthetic works, specifically, were "deceptive" in that they appeared to promote falsehood, but in actuality they were part of a grand scheme to promote the truth: "But from the total point of view of my whole work as an author, the esthetic writing is a deception, and herein is the deeper significance of the *pseudonymity*. But a deception, that is indeed something rather ugly. To that I would answer: Do not be deceived by the word *deception*. One can deceive a person out of what is true, and—to recall old Socrates—one can deceive a person into what is true. Yes, in only this way can a deluded person actually be brought into what is true—by deceiving him." Kierkegaard, *The Essential Kierkegaard*, 467.

144. Kierkegaard, *The Essential Kierkegaard*, 449–81.

the aesthetic, the ethical, and the religious in order to oppose them. The reason was to address a problem he saw in "Christendom," which was that many who supposed themselves to be Christian, or religious, were actually living in unconscious despair and delusion, that is, in the aesthetic or the ethical. To effectively address this problem, he believed only an indirect approach would work. It would do no good to immediately present an opposing perspective; rather, to dispel the delusion would require an indirect method:

> Generally speaking, there is nothing that requires as gentle a treatment as the removal of an illusion. If one in any way causes the one ensnared to be antagonized, then all is lost. And this one does by a direct attack . . . demanding that another person confess to one or face-to-face with one make the confession that actually is most beneficial when the person concerned makes it to himself secretly. The latter is achieved by the indirect method, which in the service of the love of truth dialectically arranges everything for the one ensnared and then, modest as love always is, avoids being witness to the confession that he makes alone before God, the confession that he has been living in an illusion.[145]

This principle undergirds Kierkegaard's authorship and its deceptive quality. The deception consisted in beginning with writing aesthetic, pseudonymous works that established rapport with the "crowd," drawing readers to identify with the perspective being presented, and then, at the right time, following these works with a new and shockingly contradictory perspective so as to force readers to judge between the two.

Kierkegaard believed such an indirect approach was "a true Christian invention," reflecting Christ's own way of coming to help people.[146] For one, Christ appeared in weakness and humility, concealing his authority and purpose until the right time. Christ allowed himself to be misunderstood and withstood the temptation to coerce people by his power. He did not demand people submit to his teaching but allowed them to either freely follow him or freely reject him, hate him, and even crucify him. Likewise, whoever would help people escape a delusion must give up trying to coerce them with judgment and condemnation, arranging instead for them to make the choice, by provoking them to awareness: "Compel a person to an opinion, a conviction, a belief—in all eternity, that I cannot do. But one thing I can do . . . I can compel him

145. Kierkegaard, *The Essential Kierkegaard*, 459.
146. Kierkegaard, *The Essential Kierkegaard*, 460.

to become aware. . . . By compelling him to become aware I succeed in compelling him to judge."[147]

Thus, the greatest intervention we could provide for others ensnared in false self-understanding is to compel them to become aware and to judge between multiple conflicting perspectives, which go by different names: aesthetic or ethical and religious, despair and faith, illusion and truth, or worldly wisdom and the gospel.

Thomas Merton

Now we move to Thomas Merton, who believed that human beings are called by God to discover their true selves. By dying to their false selves, they may become who they truly are in God's sight.

Merton on the Self

Meant to Be a Particular Thing

Human beings are like all creatures, according to Merton, in that God made them to glorify himself.[148] Everything that exists shares this one holy purpose: to reflect the goodness of the Creator.

In a chapter entitled "Things in Their Identity," Merton conveys his belief that a thing's identity as a creature lies in its particularity; a creature brings glory to the Creator by being itself, that is, by existing as God made it.[149] The identity of an individual created thing is not gained through its "conformity to an abstract type," but through its particularity or uniqueness.

Likewise, the way it is holy and imitative of God is not through altering itself into something different, but by simply being itself: "a tree imitates God by being a tree. The more a tree is like itself, the more it is like Him."[150] The same is true for people: to the degree that a human exists

147. Kierkegaard, *The Essential Kierkegaard*, 464.

148. Merton, *New Seeds of Contemplation*.

149. Merton, *New Seeds of Contemplation*. In his understanding of creation and its goodness and holiness, Merton had many influences, especially Augustine and Aquinas, but in his understanding of "things in their identity" Duns Scotus should probably be placed at the top of the list. See Horan, "Thomas Merton the 'Dunce,'" 149–75.

150. Merton, *New Seeds of Contemplation*, 29.

as himself or herself, to that degree will he or she be holy, reflecting God. In *individual being* lies the goodness of humans and of all creation.[151]

Choosing to Be

Human beings are different from the rest of creation, however, because they have been given the freedom to be themselves or not: "God leaves us free to be whatever we like. We can be ourselves or not, as we please. We are at liberty to be real, or to be unreal. We may be true or false, the choice is ours."[152] God's purpose in giving this freedom was not to tempt humans, but to honor them above all other creatures as his image-bearers and as those most like him, having the capacity to consciously will to exist. Because God calls humans to be themselves *consciously*, they have a special power and responsibility: to will their own existence, to participate with God in their creation. Merton says, "We are free beings and sons of God. This means to say that we should not passively exist, but actively participate in His creative freedom, in our own lives, and in the lives of others, by choosing the truth."[153] In giving humans freedom, God calls them to take responsibility for their selfhood.

Selfhood, according to Merton, refers to the individuality of all humans as unique beings. Just as no two trees are alike, so every human being is unique in his or her particularity. To be a self is to be a particular human being, who exists like a tree that gives glory to God by "spreading out its roots in the earth and raising its branches into the air and the light in a way that no other tree before or after it ever did or will do."[154] However, whereas a tree has no choice in its own particular existence, a person does. People can participate with God in their selfhood, but they can also work against it.

---

151. On the other hand, as with Augustine's view above, things are evil in so far as they lack being, or so far as they are not true to their own existence.

152. Merton, *New Seeds of Contemplation*, 31–32.

153. Merton, *New Seeds of Contemplation*, 32.

154. Merton, *New Seeds of Contemplation*, 29.

Merton on the False Self

Refusing to Be

Following Augustine, Merton believed that ever since Adam and Eve sinned in the Garden, humans have existed in a state of conflict between being and non-being, between truth and falsehood.[155] People are sinners in this regard, having forfeited their freedom to be themselves. Merton ties sin directly into his understanding of the false self:

> To say I was born in sin is to say I came into the world with a false self. I was born in a mask. I came into existence under a sign of contradiction, being someone that I was never intended to be and therefore a denial of what I am supposed to be.[156]

The false self is the godless identity of those born in sin, who have denied themselves the freedom and responsibility to be creatures that reflect God in their conscious and willing submission:

> Sin is the refusal of spiritual life. . . . It is not only a refusal to "do" this or that thing willed by God, or a determination to do what he forbids. It is more radically a refusal to be what we are, a rejection of our mysterious, contingent, spiritual reality hidden in the very mystery of God. Sin is our refusal to be what we were created to be—sons of God, images of God. Ultimately sin . . . is a flight from freedom and the responsibility of divine sonship.[157]

By rejecting the selfhood God intended for them, human beings suffer a depleted, contradictory existence, of which they are tepidly aware. Merton called this dim awareness "existential dread."[158] It is a "sense of insecurity, of lostness, of exile, of sin."[159]

Building an Illusory Self

In order to assuage this contradictory existence that is at once being and non-being—that is, living as a physical being and yet not living as a spiritual one—people construct an illusion to deceive themselves and thereby

155. See Gustafson, "Place, Spiritual Anthropology and Sacramentality," 76.

156. Merton, *New Seeds of Contemplation*, 33–34.

157. Merton, *Life and Holiness*, 4.

158. Merton, *Contemplative Prayer*, 26.

159. Merton, *Contemplative Prayer*, 26.

find peace of mind. This illusion is the false self. Categorically, the false self is a subjective construct made in order to "conceal the truth of our misery from ourselves, our brethren and from God."[160] The false self is an image of oneself that people try to convince themselves and others that they are. Although people are nothing apart from God, they have chosen to believe that they are something. To mute the truth about their nothingness or non-being, most people work so hard at building this illusion that it becomes the greatest subjective reality in their lives.[161]

Despite their refusal to be real human beings in spiritual relationship with God, people continue to be. Although they have chosen to die spiritually and to deceive themselves with an illusion (i.e., the false self), God allows them to exist still. Furthermore, although humans have forfeited their nature as creatures, God has not relinquished his role as Creator and even goes so far as to be the Redeemer.

Therefore, hope remains for human beings, because God continues to sustain and pursue them.[162] Through Christian baptism, Merton believed, God recreates a person's soul and gives it spiritual life once again.[163] Spiritual new birth is the beginning of the false self's demise and the true self's life.

Merton on the True Self

Willing to Be a Saint

Just as the false self is bound up with sin, so the true self, which is the spiritually resurrected soul born in baptism, is bound up with salvation: "For me to be a saint means to be myself. Therefore the problem of sanctity and salvation is in fact the problem of finding out who I am and of discovering my true self."[164] For Merton, the discovery of the true self is just another way of describing the Christian life. What Merton means by discovering the true self is not only about *becoming conscious* of who one really is but about *being* who one really is. The true self, therefore, is

160. Merton, *The Silent Life*, 159.

161. Merton, *New Seeds of Contemplation*, 34.

162. There is some disagreement over whether Merton believed Christianity was the only way of salvation or if other "high" religions might be also. Among those who believe the former is Carr, *A Search for Wisdom and Spirit*.

163. See Merton, *The New Man*, 73.

164. Merton, *New Seeds of Contemplation*, 31.

the saved and sanctified human being who exists as itself and who consciously wills to do so.

Returning to the analogy of the tree that glorifies God simply by existing as itself and not something else, so the true self is the human that glorifies God because he or she exists as himself or herself rather than pretending to be something else. Of course, the difference again is that a tree has no choice but to exist as itself, while a human does have a choice because of self-consciousness. Therefore, the true self is a person who exists as himself or herself by consciously willing to do so. Thus, to be clear, the true self is a person who both *exists* and *wills to so exist*. In other words, when people become or discover their true selves, two attributes qualify them: they are spiritually alive, existing as God's individual creatures who glorify God in their particularity and they consent to this existence as their identity.

In Merton's use of the term, therefore, the true self is both subject and object. On the one hand, it is a subject, or a particular person who acts and exists in the world and in relation to God and to other people. In this vein, Merton could speak about the self-forgetfulness of the true self; as one's true self, a person is not pent up with constructing a self-image, but instead looks outward in wonder and love towards creation and seeks to work with God in developing it.[165]

Discovering What Is Already Known by God

On the other hand, the true self is an object because it can be known. First, the true self is known to God, as Merton states in various ways. "The secret of my identity is hidden in the love and mercy of God."[166] In another place he says, "the real 'I' is just simply ourself and nothing more. . . . Our self as we are in the eyes of God."[167] Merton relates an experience he had on a city sidewalk in which, looking at pedestrians around him, he felt for a brief moment that he could sense what God sees in them, their true selves:

---

165. For examples of how this aspect of the true self appears in Merton's poetry, see Labrie, "Wholeness in Thomas Merton's Poetry," 41–60; Kramer, "Forgetting in Order to Find," 375–88.

166. Merton, *New Seeds of Contemplation*, 35.

167. Merton, *The Essential Writings*, 301.

Then it was as if I suddenly saw the secret beauty of their hearts, the depths of their hearts where neither sin nor desire nor self-knowledge can reach, the core of their reality, the person that each one is in God's eyes. If only they could all see themselves as they really are. If only we could see each other that way all the time.[168]

Whether he thought these people were actually Christians is beside the point, because, in Merton's thinking, although their true selves could only be substantially created at baptism, people's true selves are always visible to God in their potentiality. As an object, therefore, the true self is known first and foremost to God. God knows it completely, but people can only partially know their true selves.[169] Merton states, "My deepest realization of who I am is—I am one loved by Christ. . . . The depths of my identity are in the center of my being where I am known by God."[170] The true self is known fully by God, and in so far as God reveals it, the true self can be known to the person. The true self is

a point of nothingness which is untouched by sin and by illusion, a point of pure truth, a point or spark which belongs entirely to God, which is never at our disposal, from which God disposes of our lives. . . . It is so to speak His name written in us, as our poverty, as our indigence, as our dependence, as our sonship.[171]

Working to Put on Christ

In both senses, as a subject and object, Merton believed that the true self is gained or discovered by "putting on Christ."[172] Through union with Christ in baptism, people begin to exist as their true selves.[173] Incorporation into Christ moves one's true self from a potentiality to an actuality. However, sanctification is a temporal process, and the true self is not manifested right away. Merton explains that while the soul or true self is made alive spiritually through conversion, a person's full existence as a real human being demands more work in the person:

168. Merton, *Conjectures of a Guilty Bystander*, 142.

169. See Horan, "Thomas Merton the 'Dunce,'" 164.

170. Quoted in Faricy, "Thomas Merton," 195.

171. Merton, *Conjectures of a Guilty Bystander*, 142.

172. Gustafson, "Place, Spiritual Anthropology and Sacramentality," 76.

173. Merton, *The New Man*, 73.

> The faculties of the soul nevertheless, as well as the body with
> its senses, remain subject to the "wisdom of the flesh." This
> demands an ascetic struggle, in which our spirit, united with
> the Spirit of God, resists the flesh, its desires and its illusions, in
> order to strengthen and elevate us more and more, and open our
> eyes to the full meaning of our life in Christ.[174]

As discussed above, full existence for humans is stipulated on their
willingness to exist. Only as they understand and consent to their life
in Christ, that is, to their true selves, will they live out their true selves.
An "ascetic struggle" with the Spirit's help will be required. Merton concludes, "Finally, however, there will come a mystical transformation in
which we will be perfectly conformed to the likeness of Christ. The Second Adam will live entirely in us. We will be "the New Man" who is, in
fact, one Man—the One Christ, Head and Members."[175]

Merton on Interventions

Disposing Oneself to God

For Merton, the way to the true self begins with this foundational idea: to
discover and become one's true self, people must begin in faith set on God's
Word. Merton recommended sacred reading (i.e., *lectio divina*), corporate
singing of the liturgy, and other practices of attending to a growing conceptual, experiential, and praxis-grounded understanding of God.

The purpose and fruit of meditation is to help one assume a certain
posture, looking beyond oneself to God. For Merton the true self is not
something people make or attain but a gift received from God. Merton
explains, "We should not look for a 'method' or 'system,' but cultivate
an 'attitude,' and 'outlook': faith, openness, attention, reverence, expectation, supplication, trust, joy."[176] As we have seen, Merton used the image
of sonship to depict the true self; from the beginning, those who would
become their true selves must believe God is their Father, looking to him
for their sanctity rather than "violently overcoming" their weakness.[177]
While spiritual practices and asceticism are necessary, their purpose is

174. Merton, *The New Man*, 157–58.
175. Merton, *The New Man*, 158.
176. Merton and Steere, *The Climate of Monastic Prayer*, 49.
177. Merton, *Life and Holiness*, 31–32.

only to help cultivate a posture of reception, that is, a disposition that actively waits and expects God to be for us what he has promised to be in his Word.

Merton called this disposition or attitude "contemplation." While it begins by one placing faith in conceptual ideas revealed in God's Word, contemplation moves beyond intellectual apprehension to experiencing God's presence, which entails a new way of seeing the world, including oneself, that accords with divine reality.

Another way Merton describes contemplation is by saying that it is about experiencing God's gaze, that is, about being known and discovered by God "It is in proportion as we are known to him that we find our real being and identity in Christ."[178] Merton believed that God already knows people completely, but that is not the same as the conscious experience of being known; when Merton refers to being known by God, he means that one has stopped concealing oneself from God behind the false self and wills for God to know oneself. Yet in order to realize the truth, a person must go through the painful divestiture of falsehood. Merton says, "To reach one's 'real self' one must, in fact, be delivered by grace, virtue and asceticism from the illusory and false 'self' whom we have created by our habits of selfishness and by our constant flights from reality."[179]

Purging the False Self

Here is where asceticism comes in, because in order to be known by God one must leave behind or purge the false self. Purging the false self is painful because it has been a source of comfort and security against the dreadful awareness of one's sinful existence. The false self has taken pride of place in one's desires, and so it is not easily dethroned: "In order to become myself I must cease to be what I always thought I wanted to be, and in order to find myself I must go outside myself, and in order to live I have to die."[180]

Recognizing the true self is impossible from the side of a person's own effort to find it, because, unlike the false self, the true self is not one's own to construct. Whereas people know their false self through having crafted it themselves, they cannot know the true self in the same way

178. Merton, *Contemplative Prayer*, 104.

179. Merton, *The New Man*, 94.

180. Merton, *New Seeds of Contemplation*, 47.

because they do not make it or control it: "Contemplation is precisely the awareness that this 'I' is really 'not I' and the awakening of the unknown 'I' that is beyond observation and reflection and is incapable of commenting upon itself."[181]

Contemplation is about people being delivered from their own self-deception and false selves by willingly consenting to experience a "dark night of the soul" in which they recognize that what they have assumed as their fundamental identity is utterly worthless.[182] Contemplation or prayer helps one to expose, repudiate, and detach from the false self:

> The dimensions of prayer in solitude are those of man's ordinary anguish, his self-searching, his moments of nausea at his own vanity, falsity and capacity for betrayal. Far from establishing one in unassailable narcissism, the way of prayer brings us face to face with the sham and indignity of the false self.[183]

Merton was thankful for the emphasis he saw in Freud upon exploring the unconscious or the "whole house."[184] However, inasmuch as Merton opposed Freud's naturalism and atheism, he rejected the idea that neuroses, psychoses, and complexes derived from physiological and environmental factors were the most important aspects of the unconscious. In contemplation, in contrast to Freudian psychoanalysis, the greatest illusion being confronted is a spiritual one: the false assumption that people exist in themselves (i.e., apart from God). In contemplative prayer, people are forced to encounter the existential dread of their autonomy, which they have tried to avoid by means of their false self.

Being Alone in Nature

To the degree that people face the "sham" of their false self, they are enabled to see themselves as they really are: creatures, dependent on God. Another strategy Merton recommended was exposure to the outdoors, and he often wrote about his own contemplative experiences of nature. It was in the solitude of a forest that he found momentary freedom from

181. Merton, *New Seeds of Contemplation*, 7.

182. For a discussion of how Merton was influenced by John of the Cross and his spiritual meditations on the "dark night of the soul," see Lipsey, "The Monk's Chief Service," 170–75.

183. Merton and Steere, *The Climate of Monastic Prayer*, 35–36.

184. Merton, *Conjectures of a Guilty Bystander*, 98.

the false self: "It seems to me that solitude rips off all the masks and all the disguises. It does not tolerate lies. Everything but straight and direct affirmation is marked and judged by the silence of the forest."[185] Merton believed that contemplation is induced by encountering nature because "everything we meet and everything we see and hear and touch, far from defiling, purifies us and plants in us something more of contemplation and of heaven."[186] As people really perceive the underlying essence of things as creations of God, and as they experience real "being," they demonstrate their detachment from their illusions about themselves and the world.

Quieting Self-Consciousness

Seeing the truth about the world and oneself requires a certain abstinence from self-consciousness, because the human capacity for self-consciousness has been corrupted through its fabrication of the false self. Going about contemplation can easily become just another means of building up the false self; one can perform spiritual practices self-consciously with the intention of making a more perfect (false) self, but Merton warns, "the only way we become perfect is by leaving ourselves, and, in a certain sense, forgetting our own perfection, to follow Christ."[187]

This self-forgetfulness, however, is only in a "certain sense," that is, as it concerns forgetting one's narcissistic aim of self-construction. Detachment from self-consciousness and from signs of progress in faith and contemplation allows one to discard the false self and receive the true self.[188] The goal is not to do away with self-consciousness altogether, but to wait for God as he discloses one's true self.

Praying Contemplatively

In more pragmatic terms, Merton's conception of contemplation is just a thick description of prayer. It is prayer understood as more than petition, and as a practice, *contemplative* prayer encompasses all of life, not only set apart times.

185. Merton and Daggy, *Dancing in the Water of Life*, 278.

186. Merton, *New Seeds of Contemplation*, 25. See Labrie, "Wholeness in Thomas Merton's Poetry," 44–58.

187. Merton, *The New Man*, 27.

188. See Merton, *New Seeds of Contemplation*, 236.

Contemplative prayer happens in the midst of daily mundane activities; for Merton, prayer occurs in the liturgy sung in choir, at chores, and on the porch listening to the wind in the trees.[189] Merton said that one of the best skills for beginners in prayer to acquire is "the agility and freedom of mind that will help them to find light and warmth and ideas and love for God everywhere they go and in all that they do."[190] He continues:

> Learn how to meditate on paper. Drawing and writing are forms of meditation. Learn how to contemplate works of art. Learn how to pray in the streets or in the country. Know how to meditate not only when you have a book in your hand but when you are waiting for a bus or riding in a train.[191]

Prayer is an attitude of dependence on God and an awareness of his presence.

Prayer is of "the heart," meaning that a person prays out of "the deepest psychological ground of one's personality, the inner sanctuary where self-awareness goes beyond analytical reflection and opens out into metaphysical and theological confrontation."[192] In prayer one encounters existence, the real world.[193]

The true self is discovered through prayer, but not by focusing on oneself. Rather, prayer focuses on Christ, allowing Jesus' name to occupy one's heart.[194] The more one prays this way, or with a contemplative attitude, the more one comes to experience the spiritual life that was substantially already given in baptism: "In prayer we discover what we already have. . . . Everything has been given to us in Christ. All we need is to experience what we already possess."[195]

Conclusion

In this chapter we have explored the insights of four Christian writers, considering how their thinking helps us understand the false self and true self. In conclusion, let's draw together some common threads.

189. See Merton, *Contemplative Prayer*, 37.

190. Merton, *New Seeds of Contemplation*, 216.

191. Merton, *New Seeds of Contemplation*, 216.

192. Merton, *Contemplative Prayer*, 38.

193. Merton, *Contemplative Prayer*, 24–25.

194. Merton, *Contemplative Prayer*, 22–24.

195. Steindl-Rast, "Recollections," 2–3.

First, what function do these writers ascribe to self-understanding in their description of human beings? For Augustine self-understanding enables people to apprehend God, who created people with an innate connection to him, so that when they turn inward to know themselves they can then turn upward to know him. Similarly, for the other writers, self-understanding allows people to consciously perceive themselves in relation to God. For all the writers, by virtue of resting in this relationship people can properly be what God created them to be. To refuse to see oneself in relation to God, however, is a rejection of true humanity.

Therefore, in answer to what kind of problem false self understanding is in human life, these writers would all characterize the problem as primarily *spiritual* in nature. The cause of the false self has to do with human beings' refusal to relate themselves to God. When humans reject their true existence they have to fabricate a false one in order to subsist. For Augustine, a false or sinful existence is characterized by movement towards death, fixation on sensible experiences without faith, and pridefully "living according to man" as the ground of goodness, being, and knowledge. Although Luther did not share Augustine's Neoplatonic leanings, he agreed that humanity's problem is ultimately spiritual: people become sinners by exchanging their creaturely status for the illusion of self-sufficiency. Similarly, Kierkegaard understood despair to be a spiritual sickness that results from refusing to relate oneself to God; instead of willing to be what they were made to be, human beings despair over themselves, and gradually through various forms of self-deception, people lose awareness of their spiritual nature and conceal their despair. The wasted life, according to Kierkegaard, is the one lived without having known one's true self before God. For Merton, ever since Adam and Eve, humans have rejected their true selfhood and suffered a depleted existence. In order to cover over the "existential dread" that results, they have fabricated the false self, which is an illusory self-image that people try to convince themselves and others that they are. God allows people to continue to exist even though they deceive themselves into believing in an illusion, a false self, or an untrue existence. All of these writers, therefore, attribute the deception under which people live to the dissolution of humanity's spiritual relationship with God.

Third, as the problem is spiritual in nature, so is the solution; just as false self-understanding is caused by turning away from God, so true self-understanding is realized by returning to him, specifically through faith in Christ. Augustine described this spiritual conversion as the soul turning its gaze away from sinful attachments and directing its love towards God, so that God may be truly known. Conversion is an inward and upward turn; by looking to the inner self and learning from Christ's humility, people can find truth in their souls, particularly the truth that they are not the ground of their existence, and then looking above the soul they can find God and their salvation. Christ mediates this process by humbly dying and showing sinners the way to life. However, Augustine did not adequately uphold the necessity of fixing one's gaze on Jesus, because of his Platonic aversion to fleshly things. Luther differed from Augustine in seeing salvation not fundamentally as a turn from flesh (i.e., material substance) to spirit (i.e., intelligible truth) but as a turn from a fleshly (i.e., self-sufficient) orientation to a spiritual (i.e., dependent) orientation: salvation comes through trusting that one is justified in Christ, and thus responding to God's promise in the gospel with faith. Kierkegaard likewise pointed to faith as the cure for humanity's spiritual problem, pitting it against the spiritual sickness of despair. Kierkegaard defined faith as "resting transparently in God." This resting involves both accepting the true self that one is before God and also consenting to the ideal self that God calls one to be. The power that enables this resting is the gospel of God's gratuitous, outrageous beneficence and grace. Similarly, Merton described God's continued pursuit of his creatures, calling them to turn back to their true existence and life. Those who respond with faith "put on Christ" in baptism and experience the vivification of their true self. As people understand and consent to their true selves in Christ, they live out their true selves and reflect Christ. People discover and become their true selves by being known by God and by discarding false self. What we find in these writers is the common belief that—just as a false self-understanding has its root in refusing to identify with God—true self-understanding is gained by people embracing their identity in God.

As might be expected, these writers can be distinguished most by the interventions they employed or recommended. Each thinker emphasizes different ways to promote faith in God and foster true self-understanding. However, important similarities unite their approaches. For one, all of the writers maintained the benefit of certain biblical practices: meditation on Scripture (e.g., in a sermon, in private reading), baptism, the Lord's supper, and confession. These interventions have been the rule of the church in all its eras and across its denominations. Although the precise manners of their operations have been debated and would be articulated differently among the proponents we have studied, their permanent place in

Christian teaching and practice has long been established. But far more crucial than these forms—or "images" as Luther called them—is the reality they all serve to communicate. That reality is the gospel of Jesus Christ. The gospel is the primary intervention, and, according to most of the writers observed here, the gospel alone is capable of freeing people from their false self-understanding and enabling them to discover or realize their true humanity. Furthermore, the gospel comes personally as God's truth, word, and promise to the individual. Augustine demonstrates this personal dimension by focusing on the inward turn that each person must make in order to find God. Luther specifies that true faith consists in not just believing that the gospel applies to people in general, but to oneself in particular.[196] Likewise, Kierkegaard and Merton agree on the necessity of personally receiving God's offer or call, as a particular individual.

In conclusion, within the Christian tradition, as represented by these four writers, there exists a Christian psychological description of human beings that bears on the key questions of this study. Of pivotal importance is the spiritual nature of humanity: humans were created to exist in a conscious relationship with God; because of the obfuscation and loss of that relationship, human beings have lost touch with the truth about themselves as God's image-bearers; still, God calls people back into relationship with him through the gospel, which restores true self-understanding; the gospel can be communicated in myriad forms, but its efficacy depends on it being received by the individual and personally responded to in faith.

In the next chapter, we will observe how secular psychologists have largely missed the *spiritual* dimension of selfhood in their discussions of the true and false self. On the other hand, we will also see how they can inform Christian psychology with insights about the *developmental* dimension of selfhood.

---

196. See Luther, "First Sunday in Advent," 17–58.

4

Secular Perspectives

IN THIS CHAPTER I will present and critique the ideas of two prominent secular psychologists about the self, false self, true self, and interventions fostering the true self. Their perspectives will be considered secular, because they exclude appeals to God's involvement in psychological development and intervention. The label "secular" is not intended to describe these theorists' personal lives or private convictions, but their professional discourse. The four main questions we are considering are: (1) How does the self develop under ideal conditions? (2) What causes the formation of the false self? (3) What is the true self? (4) What interventions foster the true self? The secular stances of Winnicott and Harter significantly impact how these questions are answered according to their theories. Be that as it may, there is much to gain by examining their work and transposing their insights into a Christian perspective.

D. W. Winnicott

Winnicott (1896–1971) was a seminal representative of object-relations psychology and perhaps the first modern psychologist to extensively discuss the true self and false self. Along with other object relations theorists, Winnicott traced his heritage to Freud and psychoanalytic psychology. He was part of the "British school" of object relations theory, which set itself apart from other schools by concentrating on the first few years of life, where the foundation of personality was believed to be laid.

Winnicott on the Self

Health Starts with the Infant-Parent Relationship

Winnicott's view of healthy self-development starts with a sense of feeling real, or authenticity. Life's ultimate purpose can only be reached if one begins with this foundation: "Being and feeling real belong essentially to health, and it is only if we can take being for granted that we can get on to the more positive things."[1] Winnicott thought that this foundation is laid very early in life between infant and mother. Through their "dyadic relationship," when healthy, the infant's "core self" or ego begins to thrive, as well as the infant's innate morality that places ultimate value on authenticity and getting personal needs met rather than conforming to another's needs.[2]

Out of this beginning, individuals can gradually grow into a fuller life that includes three dimensions of health. The first is actively engaging in the external world of interpersonal relationships as well as the non-human environment (i.e., external reality). The second is enjoying one's own inner psychical reality (i.e., internal reality). The third is participating in cultural experience through creative expression (i.e., shared reality).[3] These three aspects of life or health were integral to Winnicott's system of thought. Maturing in each stage of life depends upon how the individual is related to self, others, and the space between self and other. From infancy to old age, "[individual] health can be shown to have a relationship with living, with inner wealth, and, in a different way, with the capacity to have cultural experience."[4] Before individuals can experience any of these relationships, the capacity for relating must be formed, and the first and most natural opportunity for this formation is in infancy with one's mother.

---

1. Winnicott et al., *Home Is Where We Start From*, 35.

2. Winnicott was not saying that infants think in these terms or that they are conscious of placing ultimate value on their needs getting met over against compliance to another. To an infant who has not even formed an ego, there is no "other." That is why Winnicott said the infant's morality is the fiercest morality of all: for, it is not until individuals develop a sense of self and others that they can temper their innate morality with a respect for others' needs and desires. This sense of personal sanctity, however, should always remain vital, and in health there will always be a higher value set on self-determination than compliance. See Winnicott, "Morals and Education," 102.

3. Winnicott, *Home Is Where We Start From*, 35–37.

4. Winnicott, *Home Is Where We Start From*, 36.

As a pediatrician and later as a psychoanalyst Winnicott spent thousands of hours with mothers and their children, and he focused much of his research and writing on early childhood development. In those clinical hours Winnicott saw the importance of the infant-mother relationship. What occurs in the "facilitating environment" of the mother's care sets the stage for all future relationships. Here, the self of an individual comes to be. Here, the other becomes distinguished from the self. Here, the capacity to use objects as "transitional phenomena" is first developed. In many respects, Winnicott followed the thinking of Klein, who had departed from the Freudian emphasis on the three to four-year-old Oedipal stage as the first context of meaning-making, focusing instead on the first several months of life.[5] Winnicott's unique contribution was how he defined the relationship between parent and infant.[6]

In the following passage Winnicott identifies two sides to "the theory of the parent-infant relationship":

> One half of the theory of the parent-infant relationship concerns the infant, and is the theory of the infant's journey from absolute dependence, through relative dependence, to independence. . . . The other half of the theory of the parent-infant relationship concerns maternal care, that is to say the qualities and changes in the mother that meet the specific and developing needs of the infant toward whom she orientates.[7]

In other words, the factors that determine how an individual develops boil down to either nature or nurture. Winnicott acknowledged both sides: on the one hand, development depends on "the inherited potential of the individual," but, on the other hand, it also depends on the individual's external conditions or environment, which is parental care.[8] It was to this latter side of the theory that Winnicott contributed most. His

---

5. Winnicott, "Appetite and Emotional Disorder," 33–51; Winnicott, "The Theory of the Parent-Infant Relationship," 39–42; see Tuber, *Attachment, Play, and Authenticity*, 17–18.

6. See Rodman, *Winnicott*, 7–8.

7. Winnicott, "The Theory of the Parent-Infant Relationship," 42. The first side of this theory had already been developed by Klein, but Winnicott believed the other half, concerning the mother's care, had not been appreciated. Specifically, Winnicott pointed to the absolute dependence of the infant on maternal care: "There is nothing in Klein's work that contradicts the idea of absolute dependence, but there seems to me to be no specific reference to a stage at which the infant exists only because of the maternal care, together with which it forms a unit."

8. Winnicott, "The Theory of the Parent-Infant Relationship," 43.

concern was not the infant's biological or genetic makeup, which he believed would naturally tend towards growth and development under normal conditions. Rather, he focused on the kind of parental care required to facilitate the development of the biological and genetic potential of a human being into "an infant, and thereafter into a child, a child reaching towards independent existence."[9]

Three States of Infant Dependence

Winnicott classified three states of the infant's dependence that occur in an ideal environment of parental care: absolute dependence, relative dependence, and towards independence.[10]

In "absolute dependence," which sets the foundation for future growth, infants are completely unaware of maternal care; there is no separation or distinction between self and other. Winnicott called this the "holding phase," referring to both the mother's actual physical holding of the infant and also to the infant's overall experience of the environment. In this state infants are merged with their mother and have no separating boundary between themselves and the three-dimensional environment in which they are "held." In other words, infants begin with no sense of integration, or "unit-status," but are "unintegrated."[11] Without a sense of self and other, they cannot act on their environment but only passively receive (or suffer) what it gives them.[12]

In absolute dependence, ideally, the infant scarcely notices the mother's care or physical holding, which functions as "a continuation of the physiological provision that characterizes the prenatal state."[13] As a suitable substitute for the womb, the mother's holding provides a reliable environment that adapts to the infant's needs for physiological vitality and safety, in which the infant's sensitivity to touch, temperature, sound, light, and gravity are taken into account.[14]

9. Winnicott, "The Theory of the Parent-Infant Relationship," 43.

10. See Winnicott, "The Theory of the Parent-Infant Relationship," 46.

11. Winnicott, "Primitive Emotional Development," 145–56.

12. It will be seen how the vulnerability of this state can be severely exploited in the discussion below of the false self.

13. Winnicott, "The Theory of the Parent-Infant Relationship," 49.

14. Winnicott, "The Theory of the Parent-Infant Relationship," 49.

During pregnancy, the mother feels a strong connection and "pre-occupation" with the baby growing within her, with whom she develops a high degree of identification and empathy.[15] In turn, this identification and empathy make her sense of the baby's needs very powerful, so that she is willingly and accurately attuned to giving the needed care:

> This essential maternal function enables the mother to know about her infant's earliest expectations and needs, and makes her personally satisfied in so far as the infant is at ease. It is because of this identification with her infant that she knows to hold her infant, so that the infant starts by existing and not by reacting.[16]

Through her care, the mother is enabling the infant to have a personal existence and to build up a "continuity of being," and, Winnicott says, "On the basis of this continuity of being the inherited potential [i.e., infant as biological and genetic organism] gradually develops into an individual infant."[17] In other words, maternal care or holding is the basis for the infant's ego or sense of self.

Because of the mother's provision of holding, infants can have a secure foundation from which they can confidently move from enmeshment with the environment to emergence and separation, as experiences of relating to external objects (e.g., mother or mother's breast) accumulate and become noticeable. The mother is the infant's first exposure to the world outside, and by representing a safe and reliable world she cultivates the natural maturation of the infant's intellect and apprehension of external reality:

> It is especially at the start that mothers are vitally important, and indeed it is a mother's job to protect her infant from complications that cannot yet be understood by the infant, and to go on steadily providing the simplified bit of the world which the infant, through her, comes to know. Only on such a foundation can objectivity . . . be built. All failure in objectivity at whatever date relates to the failure in this stage of primitive emotional

---

15. Winnicott, "Primary Maternal Preoccupation," 300–305.

16. Winnicott, "Ego Distortion in Terms of True and False Self," 148.

17. Winnicott, "The Theory of the Parent-Infant Relationship," 54. To clarify what he means by "continuity of being," I will continue the quotation of the passage, in which Winnicott also describes what happens if the mother's care fails to enable the infant's sense of personal existence: "If maternal care is not good enough then the infant does not really come into existence, since there is no continuity of being; instead the personality becomes built on the basis of reactions to environmental impingement."

development. Only on a basis of monotony can a mother profit-
ably add richness.[18]

When the simple but essential need for being held and feeling safe is
met through the mother's continual and "monotonous" holding—which
Winnicott said was probably the only way a mother can show her infant
love at that stage[19]—infants can start to venture out into riskier but
richer experiences in relative dependence on the mother rather than
absolute dependence.

In "relative dependence," infants become aware of needing care, and
they gradually begin to link the details of their mother's care with their
impulses. This development brings about the infant's distinguishing the
me from the not-me.

At first, however, infants live without knowing any kind of objectivity or relationship to external reality; thus, Winnicott says the infant's
experience is not first one of reality but of fantasy or illusion. The infant
is still dependent on the mother and her good care, without which the
infant cannot mature into a healthy way of relating to reality.[20]

In the ideal case, in which the mother qualifies as "good-enough,"
the continuity of her care provides the necessary facilitating environment
for the infant to come through illusion into contact with reality. How
does this happen? Winnicott describes it vividly:

> In terms of baby and mother's breast . . . the baby has instinc-
> tual urges and predatory ideas. The mother has a breast and the
> power to produce milk, and the idea that she would like to be
> attacked by a hungry baby. These two phenomena do not come
> into relation with each other till the mother and child *live an
> experience together*. The mother being mature and physically
> able has to be the one with tolerance and understanding, so that
> it is she who produces a situation that may with luck result in the
> first tie the infant makes with an external object, an object that is
> external to the self from the infant's point of view.[21]

18. Winnicott, "Primitive Emotional Development," 153.

19. Thus he wrote, "Holding includes especially the physical holding of the infant,
which is a form of loving. It is perhaps the only way in which a mother can show the
infant her love." Winnicott, "The Theory of the Parent-Infant Relationship," 49.

20. Winnicott's belief was that infants begin life psychologically enmeshed in their
mother, without any self- or other-awareness, and therefore how the mother cares for
and relates to her infant largely determines the infant's psychological maturation.

21. Winnicott, "Primitive Emotional Development," 152.

When an infant's hunger is met with the mother's milk, an opportunity is afforded in which the infant can notice the overlap of his or her sudden need for food and the mother's provision of milk. As the infant's experience of his or her instinctual urge getting satisfied is repeated, the infant "starts to build up a capacity to conjure up what is actually available."[22] In other words, infants begin to associate their urges with the satisfaction of their urges in the course of consistent maternal care. When this linkage occurs, the baby experiences an illusory sense of "omnipotence" or "magic," in which the infant's instinctual urge and "spontaneous gesture" (e.g., crying, flailing arms) seems to bring about what is wanted. Having entered into the illusion of omnipotence, the infant can enjoy and play in the illusion as long as the mother continues to facilitate it by supplying the infant's needs, so that "the infant begins to believe in external reality which appears and behaves as by magic . . . and which acts in a way that does not clash with the infant's omnipotence."[23] Having enjoyed the illusion and sensed it as reliable, infants can then handle the fact that their omnipotence was actually an illusion and that what has been meeting their needs is an "object" that stands in relation to them. The infant gradually distinguishes the me and not-me as the mother continues to present the world of objects, yet with a gradual resumption of her own independence. The mother transitions out of her intense preoccupation with her infant and her highly sensitive attunement and adaptation to the infant's needs.[24] This change in the mother helps the infant change as well, as Winnicott explains:

> You see how it is that the [mother's] sensitive adaptation to an infant's ego-needs only lasts a little while. Soon the infant begins to get a kick out of kicking, and to get something positive out of being angry because of what could be called minor failures of adaptation. But by this time the mother is beginning to restart her own life that eventually becomes relatively independent of her infant's needs. Often the child's growing up corresponds quite accurately with the mother's resumption of her own independence, and you would agree that a mother who cannot gradually *fail* in this matter of sensitive adaptation is failing in another sense. . . . It is part of the equipment of the great majority of mothers to

22. Winnicott, "Primitive Emotional Development," 153.

23. Winnicott, "Ego Distortion in Terms of True and False Self," 146.

24. Recall that Winnicott called this state "primary maternal preoccupation," which he said lasted from the beginning of pregnancy up until the first two or three weeks after birth. See Winnicott, "Primary Maternal Preoccupation."

provide graduated de-adaptation, and this is nicely geared to the rapid developments that the infant displays.[25]

Because the mother slowly ceases to provide constant and "sensitive" adaptation every time the infant feels a need, the infant begins to become aware of dependence to some degree. Although this can be distressing for infants in the first couple of years, it also enables them to become a unit with an inside and an outside, that is, "a person living in the body, and more or less bounded by the skin."[26] Now equipped with an "inside"— which we could also call a "mind"—infants have a place to store things.[27] The things stored inside include parts of the mother (e.g., breast, jewelry, hair) and eventually the whole mother as a separate person, as signified in the word "mommy." In this way, infants move from existence as an "inherited potential" in absolute dependence to a relatively dependent self who is capable of relationships.

The last stage consists of moving "towards independence" from the toddler age up to adolescence. Here children increasingly develop more complex means for doing without others' care and handling problems using their own inner resources.

Winnicott describes the child's growing ability to adapt to the external world by using what has been internalized from the mother's care. For example, the child can take in the security gained through relationship with the mother and carry it into new relationships. The child also finds security by looking at the external world in a way that lessens its strangeness by making "identifications" with it: "the child is able gradually to meet the world and all its complexities, because of seeing there more and more of what is already present in his or her own self."[28]

Moving "towards independence," therefore, consists of continually meeting new experiences and overcoming challenges by sensing one's distinction as a self, external reality's strangeness, but also—and most importantly—seeing an affinity or identification between the two. In other words, to deal with the (threatening) gap between self and other, healthy human beings find or create commonalities to bridge the gap. The challenging task of "reality-acceptance" and relating inner and outer

25. Winnicott, "From Dependence towards Independence," 86–87.
26. Winnicott, "From Dependence towards Independence," 91.
27. See Winnicott, "Mind and Its Relation to the Psyche-Soma," 243–54.
28. Winnicott, "From Dependence towards Independence," 91.

experience continues throughout life and can be accomplished in many ways, notably the arts and religion.[29]

Summary of Winnicott on the Self

Winnicott believed that by accomplishing her role, the mother provided the foundation for an infant's future psychological maturity and independence as an individual self:

> From my point of view the mental health of the individual is being laid down from the very beginning by the mother who provides what I have called a facilitating environment, that is to say one in which the infant's natural growth processes and interactions with the environment can evolve according to the inherited pattern of the individual. The mother is (without knowing it) laying down the foundations of mental health of the individual.[30]

Essential to normal human development and mental health is gaining a certain kind of self-awareness, which Winnicott described variously as a confidence in one's "aliveness," "feeling real," and "going-on-being." Given an environment of "good-enough mothering," an infant with normal physical and neurological health will be able to relate to the external world as an autonomous self who can act spontaneously, without coercion, and yet who can also live well with others. Normal psychological development entails a sense of independence from others that in turn enables relationships. In health there is a core self that is isolated from the world, never explicitly communicated or influenced by external reality, but only manifested indirectly.[31] One should ideally be "living his or her own life" and also be able to "reach towards an identification with society without too great a loss of individual or personal impulse."[32] Such a healthy sense of self and other begins developing in the environment of a healthy infant-mother relationship.

29. Winnicott conceived of the gap between the inner reality and external reality as a separate and crucial issue in understanding psychological growth. He called the area between the two "transitional space." This concept and related ideas of "transitional objects" and "play" will be developed below in our discussion of interventions. See Winnicott, "Transitional Objects and Transitional Phenomena," 239–40.

30. Winnicott, *Babies and Their Mothers*, 24–25.

31. Winnicott, "Communicating and Not Communicating," 187.

32. Winnicott, *Home Is Where We Start From*, 27.

Winnicott on the False Self

Winnicott used the term false self to describe the effect of "not good-enough mothering," in which the infant's needs are repeatedly not met, forcing the infant to react to caregiver coercion. By reacting out of a demand to comply to the parent's needs, an infant does not act truly, or spontaneously and freely, but falsely, or out of compliance to external demands:

> Through this False Self the infant builds up a false set of relationships, and by means of introjections even attains a show of being real, so that the child may grow to be just like mother, nurse, aunt, brother, or whoever at the time dominates the scene.[33]

The false self is false in the sense that it is does not act according to the person's own genuine needs, forced into falsehood by another. Because a person's parents are usually the most significant relational figures in a person's infancy, they often provide the primary relational context for the development of either the true self or the false self.

A "good-enough" parent responds to the infant's needs with adequate nurture that in turn validates the infant's sense of need. A good-enough parent thus strengthens an infant's true self, which amounts to his or her authentic expression of needs. When these needs are met, the infant's self is edified, approved, and allowed to continue unhindered in its development. On the other hand, a parent with lesser skills invalidates the infant's authentic sense of need by neglecting his or her gestures for attention and care.

Complying with Demands

Winnicott identifies two primary functions of the false self:

> If we look at the earlier stages of this process we see the infant very dependent on the mother's management, and on her continued presence and her survival. She must make a good-enough adaptation to the infant's needs, else the infant cannot avoid developing defenses that distort the process; for instance, the infant must take over the environmental function if the environment is not reliable, so that there is a hidden true self, and all that we can see is a false self engaged in the double task of

---

33. Winnicott, *The Maturational Processes and the Facilitating Environment*, 146.

hiding the true self and complying with the demands that the world makes from moment to moment.[34]

The first function of the false self is to comply with external demands. The second function explains why compliance is necessary: the true self has to be protected, so it is hidden. *In lieu* of having a true self that is accepted and allowed to be expressed, a false self will form as a defense against the true self's exploitation. For an infant to become a self he or she must be allowed to be a self, that is, to have urges, needs, and a being that is distinct from the external world or environment. The good-enough-parent facilitates the infant's realization that he or she exists by adapting to and affirming the infant's needs. However, if care is not sufficient and forces the infant to comply and adapt *to the parent*, the infant's self is essentially being rejected and threatened with "annihilation." To avoid the total loss of self, it must be defended by repressing the self's needs, urges, and instincts arising from the infant. In place of the (true) self and in its defense, a false self emerges that complies with the environment to make peace, but at the cost of the infant's sense of having a true, authentic self that is separate from the environment's demands.

Hiding the True Self by Degrees

To the degree that compliance is necessary the true self will be more or less hidden by the false self in succeeding years after infancy. The degrees of false self organization can be classified along a continuum.[35]

At one extreme, a person's false self comes to be the only self that is known to oneself and others, because it is so highly organized that it is taken to be the only real self, and the true self is completely hidden. When one's true self has been split-off at this extreme of false self organization, the only intimation of the true self would be a sense that something essential is lacking.

At the other extreme of relative wellbeing, the false self is represented by "the whole organization of the polite and mannered social attitude, a 'not wearing the heart on the sleeve', as might be said."[36] Winnicott classified five types of false self organization along this continuum:

---

34. Winnicott, "Group Influences and the Maladjusted Child," 216.

35. Winnicott, "Ego Distortion in Terms of True and False Self," 142–43.

36. Winnicott, "Ego Distortion in Terms of True and False Self," 143.

1. The false self is the only self known to oneself and others.

2. The false self hides and protects the true self, but symptoms reveal the potential of a true self.

3. The false self looks for conditions of enough safety to allow the true self to appear and grow.

4. The person identifies his or her false self with names such as "Caretaker Self."

5. The person uses the false self for the sake of social manners and propriety.

In the second type of false self organization, the true self remains hidden except for symptoms of clinical illness. This demonstrates the value of symptoms, which can signal that something is wrong. Although the false self is not recognized, a person's symptoms can indicate its existence by signaling defense and protection.[37]

There is a better prognosis for people with the third type, because they see the possibility the true self's emergence and vitality. If their environment (e.g., personal relationships) can support and adapt to their true self, then they may come to own their own existence. Because their improvement depends upon finding a safe enough environment, however, their recovery is far from assured, for if their true self meets enough resistance, that cannot be defended by the false self, the alternative is "suicide" which "in this context is the destruction of the total self in avoidance of annihilation of the True Self."[38]

In the fourth classification are those closer towards health, yet with neurotic symptoms. Their false self results from having overly identified or enmeshed with others such as family members and close caregivers. These people can identify their false self and often seek clinical help in order to find a way to enable the true self to gain vitality and dominance. They do not face the same threat of "suicide" as the previous type because their true self is more firmly acknowledged and believed in, and they have more hope than despair because their true self has been given more support and been less aversively affected by the demands of external reality.

---

37. See Winnicott, "Ocular Psychoneuroses of Childhood," 85–90.
38. Winnicott, "Ego Distortion in Terms of True and False Self," 143.

Summary of Winnicott on the False Self

In light of the foregoing, we can understand why Winnicott believed that all unhealthy types of false self organization originate in the infant-parent relationship: because it is in this relationship or environment that the infant's sense of self first forms, and if a mother interferes with its formation to a great enough degree (i.e., demanding too much compliance from the infant), then there will be repercussions for the infant's psyche. At the worst, if in the first few months the infant is not adequately cared for (or "held"), then the infant will either die physically or develop psychosis.[39] Such would be the result of severe neglect in the case of an infant still in the stage of "absolute dependence" who has not yet come to have a sense of self; without any self present, the infant has no means of defending itself except psychological withdrawal. Assuming, however, that an infant has come to a sense of self, the false self will arise to the degree that the infant is made to comply to external demands and the true self is rejected.

Winnicott on the True Self

The true self, according to Winnicott, is synonymous with the self formed in health, which was discussed in the first section. The term "true self" is mainly used for the sake of distinguishing it from the false self, as he says, "There is but little point in formulating a True Self idea except for the purpose of trying to understand the False Self, because it does no more than collect together the details of the experience of aliveness."[40] In this section, therefore, I will focus on contrasting the true self from the false self.

The True Self is Natural

First, the roots of the true self naturally precede the formation of the false self. The false self forms only because the true self comes under threat.

The natural progression of human development entails creativity, spontaneity, and feeling real. At the beginning of life, human beings are

---

39. See Winnicott, "Classification," 135–36; Winnicott, "Primitive Emotional Development," 149.

40. Winnicott, "Ego Distortion in Terms of True and False Self," 148.

alive without knowing it, but they have the intellectual potential to become conscious of their aliveness. This consciousness is the true self.

If everything goes well enough in an infant's environment, the true self will naturally develop as the primary self, and the only type of false self organization will consist of social manners.

The True Self is Mind and Body Integrated

Second, whereas the false self results from disconnection or splitting within a person, the true self results from one's integration. The true self is oriented to one's internal reality, whereas the false self is cut off from that awareness, because it is oriented to external reality.

Winnicott linked his conceptions to those of Freud: "In particular I link what I divide into a True and a False Self with Freud's division of the self into a part that is central and powered by the instincts . . . and a part that is turned outwards and is related to the world."[41]

The true self is related to the inside, and this not only includes one's thoughts but also all of one's bodily functions. The true self corresponds to the "psyche-soma," which is a state of integration between one's physical body and one's thinking.[42] In the beginning, the true self is the infantile mental awareness of one's somatic being:

> The True Self comes from the aliveness of the body tissues and the working of body-functions, including the heart's action and breathing. . . . The True self appears as soon as there is any mental organization of the individual at all, and it means little more than the summation of sensori-motor aliveness.[43]

From these beginnings, the true self remains integrated with the body and is in fact just an awareness or reflection of the body, rather than a thing in itself: "At a later stage the live body, with its limits, and with an inside and an outside, is *felt by the individual* to form the core for the imaginative self."[44]

In psychological health, self-consciousness is not a function of some localized part of the body (e.g., brain) but of the "psyche-soma." Where there is a split between mind and body, however, there is also

41. Winnicott, "Ego Distortion in Terms of True and False Self," 140.
42. Winnicott, "Mind and Its Relation to the Psyche-Soma."
43. Winnicott, "Ego Distortion in Terms of True and False Self," 149.
44. Winnicott, "Mind and Its Relation to the Psyche-Soma," 243–44.

a split between true self and false self.[45] As we have seen, this splitting results from a failure in the infant's environment to adequately respond to the infant's needs, which are both bodily and psychological: a not-good-enough parent's demands cause the infant to react with a defensive false self, which is necessarily split off from the infant's true bodily needs. Good-enough-parenting facilitates the infant's inward orientation to the body's needs, feelings, emotions, and thoughts that constitutes the integration of psyche-soma.

The True Self is Playful

Third and finally, whereas the false self is characterized by compliance and defensiveness, the true self is marked by creativity and spontaneity.

As we have seen, when an infant's spontaneous needs have been sufficiently suppressed by external demands for compliance, the infant develops a false self that complies in order to protect the true self. But by being protected and hidden the true self gets repressed, along with its creativity and spontaneity. When, on the other hand, the true self thrives, so does the person's freedom and capacity to play.

Recall that good-enough-parenting enables the infant's illusion of omnipotence, and the result is that the infant is freed to engage the world of external objects. In other words, the illusion that one has control over what happens outside, or that what is inside overlaps with what is outside (through identification), allows him or her to overcome the threatening gap between me and not-me. The challenge of accepting external reality (and its demands) without forfeiting one's internal reality (and its needs) is accomplished by relying on one's sense of competence (or for an infant, an illusory sense of omnipotence) that he or she has internalized from past successes—such as the successes afforded to an infant by a good-enough-parent.

45. Winnicott believed that in people with high intellectual potential the false self can become specifically localized in the person's mental life or mind. This happens when the mother's failure to adapt to the infant's needs, especially in the form of her erratic behavior, leads to the infant becoming overly active in mental functioning and precocious in a bad sense: "Here, in the overgrowth of the mental function reactive to erratic mothering, we see that there can develop an opposition between the mind and the psyche-soma, since in reaction to this abnormal environmental state the thinking of the individual begins to take over and organize the caring for the psyche-soma, whereas in health it is the function of the environment to do this." Winnicott, "Ego Distortion in Terms of True and False Self," 246.

Having had one's true self affirmed as competent and secure, one can approach the environment as a safe place to be creative and spontaneous. In childhood this happens through play, and in adulthood through participation in the arts, religion, and other aspects of cultural life.[46] To the degree that one's true self is strong he or she will have a greater or lesser ability to play.

Winnicott on Interventions

Not Violating Another's Hidden Self

Winnicott was both a theorist and a practitioner. In order to understand the interventions he employed as a psychoanalyst, consider the following passage where he elucidates his theory of the true self:

> I suggest that in health there is a core to the personality that corresponds to the true self of the split personality; I suggest that this core never communicates with the world of perceived objects, and that the individual knows that it must never be communicated with or be influenced by external reality. . . . At the center of each person is an incommunicado element, and this is sacred and most worthy of preservation. Ignoring for the moment the still earlier and shattering experiences of failure of the environment-mother, I would say that the traumatic experiences that lead to the organization of primitive defenses belong to the threat to the isolated core, the threat of its being found, altered, communicated with . . . [r]ape, and being eaten by cannibals, these are mere bagatelles as compared with the violation of the self's core, the alteration of the self's central elements by communication seeping through the defenses. For me this would be the sin against the self. We can understand the hatred people have of psycho-analysis which has penetrated a long way into the human personality, and which provides a threat to the

46. Winnicott also describes the link between childhood play and the cultural life of adults in terms of the capacity to use symbols: "In the healthy individual who . . . is a creative and spontaneous being, there is at the same time a capacity for the use of symbols. In other words health here is closely bound up with the capacity of the individual to live in an area that is intermediate between the dream and the reality, that which is called the cultural life." Winnicott, "Ego Distortion in Terms of True and False Self," 150.

human individual in his need to be secretly isolated. The question is: how to be isolated without having to be insulated?[47]

The reason Winnicott believed the true self must be protected from "communication" from the outside is that he believed the self must belong to oneself and be under one's own control. If someone outside were able to force through people's barriers and look into their inner reality, that person would possess or control them in a fundamental way, for then they would no longer be the one deciding who they are due to their exclusive self-knowledge, but someone else would have usurped that power. For Winnicott *this is the worst thing that could happen to a person*; it is the "sin against the self." And the threat of the self's violation explains why people resort to barricading themselves with the false self, and why many people avoid psychoanalysis.

For the true self to thrive without recourse to the unhealthy false self, it must be safe from violation, and people must be allowed to communicate or not communicate their true self on their own terms. In answer to his question about how to be isolated without having to be insulated, Winnicott says somewhat cryptically, "The answer might come from mothers who do not communicate with their infants except in so far as they are subjective objects."[48] What he is getting at is that if someone outside is to communicate or have a real relationship with a person's true self, then it must be because that person feels confident that he or she controls how much the other person knows. In other words, if people are to reveal their true self and the outcome be good (i.e., such that their true self is strengthened and defenses lessened), then it must be out of their own spontaneity and freedom and never out of coercion. And just as a good-enough-parent is able to foster the infant's true self by becoming a "subjective object" who abdicates "omnipotence" to the infant, a good-enough therapist fosters a patient's true self by holding it sacred and inviolable enough to become subject to it. Let us consider how a therapist does so.

Helping Others by Becoming Subject to Them

Winnicott was a psychoanalyst in the Freudian tradition, with ties to Anna Freud and Melanie Klein. Like others in this tradition he valued the

47. Winnicott, "Communicating and Not Communicating," 187.
48. Winnicott, "Communicating and Not Communicating," 188.

use of the transference that occurs between patient and therapist. Transference refers to the patient's unconscious carrying-over of past relationships (e.g., with mother or father) into the patient-therapist relationship. Winnicott explains transference and its usefulness:

> Here in the unconscious transference appear samples of the personal pattern of the patient's emotional life, or psychic reality. The analyst learns to detect these unconscious transference phenomena and, by using the clues supplied by the patient, is able to interpret that which is just ready for conscious acceptance at any one session. The most fruitful work is that which is done in terms of transference.[49]

His method of intervention can be grossly summarized as a two-step process: first, understand the patient's psychic reality through the transference, and then express interpretations of the transference at the optimal moments. Put this way, Winnicott's approach sounds very similar to others in classic psychoanalysis.

Winnicott, however, approached his analytic work in terms of his own system. Thus, he subsumes transference into his concept of "transitional phenomena." Like transference, transitional phenomena have to do with the way a person relates to another out of his or her psychological condition and history. A therapist works with the patient's transference in order to help him or her move from an inappropriate and neurotic (or psychotic) way of relating into a more objective and accurate view of reality.

Likewise, in an infant's development health entails gradually transitioning from a purely subjective relation to the external reality to relating objectively to perceived objects outside of the infant.[50] In both conceptualizations the movement into greater health requires a good-enough environment. For infants a good-enough parent is needed who becomes subject to the infant and meets the infant's need for "omnipotence" but also gradually becomes an object through her "misattunements" to the infant.[51]

---

49. Winnicott, "Child Analysis in the Latency Period," 117–18.

50. See Winnicott, "Ego Integration in Child Development," 57.

51. By infants having a need for "omnipotence" Winnicott meant that they must experience an illusory sense of control over their environment in order to develop well: by first realizing that their actions initiate responses (e.g., crying is followed by feeding), infants are equipped to later recognize themselves and others. From a Christian perspective, the word "omnipotence" seems odd and out of place, since it is a more fitting description of God than of a baby. As Tuber suggests, "competence" is a better label. Tuber, *Attachment, Play, and Authenticity.*

In the patient-therapist relationship the good-enough therapist is needed to fill in the gap between subjectivity and objectivity by allowing the patient to grow gradually in his or her capacity to relate to the therapist not out of transference but as a separate individual. Therapy provides a space for coming to terms with inner reality and external reality, a transitional space that exists as "a resting place for the individual engaged in the perpetual human task of keeping inner and outer reality separate yet inter-related."[52] The therapist purposively allows him- or herself to be used by the patient as a means of adapting to reality; the therapist becomes a subjective object to be used by the patient in order to eventually become an objective object:

> For me this means communicating with the patient from the position in which the transference neurosis (or psychosis) puts me. In this position I have some of the characteristics of a transitional phenomena, since although I represent the reality principle, and it is I who must keep an eye on the clock, I am nevertheless a subjective object for the patient.[53]

For Winnicott, the main task of analysis is to facilitate the competence of the patient's true self, or "ego-strength," in which "the patient begins to take for granted a feeling of existing in his or her own right."[54]

Attunement, Misattunement and Play, and Interpretation

Winnicott outlined three phases of strengthening the true self. First, ego-strength is built by being highly attuned and adapting sensitively to the patient. The therapist takes up a special role of care that is professional and reliable. Although therapists cannot show the same level of care that a mother can to her infant, they can show genuine concern and reliability if set within a professional framework, which Winnicott here describes:

> An interview must be arranged in a proper setting, and a time limit must be set. Within this framework we can be reliable, much more reliable than we are in our daily lives. Being reliable in all respects is the chief quality we need. This means not only that we respect the client's person and his or her rights to time and concern. We have our own sense of values, and so we are able

---

52. Winnicott, "Transitional Objects and Transitional Phenomena," 230.

53. Winnicott, "The Aims of Psycho-Analytic Treatment," 166.

54. Winnicott, "The Aims of Psycho-Analytic Treatment," 168.

to leave the client's sense of right and wrong as we find it. Moral judgment, if expressed, destroys the professional relationship absolutely and irrevocably. The time limit of the professional interview is for our own use; the prospect of the end of the session deals in advance with our resentment, which would otherwise creep in and spoil the operation of our genuine concern.[55]

These practical guidelines flow directly from Winnicott's theory. The time limit, as he says, is for the therapist's use; it serves to ensure that the therapist only has to be greatly attuned and adapting for a set time, so that genuine concern or love for the patient is not overcome by the strain of having to care past one's limit. *In lieu* of having the mother's capacity for "primary maternal preoccupation" the therapist utilizes a time limit, so that, if only for an hour, the patient can receive reliable and genuine care.

The therapist also must eschew expressing moral judgment.[56] To cast judgment is analogous to a non-adaptive mother's impingement on the baby's true self, and it will foster the false self. The first stage of therapy must begin to build support for the patient's self through a high degree of reliability, genuine concern, and a complete absence of coercion in the form of moral judgment.

In the second phase the patient experiments in being less dependent on the therapist for ego-support.[57] This corresponds to the infant's transition from absolute dependence to relative dependence. The patient may begin to become more aware of the therapist as an objective object, and the therapist can enable this by subtly dispelling the patient's illusion of his perfect attunement. Thus Winnicott says he would sometimes use verbal interpretations in order to call attention to his misattunement: "If I make none [i.e., interpretations] the patient gets the impression that I understand everything. In other words, I retain some outside quality by not being quite on the mark—or even by being wrong."[58] Because confidence has already been established in the therapist's reliability and support, the patient can handle recognizing the therapist's misattunements, and though the gap between patient-therapist becomes more clear, it is not threatening enough to keep the patient from playing within it.

55. Winnicott, "Advising Parents," 174–75.

56. By this assertion Winnicott does not mean that therapists should eschew morality but just the expression of stated judgments about patients' morality.

57. Winnicott, "The Aims of Psycho-Analytic Treatment," 168.

58. Winnicott, "The Aims of Psycho-Analytic Treatment," 167.

For Winnicott, play is very important in therapy. Winnicott thought it was essential to therapeutic intervention because play is the domain of the true self. In play, the patient can explore the gap between his or her inner reality and the outer reality that is gradually becoming identified with the therapist. The patient starts to notice and even appreciate the therapist's separateness because it does not force itself onto the patient (e.g., by coercive interpretations) but plays and leaves the interpreting mainly to the patient.

One of Winnicott's preferred techniques for child analysis was "the squiggle game," in which he and the child would take turns drawing a picture together. Twenty or thirty drawings might take up a session, and in that time Winnicott would facilitate the child's analysis using the draw-ings and the meaning expressed in them. Knowing his patient's problems and conflicts, he might present themes for the patient to address in the play/drawing. As Tuber notes, however, the play enabled his patient to do the meaning-making and call the shots on interpretations:

> Play is meaningful precisely because it is an original production of the child or a spontaneous duality between two partners. . . . Interpretation from the therapist, if it is in a directed, forced form, is thus the obverse of play. Winnicott therefore may pres-ent themes for [the child] to play with, which can shape her play in the direction of conflicts he wants to see if she can address, but he will leave the meaning-making to her, so that it remains *her* play, thus respecting her boundaries and her True Self.[59]

To the degree that the therapist makes therapy a kind of play, the patient will have the freedom and safety necessary to better recognize and ap-preciate his or her world and the objects (including people) within it. Through playful exploration of their world, patients become more ad-ept at navigating its challenges and less dependent on the therapist for ego-support.

In the third and final phase, the therapist will find the patient has become comfortable with his or her independence and true self.[60] Be-cause the patient's sense of self is strong enough to respond with freedom and competence, the therapist may venture an interpretation in order to call the patient to take conscious control of his or her own reality. Winn-icott says, "Verbalization [i.e., interpretation] at exactly the right moment

---

59. Tuber, *Attachment, Play, and Authenticity*, 133.

60. Winnicott, "The Aims of Psycho-Analytic Treatment," 168.

mobilizes intellectual forces."[61] The goal, however, is not a "clever inter-pretation" by the therapist.[62] Rather the therapist seeks to help the patient arrive at a place of ego-strength and a predominant sense that he or she is authentically relating to the world.

Maintaining a Professional Relationship

One last important aspect of Winnicott's approach to therapy concerns the issue of countertransference. The task of the therapist is a difficult one and the strain of bearing with sick people can tempt one to seek a payoff in the patient-therapist relationship. As just mentioned, the therapist's clever interpretations can be used in this way. Not only is it tempting to seek to meet one's own needs from work with patients, but patients are often very willing to comply, especially if their need is to enmesh with the therapist or to fall in love. For this reason, Winnicott emphasizes the necessity for a professional relationship with patients, modeled in antiq-uity by Hippocrates: "He perhaps founded the professional attitude. The medical oath gives a picture of a man or woman who is an idealized ver-sion of the ordinary man or woman in the street. . . . Included in the oath is the promise that we do not commit adultery with a patient."[63] A pro-fessional attitude establishes a protective barrier between therapist and patient, but it does more than protect from malpractice or a lawsuit. The professional attitude protects the true self of both therapist and patient. For the patient's true self to thrive, the therapist must respect the patient's ultimate need to be a separate individual. If the therapist lets unconscious feelings affect the analysis and interpretation, the patient's ego will not be strengthened. On the other hand, the therapist's true self can only thrive if he can also be separate. The professional attitude allows the therapist to acknowledge his emotions and feelings without letting them intrude on the patient's work:

61. Winnicott, "The Aims of Psycho-Analytic Treatment," 167.

62. The greater a patient's pathology the greater a therapist's restraint must be in making interpretations: "In our work, especially in working on the schizoid rather than the psycho-neurotic aspects of the personality, we do in fact wait, if we feel we know, until the patients tell us, and in doing so creatively make the interpretation we might have made; if we make the interpretation out of our own cleverness and experi-ence then the patient must refuse it or destroy it." Winnicott, "Communicating and Not Communicating," 182.

63. Winnicott, "Counter-Transference," 160.

Ideas and feelings come to mind, but these are well examined and sifted before an interpretation is made. This is not to say that feelings are not involved. On the one hand I may have stomach ache but this does not usually affect my interpretations; and on the other hand I may have been somewhat stimulated erotically or aggressively by an idea given by the patient, but again this fact does not usually affect my interpretative work. . . . The analyst is objective and consistent, for the hour, and he is not a rescuer, a teacher, an ally, or a moralist. The important effect of the analyst's own analysis in this connexion is that it has strengthened his own ego so that he can remain professionally involved, and this without too much strain.[64]

By remaining professional, the therapist ensures that the goal of therapy is attained: to foster the patient's true self, wean the patient from the false self, and facilitate the patient's growth towards independence so that he or she can relate authentically and competently with the world.

Susan Harter

Susan Harter (1939–2020) was a developmental psychologist whose research focused on the cognitive and social construction of the self. In the second edition of *The Construction of the Self*, she expresses one of her central concerns: "how the authenticity of the self, the ability to act in accord with one's true inner self, can become compromised over the course of development."[65] To begin, we will examine her theory of the self and its development.

Harter on the Self

Harter maintains that the self is both a cognitive and social construction. The picture people form of themselves is a product of their own thinking and others' influence.

In her basic definition of the self, Harter employ's William James' distinction between the I-self and Me-self.[66] The Me-self can be thought of as a cognitive construction, self-theory, self-portrait, self-representation,

---

64. Winnicott, "Counter-Transference," 161–62.

65. Harter, *The Construction of the Self*, 329.

66. Harter, *The Construction of the Self*, 16–22; see James, "The Principles of Psychology."

self-concept, or self-structure. The I-self is the self-reflector and the constructor of the Me-self, and as the I-self develops in cognitive capabilities, its construction of the Me-self is impacted. Harter refers to the I-self whenever she considers the cognitive capabilities that shape the structure and content of the Me-self and how it is described and evaluated differently at different stages.[67] Harter's research focuses on the Me-self, especially the evaluated or judged Me-self. However, the I-self is also of central concern, since through it the Me-self is formed and evaluated.

Representing Oneself with Increasing Complexity

Harter is particularly interested in how people articulate their understanding and evaluations of themselves through verbalized self-representations. She defines self-representations as "attributes or characteristics of the self that are consciously acknowledged by the individual through language."[68] Thus self-representations are conscious, cognitive constructions that can be verbalized.

The ability to make simple self-representations begins in early childhood between ages two and four and grows in greater complexity, starting with specific abilities and activities (e.g., "I can run!") and eventually widening out to generalizations across particular domains (e.g., "I am athletic") and to global descriptions and evaluations (e.g., "I am a good person").

As a person's cognitive capabilities develop through childhood and adolescence, the complexity and coherence of one's self-representations grow until they form an overall theory of the self (i.e., the Me-self). Harter writes, "The particular cognitive abilities and limitations of each developmental period (I-self processes or the self as subject) will represent the template that dictates the features of the self-portrait to be crafted (the Me-self or the self as object)."[69] Harter identifies four different I-self processes that function to form self-representations and that develop as a result of age-related cognitive advances: self-awareness, self-agency,

---

67. Along with James and several newer "postmodern" theorists, Harter assumes the possibility of persons constructing multiple Me-selves as they develop the capacity for describing themselves in different contexts. See Harter, *The Construction of the Self*, 6, 97, 296.

68. Harter, *The Construction of the Self*, 19.

69. Harter, "Development of Self-Representations," 613.

self-continuity, and self-coherence.[70] As these processes develop, so does one's self-theory.

Harter maintains that the self is both a cognitive and social construction. On the one hand, forming a self-theory requires certain cognitive capabilities or I-self processes that develop with age, and these "cognitive-developmental antecedents" of the self make it possible for one to form self-representations and attain an overall conceptualization of the self.[71] On the other hand, how one describes and evaluates oneself is also a product of "socialization experiences" that "influence the particular content and valence of one's self-representations."[72]

To explain the social aspects of the self's construction, Harter recalls the social interaction theories of Baldwin, Cooley, and Mead:

> As the symbolic interactionists observed, the self, as a social construction, develops within the crucible of interpersonal relationships with caregivers. One outcome is that the child comes to adopt the opinions that significant others are perceived to hold toward the self. These reflected appraisals come to define one's sense of self as a person. Through an *internalization* process, the child comes to own these evaluations as his/her own judgments about the self. Internalization must itself develop according to a predictable sequence of stages; there are prerequisites to the emergence of the looking-glass self.[73]

Other's opinions about oneself can become incorporated into one's own self-representations, resulting in a "looking-glass self" and changing how one describes and evaluates oneself. For Harter, the normative or ideal impact of socialization experiences would be to support the self-representations that a child or adolescent feels truly define him or her.[74]

By tracing the normative development of I-self processes in the stages and substages of childhood, adolescence, and emerging adulthood, Harter elucidates the differences in self-representations that occur as people develop as well as the influence of socialization experiences.[75]

---

70. Harter, *The Construction of the Self*, 16–17.

71. Harter, *The Construction of the Self*, 9–11.

72. Harter, *The Construction of the Self*, 11.

73. Harter, *The Construction of the Self*, 11–12; see Baldwin, *Mental Development of the Child and the Race*; Cooley, *Human Nature and the Social Order*; Mead, *Mind, Self & Society from the Standpoint of a Social Behaviorist*.

74. Harter, *The Construction of the Self*, 11–12.

75. Harter, *The Construction of the Self*, chap. 2–4.

Harter's substages of childhood are very early childhood (ages 2–4), early to middle (ages 5–7), and middle to late (ages 8–10). Before turning to her model, however, her observations on infancy must be considered.

Infancy

Harter draws out four key points on infant self-knowledge.[76] First, knowledge of self and knowledge of other develop at different times depending on the situation. Infants come to a knowledge of self *before* knowledge of other when it pertains to a sense of agency; infants must first learn that they are "active causal bodily agents" before they can appreciate this quality in other people.[77] On the other hand, knowledge of other precedes knowledge of self when it pertains to visual recognition and labeling: "The infant learns to recognize Mommy and Daddy before it can recognize the self, and learns the labels "Mommy and "Daddy" before learning its own name."[78]

Second, Margaret Mahler's stages of separation-individuation in infancy suggest that infants' healthy development of self depends on the development of "maternal object constancy": "That is, the infant must develop a stable or constant intrapsychic representation of mother that can be emotionally comforting to the infant in the mother's absence."[79]

Third, the stage model formulated by attachment theorists corroborates Mahler's stages and also identifies three types of attachment (i.e., avoidant, attached, and resistant) that may correlate with how well infants develop a sense of self.

Fourth, Sander's model of mother-infant interaction sheds light on the infant's role in the development of self-recognition. What infants do in relation to their mother plays a part in their emerging sense of self; for example, toddlers in the "terrible twos" become aware of their self-constancy (i.e., continued existence) when they can oppose mommy and still remain.

Finally, Harter concludes her examination by asserting that these frameworks for infant development (visual recognition studies, Mahler's phases of separation-individuation, Ainsworth's phases of attachment,

---

76. Harter, "Developmental Perspectives on the Self-System," 279–92.

77. Harter, "Developmental Perspectives on the Self-System," 284.

78. Harter, "Developmental Perspectives on the Self-System," 285.

79. Harter, "Developmental Perspectives on the Self-System," 292.

and Sander's stages of mother-infant interaction) need to be further integrated "in order to provide a comprehensive model of the development of self-understanding."[80]

Very Early Childhood (Ages 2–4)

Before reaching two years of age, toddlers have become adept at bodily awareness and can recognize and distinguish their own bodies from others. However, a shift occurs when they start to use self-referential language around age two. Now for the first time they can describe the self verbally. Self-representations include descriptions of one's body ("I have brown eyes"), physical activities ("I can run fast"), social relationships ("This is my grandma"), and possessions ("I have a doll"), but these descriptions are limited to concrete, observable phenomena. Children at this stage lack the ability to make abstract generalizations about themselves (e.g., "I am athletic") or to bring their descriptions of themselves into a coherent picture: "the young child is incapable of integrating these compartmentalized representations of self. . . . This lack of coherence is a general cognitive characteristic that pervades the young child's thinking across a variety of domains."[81]

Children at this stage have an "all-or-none thinking" and cannot relate or hold together opposing attributes.[82] They also conflate how they want to perform with how they actually do: "young children cannot yet formulate an ideal self-concept that is differentiated from a real self-concept."[83] Due to these and other limitations in their cognitive capabilities, children at the stage of very early childhood form inaccurate evaluations of self attributes.

These exaggerated descriptions are normally positive. For example, a young child who says, "I can run faster than anyone," typifies the vaunted self-evaluations of very early childhood. This feature, however, is normal and part of healthy development, according to Harter, who argues that it accomplishes a protective function:

> Self-enhancement can serve to avert feelings of helplessness in
> the face of daunting challenges that accompany the master of

80. Harter, "Developmental Perspectives on the Self-System," 292.
81. Harter, *The Construction of the Self*, 30–31.
82. Harter, *The Construction of the Self*, 32.
83. Harter, *The Construction of the Self*, 31.

many developmentally appropriate skills (e.g., learning to throw a ball, read, understand written language, understand complex social rules).[84]

Harter adds that the adaptive function of inaccurate self-evaluations is not only a result of normal cognitive development but also of good parental support. As parents allow for and encourage the young child's self-enhancement they promote his or her well-being. On an immediate level, parental support affirms the child's verbalized over-confidence in his or her abilities and so motivates the child to keep meeting new challenges. On a deeper level, parental support affirms the child's pre-verbalized sense of confidence or esteem in his or her whole self.

Although children at this stage can only evaluate separate attributes and cannot verbalize global self-evaluations (e.g., one's worth as a person), Harter observes that the antecedents to such evaluations are already in play, namely, "concrete acknowledgement of parental affection."[85] In other words, very young children can absorb overall evaluations from significant others and respond to them with behavior that reveals a latent, pre-verbal sense of self-esteem. The healthy overall self-confidence that one will need later in development (i.e., adolescence and adulthood) depends upon the over-confidence in one's abilities as a child that cognitive limitations and parental support facilitates.

To summarize, what Harter argues is that in healthy psychological development very young children have an unrealistic view of their abilities that is enabled by their cognitive capacity and fostered by parental support. One of the main reasons that this is healthy is because it serves to protect children from being stifled in their exploration and growth. Another reason is that it lays the foundation for a healthy self-esteem and self-confidence in later stages. While the exaggerated boasts of young children are inappropriate for adults, who should be able to feel confidence in themselves without lying to themselves, such boasting is good for children, who need "delusions of grandeur" in order to move ahead.

Early to Middle Childhood (Ages 5–7)

In the next stage of development, which Harter labels "early to middle childhood," children continue to display unrealistic evaluations of their

---

84. Harter, *The Construction of the Self*, 33.
85. Harter, *The Construction of the Self*, 34.

performance, yet with more self-awareness.[86] A major advance in years 5–7 is the ability to verbalize opposites (e.g., tall versus short). Thus, children at this stage go beyond describing their attributes to verbally qualifying themselves as good or bad. This advance reinforces children's over-estimations of their abilities: "These [over-confident] beliefs are even more intractable than in the previous period given cognitive and linguistic advances that bring such beliefs into consciousness, allowing them to be verbalized, and given benevolent adults who support such positivity."[87]

Increased ability to describe the self verbally combined with continued affirmation from parents and others results in the child's firmer confidence. However, due to other remaining cognitive limitations, children at this stage do not apply positive or negative evaluations in terms of more general, continuous "traits":

> Although children may describe themselves in such terminology as good or bad, nice or mean, smart or dumb, these characteristics do not represent "traits." . . . From a cognitive-developmental perspective, traits represent *higher-order generalizations*, as we see at the next stage where abilities in specific school subjects combine to represent the inference that one is smart. From the perspective of *personality* theorists, traits represent characteristics that are stable across time and situation and typically converge with external ratings or manifestations.[88]

Middle to Late Childhood (Ages 8–10)

In the final substage of "middle to late childhood," children begin to describe themselves in terms of traits, such as being smart, popular, or nice. Children become more adept at describing their emotions and begin to leave behind their unbalanced all-or-none thinking: "Thus, the child develops a representational system in which positive emotions (e.g., "I'm usually happy with my friends") are integrated with negative emotional representations (e.g., "I get sad if my friends aren't there to do things with")."

Further, children at this stage can experience emotions about themselves, reflecting their growing capacity for self-evaluation; the

---

86. Harter, *The Construction of the Self*, 49–54.

87. Harter, *The Construction of the Self*, 55.

88. Harter, *The Construction of the Self*, 52.

"self-conscious emotions" of pride and shame become part of the child's experience for the first time.

Two other major advances regard socialization experiences: children can consciously incorporate their parents' evaluations of them, and they can compare themselves with others in order to judge their own competence in various traits.

Altogether these advances enable children to discern holistic evaluations of themselves, as Harter explains:

> One's overall worth as a person can now be expressed verbally. Prior to this age level, children could only formulate self-perceptions within specific domains . . . but could not yet integrate these self-appraisals into an overall evaluation of their self-esteem. In mid- to late childhood, children come to appreciate that success in domains of personal importance promotes high self-esteem. . . . Moreover, [a child] realizes that the approval of both parents and peers also contributes to her liking herself as a person, consistent with Cooley's looking glass self-theorizing.[89]

Early Adolescence (Ages 11–13)

The arrival of adolescence brings with it a "proliferation of selves."[90] In the first substage which Harter calls "early adolescence," youth ages 11–13 begin to understand themselves in terms of holistic generalizations that combine various traits. "For example," Harter says, "one can construct an abstraction of the self as "intelligent" by combining such traits as smart, curious, and creative."[91]

However, these characterizations of the self do not take into account opposing traits that appear at separate times, and so Harter continues, "Alternately, one may create an abstraction that the self is an "airhead" given a situation where one feels dumb and "just plain stupid.""[92] Young adolescents tend not to relate such opposing evaluations, but instead they "think about compartmentalized self-attributes, one at a time, but

---

89. Harter, *The Construction of the Self*, 63.

90. Harter, *The Construction of the Self*, 76.

91. Harter, *The Construction of the Self*, 77.

92. Harter, *The Construction of the Self*, 77.

not simultaneously."[93] Interestingly, early adolescent experience entails bifurcated, all-or-none thinking similar to a young child's.

The cognitive advances of adolescence, therefore, result in a return to unrealistic self-evaluations as in very early childhood, but at this stage the evaluations focus on abstract generalizations (e.g., "I am so intelligent"), rather than concrete skills (e.g., "I can run fast"). Also, social influences can take on greater meaning because adolescence brings a heightened sensitivity to the opinions of others, including one's peers.

Middle Adolescence (Ages 14–16)

"Middle adolescence" occurs during ages 14–16.[94] With the cognitive facility to discern the various roles that one has, youth at this substage may wonder which role truly defines them. Youth now start to relate the opposing generalizations that they ignored previously in early adolescence. However, although they can compare opposing attributes that show up in different contexts (e.g., home, school, part-time job), they cannot resolve the oppositions. "Self-awareness, therefore, is quite intense; however, the images are not stable or enduring. . . . By analogy, awareness quickly shifts from role to role where one's image of self is defined quite differently."[95]

Ideally, parents and other significant adults will support adolescents at this time by providing accurate opinions that present a more balanced picture of the adolescent's self than he or she is able to recognize.

Late Adolescence (Ages 17–19)

In "late adolescence" the stalemate between opposing self-generalization in the previous substage is overcome. Youth are able to resolve tensions between various self-representations through the use of abstractions even broader than those made before. Harter gives the example of a student leaving for college who integrates feelings of excitement about going away with feelings of sadness about leaving parents; the mature adolescent can mitigate the opposition between excitement and sadness by describing the experience as "bittersweet."[96]

---

93. Harter, *The Construction of the Self*, 78.

94. Harter, *The Construction of the Self*, 94–108.

95. Harter, *The Construction of the Self*, 96–97.

96. Harter, *The Construction of the Self*, 121.

Moreover, they are not bothered about the seeming contradictions that appear in their various roles because they can see the variances as normal and adaptive. Ideally, parents and significant adults will support the more balanced conclusions that adolescents draw by virtue of their ability to reconcile real or seeming inconsistencies in themselves.

Emerging Adulthood (Ages 18–25).

Moving to another stage of development, Harter examines "emerging adulthood" which includes persons in the range of 18–25 years of age.[97] Ideally, in these years one will achieve a conscious sense of having a firm identity. This achievement is won by considering different future selves and thoughtfully deciding on a plan for their adult life, especially as it regards occupational and romantic commitments. Referring to people in America (and other culturally alike countries), Harter asserts that emerging adulthood is "a necessary developmental phase" and that for most people it is one they "will eventually navigate with relative success."[98]

Ideally, persons in this phase of big decision-making will have the benefit of "responsible adult role models" who can offer guidance as to where and how these persons should direct their interests and establish their identity.[99]

This stage's challenge constitutes no less than an integration of all one's life choices:

> The task at this stage is not only to explore and experiment with possible life choices in the realms of occupational and educational options, social and romantic decisions, and belief systems (e.g., moral, religious, political). One must also *integrate* the

97. Harter notes that debate exists over whether emerging adulthood should be considered a stage at all, citing evidence that in cultures outside America and other western countries (e.g., China) people in this age range demonstrate different characteristics. While noting the differences, Harter seems to assume the value in assigning at least some people to this stage. Therefore, as to the question of whether "emerging adulthood" should be considered a universal "stage" in all cultures or a contingent "process" for some persons, she concludes, "As with many debates that have dominated our field over the years (e.g., nature vs. nurture), the truth would appear to lie somewhere in between." Harter, *The Construction of the* Self, 146.

98. Harter, *The Construction of the Self*, 147.

99. Harter, *The Construction of the Self*, 149–50.

outcomes of such explorations in a manner that brings meaning and coherence to one's identity.[100]

The emerging adult must construct an elaborate self-system that integrates all that one knows and is coming to know about oneself and one's world. Harter concludes that adult maturation is not a quick or easy attainment:

> This is a lengthy process that requires extensive life experiences, considerable reflection, the support of more mature individuals, and the cooperation of neurological development, in order to reach such a teleological end state. Many adults never achieve this cognitive-developmental nirvana.[101]

Thus, in describing the goals and tasks of emerging adulthood, Harter seems to be positing that adulthood is always "emerging."

Summary of Harter on the Self

To summarize, Harter traces the development of the self's construction through seven developmental stages: very early childhood, early to middle childhood, middle to late childhood, early adolescence, middle adolescence, late adolescence, and emerging adulthood. Developmental advances throughout the stages depend upon both cognitive and social factors. Every stage can be understood as a cognitive advance upon those before because of an increasing ability to generalize or abstract out from previous self-descriptions and self-evaluations. As individuals mature in their cognitive capacity to relate and integrate separate attributes, they come to understand themselves at higher and more abstract levels. Ideally these advances, aided by social experiences that support an authentic sense of self, will result in firmer self-coherence and more accurate self-descriptions and self-evaluations, enabling psychological health and well-being.

Harter on the False Self

Along with tracing the self's normative construction, Harter also describes how certain cognitive-developmental liabilities and potentially harmful social experiences can give rise to pathological forms of

---

100. Harter, *The Construction of the Self*, 136.

101. Harter, *The Construction of the Self*, 136.

self-construction, including negative self-esteem, narcissism, and maladaptive self-enhancement strategies.

On the one hand, Harter seeks to demonstrate that the human capacity for self-construction (i.e., forming a Me-self) has many positive functions that can be categorized as "organizational," "motivational," and "protective."[102] Thus, the I-self processes that occur at various stages of development can serve good ends, such as *organizing* one's reality and enabling one to "interpret and give meaning to life experiences and to maintain a coherent picture of oneself in relation to one's world."[103] I-self processes can also provide *motivational* impetus by enabling one to set up goals to accomplish and an ideal-self to attain, and they can *protect* one from painful affect by "maintaining favorable impressions of one's attributes."[104]

On the other hand, cognitive I-self processes hold certain liabilities that, if exploited, can lead to pathology. These liabilities exist because the self is not only cognitive but social; the self is formed, in part, when we internalize others' opinions of us, and so our psychological health depends not only upon our cognitive makeup or "hardware" but also upon the social influences or "software" that we incorporate into our self-understanding. Harter explains how healthy self-construction is contingent on the looking-glass self reflected in others:

> Benevolent socializing agents will readily provide the nurturance, approval, and support that will be mirrored in self-evaluations that are positive. Approval, in the form of the reflected appraisals of others, is, therefore, internalized as acceptance of self. However, in the search for his/her image in the social mirror, the child may well gaze through a glass darkly. Caregivers lacking in responsiveness, nurturance, encouragement, and approval, as well as socializing agents who are rejecting, punitive, or neglectful, will cause their children to develop tarnished images of self.[105]

In consequence of such poor socialization experiences, people can form a self that is deficient in positive self-affect and marked by a sense of shame, leading to depression and other disorders.

---

102. Harter, *The Construction of the Self*, 13.
103. Harter, *The Construction of the Self*, 13.
104. Harter, *The Construction of the Self*, 13.
105. Harter, *The Construction of the Self*, 12.

Socialization that Compromises the True Self

In particular, Harter recognizes the potential for harmful experiences with others that diminishes one's sense of authenticity. Again, she contrasts healthy and unhealthy forms of socialization and their results, but specifically in terms of the true self and false self:

> if significant others provide support for who one is as a person, for attributes that the child or adolescent feels truly define the self, then one will experience the self as authentic. However, the construction of a self that is so highly dependent upon the internalization of others' opinions can, under some circumstances, lead to the creation of a false self that does not mirror one's authentic experience. False-self behavior is particularly likely to emerge if caregivers make their approval contingent upon the child's living up to his/her own unrealistic standards of behavior, as the child must adopt a socially implanted self.[106]

Thus, if our influential figures (e.g., parents) refuse to affirm the self we think we are, we will attempt to reconstrue the self into a form that does win affirmation, but at the cost of our sense of authenticity (i.e., the true self).

As we shall now see, Harter demonstrates how the loss of the true self can occur at each stage of development through the exploitation of normative I-self processes by harmful socializing experiences.

Compromising the True Self in Childhood

First, one's true self can be compromised in childhood.

Very young children may begin to construct a false self because others distort their self-narrative. The social danger is that, as Harter says, "Caregiver's renditions of their child's narrative can distort the child's experiences, planting the seeds of an inauthentic self, if the child accepts the falsified version of his/her life story."[107] There is also the danger that the child will use his newly acquired language abilities to build a false self through verbal self-representations.

The construction of the false self can continue on from early to middle childhood if parents contribute inflated images of their child as

---

106. Harter, *The Construction of the Self*, 13.
107. Harter, *The Construction of the Self*, 330.

special, exceptional, and better than the child's peers. At this stage, the child is the victim of all-or-none thinking, which promotes unrealistic self-perceptions.

Finally, in middle to late childhood, children develop the ability to distinguish between their real and ideal self. Harter says, "This realization can potentially lead to negative self-evaluations."[108] In order to counter this threat and feel better about themselves, children may blur the distinction between the real and ideal self, or between what they are and what they want to be. By inflating their self-perceptions, they may feel better, but in the process their true self gives way to false self behavior.

Compromising the True Self in Adolescence

Second, one's true self can be compromised in adolescence. The perspective of one's peers begins to play a greater role, and when one's self-construction depends too much upon the opinion of others, one's authentic experience is sacrificed. As adolescents try to manage how they appear to others (i.e., "impression management"), they will eventually realize they are acting falsely, adding to their distress about figuring out who they really are. Caregivers can exacerbate adolescents' false self behavior by setting unrealistic standards in order to gain approval. Harter says this "conditionality" aids the construction of the false self and also lowers self-esteem.[109]

Those experiencing middle adolescence will have more trouble discerning their true self, because they have so many possible selves to choose from due to the many roles demanded of them. Harter says, "These contradictory self-attributes contribute to unstable self-representations that cannot be integrated into a unified sense of self."[110] Not only is it difficult to make sense of one's multiple selves, but discerning what comprises one's true self may seem like an arbitrary choice.

In late adolescence, youth internalize the standards and opinions they have received and formulated, but they may not be sure if their thinking is authentic or not. They are liable to adopt a false self that lends a sense of competency as a way of coping with their uncertainty.

---

108. Harter, *The Construction of the Self*, 331.
109. Harter, *The Construction of the Self*, 331.
110. Harter, *The Construction of the Self*, 332.

Compromising the True Self in Adulthood

Third, one's true self can be compromised throughout adulthood.

In emerging adulthood, failure to establish a firm sense of identity increases the likelihood of false self behavior, which in turn can "compromise the formation of meaningful, intimate relationships."[111] In an effort to assuage their shame for failing to meet their own expectations and those of society, emerging adults may rely on the false self and other forms of self-deception.

Harter cites several studies that reveal the prevalence of self-enhancement strategies and self-serving biases among adults. For example, she cites Leary who says that perhaps the most common self-enhancement strategy is to overestimate one's positive qualities.[112] People may describe their strengths as heavily outweighing their weaknesses. As Greenwald describes it, this strategy is akin to the practice among totalitarian regimes that rewrite history in order to emphasize the positive qualities of a dictator or government.[113] Harter also cites research revealing that many adults are overly optimistic about their characteristics and base their self-evaluations on snap judgments rather than sustained reflection.[114] Related research also suggests that such adults are largely unaware of the fact that their self-assessments are inaccurate.[115] The complexity and efficacy of false self behavior reaches its zenith in adulthood, because adults' false self behavior is able to obscure not only their true self but even the fact that they are behaving falsely.

Motives and Skills for Maintaining the False Self Expand

Harter observes that as individuals move from early childhood to adolescence, they gradually develop and strengthen the motives and skills necessary for self-enhancing strategies. Very young children, like adults who exhibit false self behavior, promote an unrealistic view of themselves for self-protective purposes. One major difference between the adult who acts falsely and the young child, however, is that a child's positive sense of

111. Harter, *The Construction of the Self*, 151.

112. Leary, *The Curse of the Self*.

113. Greenwald, "The Totalitarian Ego," 603–18.

114. Gilovich et al., "Shallow Thoughts about the Self," 67–84.

115. Krueger and Dunning, "Unskilled and Unaware of It," 1121–34; Hodges et al., "Difficulties in Recognizing One's Own Incompetence," 87–89.

self is strong and certain, but a hypocritical adult's sense of self is fragile and liable to exposure. Young children who speak unrealistically about themselves are usually being thoroughly authentic, while adults displaying the same behavior are not. Very young children are also different from adults in that they do not possess the skills that underlie many of the self-serving biases exhibited by adults.

Older children develop the ability to assess the opinions of others, making them vulnerable to a loss in self-esteem. Harter regards this period as a critical stage in development, "because those children with negative self-views now begin to possess a *motive* to engage in self-protective strategies."[116] Also, due to newly realized cognitive skills, they begin to utilize some premature self-enhancing strategies, such as considering themselves better than others by comparison.

Adolescent development brings self-enhancing skills almost to an adult level of deftness, while experiences among peers and competitive social contexts increase one's motivation to defend against the loss of self-esteem.

Through the course of these stages, both the motive for false self behavior and the skills necessary to accomplish it advance in strength and efficacy.

According to Harter, developing and maintaining false self behavior is maladaptive in the long run. As a case in point, she seeks to demonstrate the fact that false self behavior promotes narcissism. Inevitably, false self behavior will compromise one's ability to thrive and meet the challenges of life. Citing Leary, she says, "Moreover, self-serving illusions blind people to their shortcomings that will, in turn, interfere with their motivation to confront and improve upon their less than desirable characteristics."[117] Anxiety and unhappiness will plague individuals who eschew authenticity for the sake of covering their deficiencies.

Harter on the True Self

Let us now briefly consider Harter's understanding of the true self, particularly focusing on why she identifies it with psychological health. For people to have a sense that their self is true means that they feel authentic. This feeling of authenticity looks different in every stage of development.

---

116. Harter, *The Construction of the Self*, 337.
117. Harter, *The Construction of the Self*, 338–39.

The True Self in Early Childhood: Inaccurate but Authentic

In early childhood, children are not able to grasp or verbalize high-level generalizations of themselves, much less a self-theory, so the true self is not conceptually discerned in the same way that it is in adulthood. However, the true self appears in the young child's natural, spontaneous behavior, and to the degree that parents approve the child's authentic self-expressions the true self will be fostered. Children's capacity to use language allows them to objectify themselves, and while Harter notes that this can result in inauthentic self-representations, the opposite is also possible: children can use language to describe and represent themselves authentically.

We must observe that the authenticity of a young child's self-representations does not necessarily equate with accuracy; for example, children may describe themselves in exaggerated terms (e.g., "I can run forever!") yet be perfectly authentic. In addition, distortions in one's self-descriptions derived from evaluations of the self by one's parents may lead to "the formation of a self that is perceived as unauthentic if one accepts the falsified version of experience," and since children typically absorb whatever evaluations they are given by significant others, the way is paved for the false self.[118] On the other hand, if parents accurately mirror their child's experience and support their authentic self-representations, then the true self will be confirmed and strengthened.

The True Self in Later Childhood: Accurate Perceptions and Optimal Self-Esteem

As children enter middle to late childhood and their self-evaluations become more accurate, healthy or "optimal" self-esteem will shift from being based on authentic (but often overly-positive) self-evaluations that skilled parents affirm to being based on more accurate self-evaluations that parents affirm but also sensitively improve.

Because older children have attained the capacity to take others' perspectives and realize that other people are evaluating them, they can begin to be tempted to engage in pretense in order to please others and maintain high self-esteem. Being conscious of the difference between their internal hidden self and the self they present before others, older

118. Harter, *The Construction of the Self*, 47.

children begin to recognize that they can fool others into accepting an enhanced and inaccurate opinion of them. Children at this stage not only have a heightened ability for intentional false self behavior but they also have a potentially greater motive: they can now compare their positive qualities with their negative ones. Social comparison as well as the ability to compare the real and ideal self mean that these children are more balanced and accurate in their self-evaluations.

At this stage, true self behavior appears in the child who responds adaptively to these advances by accepting his or her perceived failures without recourse to self-protective or self-enhancing strategies. This child is able to act authentically because "optimal self-esteem" has been fostered throughout his or her development:

> Optimal self-esteem is grounded in reality, based on a balanced perspective of one's personal strengths and weaknesses. . . . It reflects an inherent sense of the self as worthy . . . and is relatively stable. It does not become inflated when one succeeds nor does it crumble in the face of failure. Furthermore, it is characterized by greater personal integrity and authenticity.[119]

As opposed to "contingent self-esteem," in which a child's sense of worth depends upon the approval of others, optimal self-esteem is not dependent on outside support, because it is grounded in a sense of worth that has already been internalized. Because of adequate approval and love throughout the child's development, by the time middle to late childhood arrives he or she is able to handle its challenges in a relatively independent way. Assuming that parents have adequately fostered the child's true self up to this point, what is most needed from them and other significant adults is that they help the child accurately perceive and adaptively integrate his or her positive and negative qualities.

The True Self in Adolescence: A Real "Me" Within

For adolescents grappling with the contradictory ways they relate to others in their various roles, the true self is the "real me" that lies underneath their inconsistencies.[120]

In early and middle adolescence youth lack the cognitive capabilities to totally resolve all their contradictory selves and solidify a sense of

119. Harter, *The Construction of the Self*, 69.
120. See Harter, *The Construction of the Self*, 115, 296–97.

their true self, but it can be protected and nurtured if others sufficiently support authentic self-expression; the higher the support, the higher the sense of authenticity.

Further, Harter links a sense of authenticity with self-esteem: adolescents value the parts of themselves that seem authentic but feel unhappy or ashamed about the parts that seem false. Interpreting research data on authenticity in adolescence, Harter sees a definite relationship between higher support from others, a greater sense of authenticity, and higher self-esteem.[121]

The ideal outcome of development in adolescence is a firmer sense of authenticity that will promote confidence in oneself and eventually develop into an established idea of who one is in the world: "Teenagers who successfully navigate the journey of self-development should acquire a clear and consolidated sense of true self that is realistic and internalized, one that will lay the basis for further identity development."[122]

The True Self in Adulthood: Authentic Sense of Identity

Finally, the true self in adulthood appears in those who have achieved an authentic sense of identity. At this stage, authenticity is linked with positive benefits such as high self-esteem that is genuine and stable, realistic self-appraisals, the pursuit of self-determined goals, and genuineness and honesty in close relationships.[123]

Regarding relationships, two further points should be mentioned. First, Harter observes that authenticity and well-being are fostered most when one maintains a healthy balance between "autonomy" and "connectiveness."[124] Persons with a strong and healthy sense of individuality will also demonstrate relatedness and empathy with others, and through this combination the true self will thrive. In other words, people who are able to validate their true self and who also receive validation from others will experience a vibrant sense of authenticity.

Second, Harter asks if it is possible to be too authentic. She answers that, yes, if one's honesty goes uncensored, it can sometimes result in harm to a relationship. Citing Lerner's distinction between honesty and

---

121. See Harter et al., "Lack of Voice," 153.

122. Harter, "Self and Identity Development," 354.

123. Harter, The Construction of the Self, 363–64.

124. Harter, The Construction of the Self, 308–10; Harter, "Authenticity," 389.

truth-telling, she says that whereas honesty sometimes represents "the uncensored expression of negative thoughts and feelings," truth-telling means communicating one's authentic opinion in a way that demonstrates "thought, timing, tact, and empathy for the other person's position."[125] She concludes, "Honesty, therefore, is often not the best policy if it does not contain the elements of truth-telling that will facilitate, rather than jeopardize, relationships."[126]

Harter on Interventions

In this section, interventions will be examined that Harter proposes for fostering the sense that one is living as his or her true self. Harter is especially interested in interventions that aim to strengthen realistic self-perceptions, authenticity, and true self-esteem.

First, let's look at interventions Harter recommends during childhood and adolescence.

Helping Children and Adolescents: Verbal Validation, Listening, Unconditional Support, and Objective Standards

As we have seen, although the distinction between the true and false self does not become consciously salient until adolescence, Harter asserts, "The foundations of authenticity, however, are laid down in early childhood."[127] One way this occurs is through the use of language and the construction of narrative. Around age two, children begin to use language to describe themselves and their experiences; this capacity to capture one's self-narrative in "autobiographical memory" can strengthen one's sense of self.[128] Harter recommends that parents be encouraged to "verbalize their children's reality, rather than their adult agenda."[129] Parents should validate the child's own viewpoint and perspective of his or her experience. Of course, the child's viewpoint will be restricted according to cognitive-developmental limitations, and as we have seen, preschool children tend to have exaggerated perceptions and evaluations

125. Harter, "Authenticity," 391; see Lerner, *The Dance of Deception*, 16.
126. Harter, "Authenticity," 391.
127. Harter, "Authenticity," 386.
128. Harter, "Authenticity," 386.
129. Harter, "Authenticity," 391.

of themselves. However, since their perceptions are true *for them*, parents should validate and respect the child's experience as he or she perceives it rather than trying to reject or replace it.

Parents should appreciate that a child's authentic experience includes his or her affective reactions; reminiscent of Winnicott's thinking, Harter writes:

> To the extent that children capitulate and accept the mother's interpretation of their emotions, in order to please them or avoid disapproval, they are distorting this true-self experiences [*sic*]. Alternatively, if parents accept children's accounts of their emotional reactions, such validation will promote their sense of authenticity and reinforce their trust in the personal reality of their affective experiences . . . if parents encourage their children to construct a narrative based on their own memories of events, thereby validating the children's own experience, then the groundwork for authentic self-representations will be laid.[130]

Thus Harter also recommends that parents afford children a central participatory role in telling about their experience and using their voice, so as to promote their becoming "instrumental authors of their own true life stories."[131]

In order to have confidence in their true self and to cement their authenticity, children and adolescents need their parents to validate them through listening: "By listening, one communicates that a child's thoughts, opinions, and feelings are respected. In turn, children and adolescents come to express themselves authentically."[132] Harter's empirical studies on "voice" in adolescence lend support to these recommendations by revealing that the stronger one's level of voice (i.e., the more freely adolescents feel they can speak their mind in various contexts), the greater one's sense of authenticity.[133]

Harter's research on "perceived support" in adolescence confirms another important aspect of good parenting that is required to foster authenticity: unconditional support.[134] In Harter's studies, teenagers reporting the highest levels of true self behavior also reported the highest levels of the unconditional support from their parents. Therefore, Harter

130. Harter, "Authenticity," 386.

131. Harter, "Authenticity," 391.

132. Harter, "Authenticity," 392.

133. Harter et al., "Lack of Voice."

134. Harter and Marold, "A Model of the Effects," 360–74.

hails the critical necessity of communicating to children and adolescents what Rogers called "unconditional positive regard."[135] One form this support takes is telling children that their strengths and overall personality are valued. Going a step further, Harter insists that parents help their children learn to validate themselves by teaching them to recognize and own their strengths:

> approval must be communicated so that the child comes to internalize or actively own the positive attributes rather than remain dependent on the external feedback of socializing agents. For example, when a child or adolescent engages in a commendable behavior, telling him or her that "you must be very proud of yourself for what you did" will be more likely to foster internalization than will a comment to the effect that as a parent you are glad that the child did what you wanted.[136]

Harter compliments her emphasis on unconditional support with a caveat on discipline:

> Clearly effective child-rearing practices require that parents clarify standards, provide expectations, and specify the consequences of behavior. However, if these practices are exercised within an atmosphere of nurturance, genuine concern for the child, and respect for who the child is as a person, not only will there be more compliance but the child will come to value the behaviors that parents would like to instill. To the extent that these values are internalized, they will eventually come to be perceived as true-self behavior.[137]

Cultivating a child's true self does not mean that parents should let children run amuck without rules or discipline. Rather, parents must take care to pass along values and norms of behavior in a way that communicates their unconditional support and validation of the child's own authentic experience.

The therapeutic value of providing children with an environment of unconditional support *and* objective standards is further confirmed in Harter's evaluation of the self-esteem movement in public schools.[138] Harter addresses how programs in the United States (particularly in

135. Harter, "Authenticity," 387; see Rogers, *Client-Centered Therapy.*
136. Harter, "Authenticity," 391.
137. Harter, "Authenticity," 391–92.
138. Harter, *The Construction of the Self,* 353–60.

California) aimed to raise students' self-esteem in order to improve academic achievement have not produced the desired effects. Citing opponents of these programs, Harter observes that efforts to raise self-esteem have resulted in *inflating* self-esteem without improving student achievement, and also these efforts have distracted teachers and students from focusing on mastering skills.[139]

On the one hand, there seems to be little statistical support for the benefits of inflating students' self-esteem. Rather, evidence points to the potential harm it can produce. Harter largely agrees with those who argue that "educators should not provide positive feedback that has not been earned."[140] Teachers should strive to give students accurate feedback that promotes a realistic self-view.

Harter adds, however, that this should not preclude encouraging students towards aspirations for which they do not yet have the requisite skills, if it is possible for them to work towards attaining those skills.[141] In other words, students need both accurate and adaptive self-views; they need affirmation that although the truth tells them that they are not all they wish they were (i.e., their ideal self), success and improvement is possible.

Self-esteem programs have often employed direct, simplistic interventions such as promoting positive self-evaluations (e.g., "I am special") but have neglected to target the causes of self-esteem. This approach is insufficient to meet students' need for authenticity and can actually promote inflated and inaccurate self-esteem. By divorcing self-esteem from an accurate evaluation of student achievement, self-esteem programs may be complicit in promoting self-enhancement strategies that, in the long run, are characterized by bad decision-making, anxiety, and unhappiness. Harter observes that other correlates or consequences of inflated

---

139. See Baumeister et al., "Does High Self-Esteem Cause Better Performance, Interpersonal Success, Happiness, or Healthier Lifestyles?" 1–44; Baumeister, "Should Schools Try to Boost Self-Esteem?" 14–19.

140. Harter, *The Construction of the Self*, 357.

141 It might be helpful to note that some students will need more or less accurate feedback depending on their age. In line with Harter's agenda, interventions for students should be designed and administered with sensitivity to different needs among children and adolescents; one could apply this point by saying that students in early to middle childhood typically need more emphasis on praise and affirmation (e.g., "You are a good worker!) than accurate self-views (e.g., "Your reading level is below average"), whereas older students need accurate feedback along with encouragement to keep pursuing their goals.

self-esteem may include fragile self-esteem, egotism, narcissism, lack of empathy, and violence.

Harter points out the problem with the self-esteem movement is not the aim of helping students attain high self-esteem but the distractive emphasis on self-esteem that has obscured its underlying determinants, especially the achievement of self-determined goals. Research done by self-determination theorists supports the conclusion that when people pursue goals that hold intrinsic value for them, optimal self-esteem is the result.[142] Harter concludes that students should be directed to focus on *learning* and to satisfy the aspirations, curiosity, and internal motivation they have for *mastering certain skills*.

Doll Play Therapy for Children

Although Harter's recommended interventions for children in *The Construction of the Self* and other works tend to be on a general level (e.g., good parenting practices, school programs), she has also written up a more clinical viewpoint.[143] In this article she describes a two-phase model of doll play therapy she devised.

The first phase is diagnostic; the therapist approaches play with the child in order to better understand the presenting problems. During the diagnostic phase, the therapist is a "participant observer" and follows the lead of the child, who decides what the doll-play will be about, its characters, who will portray each character, and so on. Harter notes that, as a general principle, the child plays the roles of the significant adults in his or her life, while the therapist is directed to play the roles of the children. Next, the child is encouraged to begin the dialogue between the dolls. When the therapist's turn comes to speak, Harter emphasizes the importance of pausing to ask the child what should be said; in this way, the therapist learns more about the child's view of self and others:

> By engineering the dialogue in this fashion, my client thus speaks for all the characters present. . . . Thus, I can begin to piece together a picture of the family dynamics which might illuminate her problems. . . . Its effectiveness lies in having the child create

142. Ryan and Brown, "What Is Optimal Self-Esteem?" 120–31.

143. Harter, "Cognitive-Developmental Considerations in the Conduct of Play Therapy," 117–21. Harter suggests that this model can also be applied in other forms of play therapy in which dialogue between characters is used, such as puppet play.

the entire scenario, rather than having the therapist create part of the dialogue which may or may not be relevant, given the lack of information during the earliest phases of treatment.[144]

In the second phase, the therapist becomes more active in the play and gradually begins to express his or her own perspective for the child to consider. This interpretive phase consists of four sub-phases: (1) "interpretations by characters within the play scenario," (2) "interpretative link between a play character and the actual child," (3) "indirect interpretation about the child himself or herself," and (4) "direct interpretation to the child." As can be imagined, in the first sub-phase the therapist uses his or her characters as mouthpieces for interpretations about the character representing the child. Harter explains the interaction with this example:

> With my client, K., at this point in treatment, I had pieced to-gether a picture of her fear of going to school, given what she perceived to be censure from the teacher and ridicule from peers. Thus, during one session of our doll play, I took the initiative and spoke for the brother doll who said to the sister doll: "Sissy, I think the reason you don't want to go to school is because the teacher gets mad at you for not doing your work, and the kids make fun of you." I then ask my client, K, stepping outside of the play, what Sissy says in return. From K's response, I can determine whether she is willing to accept such an inter-pretation within the play, or whether even this is too threatening to think about. In K's case, the interpretation was sufficiently distanced in the form of the play characters that she could have Sissy acknowledge that the teachers and the other kids really did upset her. . . . However, if I attempted to suggest to K directly that she might be experiencing these feelings, she would not ac-cept my interpretation.[145]

In the second sub-phase the therapist comments to the child about the similarity between the doll character representing the child and the actual child. If the child accepts this linkage, it may indicate willingness to hear the therapist's interpretations apart from play activity. Thus, in the third sub-phase the therapist tells the child about a "friend" who seems identi-cal to the child and then makes an interpretation. If the child indicates

---

144. Harter, "Cognitive-Developmental Considerations in the Conduct of Play Therapy," 119.

145. Harter, "Cognitive-Developmental Considerations in the Conduct of Play Therapy," 120.

tacit acceptance of this indirect move (e.g., with a "whimsical smile"), the therapist can move to the fourth sub-stage and talk with the child in a direct manner about the child's problems and possible solutions.

In this piece Harter demonstrates how she thinks play can help children drop their psychological defenses and take on a true self stance. To facilitate this process, she as the therapist becomes a participant in the play and allows the client the power and freedom to determine how the play will proceed. The therapist makes interpretations gradually and indirectly at first, in a way that neutralizes the client's sense of a threat.

Helping Adults: Realistic Self-Perceptions, Pursuing One's Authentic Self, and Mindfulness

Regarding interventions for adults, Harter says, "Primary are the fostering of *realistic* self-perceptions, engagement in *mindfulness*, and the pursuit of one's *authentic self*."[146] Let us begin with "realistic self-perceptions" and "the pursuit of one's authentic self."

Harter emphasizes the therapeutic value of realistic self-perceptions and a sense of authenticity that support true self-esteem and confidence, as contrasted with unhealthy self-enhancement strategies that make self-worth contingent on the approval of others. True or optimal self-esteem, which is stable and long-lasting, is founded on a sense of authenticity that exists in conjunction with "realistic appraisals of one's strengths and weaknesses."[147]

Harter warns against a preoccupation with enhancing one's self-esteem, and instead she recommends attending to outward experiences and fulfilling one's goals in life. By striving to meet self-determined goals and by maintaining a balance between autonomy and relatedness with others, people are much more likely to achieve an optimal evaluation of themselves than by trying to earn approval through meeting others' expectations. Self-esteem that is based on the opinion of others, writes Harter, "is unstable and invariably very fragile. Thus in the face of a setback, it can plummet and/or lead to desperate attempts to regain favor in the eyes of evaluating others."[148]

---

146. Harter, *The Construction of the Self*, 375.
147. Harter, *The Construction of the Self*, 346.
148. Harter, *The Construction of the Self*, 347–48.

She continues by contrasting the instability of contingent self-esteem against the reliability of an internalized sense of self-worth that is neither much abated nor increased by accurate self-evaluations:

> In contrast, *true self-esteem* is a sense of self as worthy, not by virtue of external trappings or specific accomplishments, but because one experiences self-worth as inherent. . . . It does not become inflated when one succeeds, nor does it crumble in the face of failure.[149]

Ideally, people will have already internalized unconditional support from parents and other significant caregivers during childhood and adolescence, and from this reservoir they can draw the confidence they need to face difficulties and reach their goals. Further, such people will have already learned to see themselves accurately and will have experienced the greater happiness and fulfillment that comes through authenticity. Harter recognizes, of course, that many adults have not experienced ideal psychological development. Therefore, besides encouraging adults to form accurate self-appraisals and authenticity, she also recommends several other interventions.

Assuming that a person has come to value self-accuracy and authenticity, Harter advises that it may be helpful to pursue various qualities that one desires but does not yet feel are authentic to oneself. She asserts that one may embrace a true self attribute in a therapeutic way so that it becomes a true self attribute. Harter cites Lerner who says, "Sometimes pretending is a form of experimentation or imitation that widens our experience and sense of possibility; it reflects a wish to find ourselves in order to *be* ourselves."[150] Although the attribute one tries to incorporate may feel inauthentic (e.g., feeling peaceful in a stress-inducing workplace), the desire for it can be authentic and reflective of the desires of one's true self. In the beginning, working out the attribute may induce the same sense of phoniness that accompanies other true self behaviors, but as it becomes ingrained through habit and starts to fulfill one's true self desire it takes on the quality of a true self behavior:

> Thus, over time, the practice of desirable false-self behaviors becomes more natural, and, through repetition, these novel thoughts and behaviors become more embedded in the person's new life narrative as genuine-self attributes. In time, such

149. Harter, *The Construction of the Self*, 348.
150. Lerner, *The Dance of Deception*, 16; quoted in Harter, "Authenticity," 392.

authenticity becomes part of what Snyder and Higgins (1997) have described as a person's negotiated reality.[151]

In some cases, pharmaceutical medication should also be used to foster the true self. Harter gives the example of a person diagnosed with depression: "People with physiologically induced symptoms of depression may need to be counseled that their more cheerful self *on* the drug is their true self that the drug is allowing them to manifest."[152] Harter applies the thinking to hyperactive children who may need a drug such as Ritalin in order to enable them to experience their true self.

Harter proposes an additional solution to the false self that is based on a Buddhist perspective. Buddhist scholars say that people attempt to convince themselves that they have a solid, continuous self, even though no such self exists. People do this by turning attention to a fabricated self-construct and occupying their time with self-enhancing strategies. Expounding on this idea, Harter applies William James' distinction between the I-self and the Me-self:

> From the perspective of Western psychology, the I-self should be gainfully employed in protecting the Me-self, packaging it as a valued commodity in the social marketplace. From a Buddhist perspective, far more fringe benefits will accrue if the I-self averts its myopic gaze, which represents a distorted lens that obscures one's true nature.[153]

Therefore, "The I-self," Harter says, "should direct its energies outward, exercising its capacity to enjoy life experiences openly, rather than turning inward in its preoccupation with the construction of a Me-self fitfully designed and distorted in order to be acceptable to the society at large."[154]

Another way of describing this outward turn is mindfulness. Harter describes mindfulness as "living in the moment" but not "for the moment." It involves attentiveness to the world one lives within so that a person can make the most out of the present moment instead of being pent up with one's self-dramas in the past or future. Mindfulness is achieved through meditation. Meditation helps achieve an accurate perception of oneself by quieting the ego: "Simply sitting for some period of

151. Harter, "Authenticity," 392; see Snyder and Higgins, "Reality Negotiation," 336–50.

152. Harter, "Authenticity," 392.

153. Harter, *The Construction of the Self*, 369.

154. Harter, *The Construction of the Self*, 369.

time, dropping one's self-protective armor, clearing out the underbrush of negative thoughts, of self-aggrandizing illusions, paving the way for the true self to make a visit."[155]

Harter makes it clear that this discussion need not be bound to "religious trappings."[156] After her foray into the Buddhist perspective, she calls up some of the recent psychological literature on mindfulness and the quieting of the ego in order to set the discussion once again in terms of her secular worldview. For her, the major distinction is between a Western self and an Eastern self, not a religious versus non-religious. The excesses of the Western self need to be curtailed and conformed to an Eastern style that cultivates self-compassion, humility, and compassion towards others. These attributes have been the subject of the research and theory of many scholars in mainstream, secular psychology; Harter cites the work of Neff, Bauer and Wayment, Tangney, and McAdams.[157]

Critique

I will now critique the theories held by Winnicott and Harter. For the most part, I am evaluating ideas they held in common, but I will also judge some important emphases particular to each. My goal is to identify elements in their theories that cannot be assimilated into a Christian perspective or that require modification.

"A Cognitive and Social Construction" That Omits God

From a Christian perspective, a secular theory of self-understanding is inadequate, because it does not take the spiritual order into account as the most important order of human life and the most basic in reality. Rather, it reckons primacy to the psychosocial order. Though Winnicott and Harter differ in how they express this secular assumption, both of their writings manifest a disregard for God's role in psychological development, with supreme regard for the role of the individual and the social environment.

---

155. Harter, *The Construction of the Self*, 371.

156. Harter, *The Construction of the Self*, 371.

157. Neff, "Self-Compassion," 95–106; Bauer and Wayment, "How the Ego Quiets as It Grows," 199–210; Tangney, "Humility," 483–90; McAdams, "Generativity, the Redemptive Self, and the Problem of a Noisy Ego in American Life," 235–42.

Winnicott: Religion Has Benefits, but Psychosocial Is Primary

In Winnicott's case, it should be noted that he may have included more room for God in his personal beliefs than his professional writings show. In a paper describing the religious influences behind Fairbairn and Winnicott, Hoffman concludes that Winnicott's theorizing was undoubtedly shaped by the Christian narrative he received under his Wesleyan upbringing.[158] Hoffman portrays him as the "John Wesley of psychoanalysis," in that, just as Wesley prescribed the practical methods of facilitating spiritual growth, Winnicott "described the need and detailed the practical methodology for an ever-increasing maturational experience."[159] Furthermore, Hoffman delineates how the philosophical roots of Winnicott's psychological thinking—and of object relations in general—were not wholly Darwinian, but Christian: his emphases on human personhood and relationship stem from the Judeo-Christian narrative, in which God made humans as persons who, like himself, live in relationship.[160] Winnicott's implicit dependence on the Christian narrative is demonstrated in his description of certain concepts like the true self, which seems, says Hoffman, "strikingly close to a Biblical description of the 'soul.'"[161] Hoffman goes on to say that Winnicott's true self is "a silent wellspring of creative and authentic living, a source of goodness not entirely unlike the human soul made in the image of God."[162]

Despite these examples and other evidences from his extraprofessional writing, such as his letters and poems, in which it is clear that Winnicott had a personal interest in religion and especially with the figure of Christ, Winnicott shied away from explicity grounding his theories in Christianity or religion in general. Rather, he seems to have followed the prevailing assumptions of his guild by working within the confines of "methodological atheism," while also holding to a soft determinism.[163] In a telling analogy, Hoffman expresses that, despite how Winnicott (and other psychoanalysts) presented his theories without tying them to the Christian narrative, they are nevertheless tethered together due to the shaping influence of his religious heritage: "For better or worse,

---

158. Hoffman, "From Enemy Combatant to Strange Bedfellow."

159. Hoffman, "From Enemy Combatant to Strange Bedfellow," 794.

160. Hoffman, "From Enemy Combatant to Strange Bedfellow," 794.

161. Hoffman, "From Enemy Combatant to Strange Bedfellow," 792.

162. Hoffman, "From Enemy Combatant to Strange Bedfellow," 793.

163. Parker, *Winnicott and Religion*.

formational narratives cradle the polished floorboards of our meticu-
lously crafted adult edifices."[164] If Winnicott went so far as to privately
acknowledge a role for God in human development, he refrained from
openly declaring that role in his theorizing. Therefore, while it may be
exaggerating to designate Winnicott as a pure atheist or strident Darwinian, it is important to recognize that his professional writings more
strongly intimate a naturalistic worldview than a Christian one, and that
his theorizing seems to discount a spiritual order of human life in which
God plays a real, active part.

Accordingly, he considered God to be a "projection" of certain moral qualities of the individual, and he inferred that religion arose solely out
of human nature.[165] The idea of God arises naturally in normal human
development, according to Winnicott, and given a certain environment
children will acquire a readiness to believe in God or whatever religious
system their parents offer. Religious belief is a product of natural psychological development that comes from within the individual and not from
outside; man makes God in his own image, not vice-versa.

Winnicott maintained some positive functions for religion, but not
in any spiritual or supernatural sense: "It is not possible for me to throw
away religion just because the people who organize the religions of the
world insist on belief in miracles."[166] Ideally, in Winnicott's view, religion
serves as an expression of people's innate sense of morality that develops

164. Hoffman, "From Enemy Combatant to Strange Bedfellow," 801.

165. God is a projection of human individuality: "So when people first came to the
concept of individuality, they quickly put it up in the sky and gave it a voice that only a
Moses could hear." Winnicott, *Home Is Where We Start From*, 57. God is a projection
of man's goodness: "The saying that man made God in his own image is usually treated
as an amusing example of the perverse, but the truth in this saying could be made
more evident by a restatement, such as: man continues to create and re-create God as
a place to put that which is good in himself, and which he might spoil if he kept it in
himself along with all the hate and destructiveness which is also to be found there."
Winnicott, "Morals and Education," 94. Religion is something humans create rather
than the human response to divine revelation: "May I say that it seems to me that what
is commonly called religion arises out of human nature, whereas there are some who
think of human nature as rescued from savagery by a revelation from outside human
nature." Winnicott, *Home Is Where We Start From*, 143.

166. Winnicott, *The Spontaneous Gesture*, 170. Winnicott was discreet in his rejection of a real God and other orthodox Christian beliefs, and this was probably done in
order to keep from harming his professional work with clients of religious persuasion.
He wrote, "One must be able to look at religious beliefs and their place in psychology
without being considered to be antagonistic to anyone's personal religion." Winnicott,
The Spontaneous Gesture, 74.

in infancy. He called this moral sense "belief in."[167] Religion of the best kind depends upon the early development of this moral sense, which enables guilt and "the setting up of an ideal."[168] As right and wrong become distinct, preparation is made for parents to provide a more fully defined system of morality, with certain ideals.[169] An infant's moral sense is cultivated through the loving care of the mother, which builds up the infant's awareness and concern for the other, leading to a sense of responsibility and guilt.[170] Religion serves to refine innate morality: "In order to complete that which has been started up, someone must let the child know what we in this family and in this bit of society at the present time happen to believe in."[171] According to Winnicott's naturalistic understanding, religion can help individuals fit into society while also benefiting the individual's growth. Religion can enrich the nascent morality of human beings and give people a code of conduct for mutual well-being. Religious practice, along with art and other forms of creative expression and play, also helps integrate and unify one's personality.[172] At its best, religion passed along by parents helps refine the infant's morality, which is more important but which needs moderation: "the infant's and the small child's innate moral code has a quality so fierce, so crude, and so crippling. Your adult moral code is necessary because it humanizes what for the child is subhuman."[173] The infant's "moral code" insists on freedom from coercion and consists of a "hatred of compliance at the expense of a personal way of life."[174] Wanting this freedom and experiencing it is essential to human growth and flourishing and corresponds to Winnicott's understanding of the true self. It must be "humanized," however, because people have to get along in society, which requires some measure of compromise. The freedom to live authentically and the responsibility to adapt to social mores must be held in balance in order to live in health.[175] In so far as religion supports this

167. Winnicott, "Morals and Education," 93–94.

168. Winnicott, "Morals and Education," 93.

169. Winnicott, *The Child, the Family, and the Outside World*, 93–97.

170. Winnicott, "The Development of the Capacity for Concern," 73–82.

171. Winnicott, "Morals and Education," 94.

172. Winnicott, *The Child, the Family, and the Outside World*, 145.

173. Winnicott, "Morals and Education," 101.

174. Winnicott, *The Child, the Family, and the Outside World*, 97.

175. "Let us say that in health," Winnicott says, "a man or woman is able *to reach towards an identification with society without too great a loss of individual or personal impulse*. There must, of course, be loss in the sense of control of personal impulse,

balance and aids human maturation, it is good.[176] Thus, in so many ways, religion is helpful, thought Winnicott, but not necessarily because it had something to do with divine revelation or a relationship with God.

So, Winnicott clearly saw a place for religion and morality in terms of individual growth and maintaining relationships with others, but he did not suggest, at least in his written work, that either religion or morality ought to be grounded in one's relationship with God. The "innate morality" of the individual, as well as the norms added to the individual's beliefs by parents and society, account for the moral and spiritual orders of human life in Winnicott's system, and neither God's existence nor activity is necessary to make sense of these orders. Albeit, strains of Winnicott's approach to pscyhoanalysis seem to parallel the Christian narrative and to reveal a private openness to God in Winnicott's thinking; for instance, the portrayal he gives of the ideal analyst as one who waits and bears the patient's attacks (i.e., "destruction") has understandably been understood to resemble the figure of Christ, who willingly suffered under those he was trying to save.[177] These strains are certainly consonant with a Christian perspective. However, because Winnicott abstained from relating the work of psychoanalysis to God's work in Christ in his discourse, his approach should not be confused with an explicitly Christian approach.

While Winnicott demurred over God's active role in the self's development and neglected to ground people's sense of morality in God, he did not hesitate to opine on the biological and psychosocial orders, with the former being the most foundational for existence (i.e., because matter is the ultimate reality), and the latter as most important for enjoying life. The psychosocial order arises from the biological, according to Winnicott: "the soul is a property of the psyche . . . and it too depends on brain function."[178] As a consequence, he denounced lobotomy as "a price too big to pay for relief or suffering, since it alters irrevocably the basis for the existence of the psyche, soul included; and there is, after the

---

but the extreme identification with society with total loss of sense of self and self-importance is not normal at all." Winnicott, *Home Is Where We Start From*, 27.

176. In the following passage Winnicott reveals what he values most in religion, particularly Christianity: "Religious people of Christian persuasion use the phrase whose service is perfect freedom, which is the same as the sonnet form accepted by Shakespeare or Keats which allows of spontaneous impulse, and the unexpected creative gesture. This is what we wait for and highly value in our work." Winnicott et al., *Thinking about Children*, 278.

177. Hoffman, "On Christianity, Psychoanalysis, and the Hope of Eternal Return."

178. Winnicott, *Human Nature*, 52.

treatment, no longer a whole person, psyche or soul, left."[179] This statement shows both the ultimacy of the biological order in his view, as well as the primacy of the psychosocial for a life worth living: lobotomy is wrong, he asserts, because it takes away the person. This idea is in direct conflict with a Christian worldview, which holds that the soul does not depend on brain function but on God's will for it to exist. Winnicott upheld the primacy of the psychosocial order, because he thought that by maturing in one's awareness of self, other, and transitional space between, reality could be better understood and enjoyed. In his view, health was the product of adequately relating three factors: enjoying one's own inner psychical reality (self), engaging the external world (other), and participating in cultural experience (transitional space). The real God—not the projection that Winnicott allowed for—is not included in this paradigm of health.

Harter: Religious Trappings Can Be Stripped

Harter more tacitly asserts her secularism, expressing ambivalence towards God's existence and influence. She repeatedly cites Buddhist scholar Thich Nhat Hanh, who advocates a religious viewpoint that Harter holds up as a good example for promoting authenticity.[180] Yet, although she can recommend a Buddhist perspective on meditation and mindfulness, she also says that these practices can be stripped of their "religious trappings" without losing their effectiveness.[181]

The secular vantage that Harter takes toward the self is implicit in her thesis that the self is a "cognitive and social construction."[182] Cognitive processes that develop with age enable one to form self-representations and attain an overall conceptualization of the self. These self-representations are also a product of others' influence. Thus, in Harter's schema, the formation of the self, as well as the degree to which people's self-portraits are true or false, depend solely upon the interaction between these two factors, with no acknowledgement of causative agents in the spiritual order (i.e., God, Satan, angels). One fatal result is that, in an otherwise deft presentation of psychosocial development, Harter's treatment of the moral and spiritual aspects of growth is not only void of

179. Winnicott, *Human Nature*, 53.

180. Harter, *The Construction of the Self*, 372.

181. Harter, *The Construction of the Self*, 368–71.

182. Harter, *The Construction of the Self*.

religious trappings but dismissive of the *raison d'être* of self-development, the greatest hindrance to its fulfillment, and the only sufficient pathway to its remediation: self-conscious grounding in God, the impediment of sin, and God's gracious intervention, respectively.

Missing an Entire Order of Reality

That Winnicott and Harter exclude God and the spiritual realm from their discourse is not only impermissible in a Christian perspective but crippling to their theory of health. Failing to take into account an entire order of reality, they drastically limit their theory.

By replacing God as the ultimate source of existence and wellbeing with biological health and psychosocial maturity, the secular viewpoint is blinded to the root cause of psychological pathology, including the false self, as well as to the necessity of God's gracious intervention. While they rightly discern the importance of the psychosocial order, by making it primary they end up missing the real problem and its solution. False self-understanding is due to humanity's fallen condition, which is a fundamentally moral and spiritual issue. The remediation of the false self and the discovery of the true self are, likewise, brought about ultimately through divine grace, though God does work within the psychosocial order.

Another serious flaw that stems from ejecting God is that the secular perspective purports that the final goals of true self-understanding are to enjoy experiences of self, other, and engaging in culture. But these are subordinate goals in a Christian perspective: growth in these areas is not an end in itself but a means of growing more aware of God and receptive of his love. By only speaking of God as an epiphenomenon and religion as a cultural practice with potential benefits, the secular theories held by Winnicott and Harter fail to provide an adequate definition of self-development as God designed it, of its corruption due to sin, and of its restoration through God's grace.

"Autonomy and Connectedness" without God as Criterion

Winnicott and Harter share the view that healthy self-development entails a balance between "autonomy and connectedness," as Harter puts it.[183] Winnicott similarly speaks of the fundamental need to complement "communication with non-communication."[184]

When they speak of "autonomy" or "non-communication" as essential to health, they mean that in order to feel authentic or real, people must sense that they are living according to values that they willingly embrace, but not according to values forced upon them. The true corresponds to the non-coerced self, and if people's personalities express their core needs, then they are living life at its most authentic and best.

However, when Winnicott and Harter link this aspect of health with connectedness or communication, they indicate that people also need to feel relatedness with others, and this includes sharing others' values. Individuals are healthiest when they experience "an identification with society without too great a loss of individual or personal impulse."[185] This "identification" includes the internalization of others' cultural, moral, and religious values. For persons' "individual or personal impulse" to go uncompromised, they must willingly accept these values as their own. Persons may depend upon others (e.g., parents) to provide them with social mores, as long as they still possess their autonomy—that is, as long as they can approve the values they are given, either because they were not forced to do things against their will, or, if they were forced to act in certain ways (e.g., forced to take baths when a three-year-old), because they eventually adopted these values. Either way, the criterion for autonomy, and thus authenticity, is people's own felt sense that their behaviors are right and true to themselves.

The problem with this criterion is that it places the moral and epistemological center of human beings in themselves. From a Christian standpoint, the ultimate criterion for right and wrong and for the true self and false self is not self-validation but God. As humanity's good creator, God gives people rules of conduct to help them experience wellbeing and to direct them away from evil. He is the final arbiter between good and bad behavior. Since he is omniscient and knows each individual comprehensively, God is also the preeminent judge of truth and falsehood, and he alone can say whether one is behaving authentically or not. While people can sense whether they are being fake or genuine, their self-reflection is no surety that their actions are right or good, since it is possible to

---

183. Harter, *The Construction of the Self*, 308–10.

184. Winnicott, "Communicating and Not Communicating."

185. Winnicott, *Home Is Where We Start From*, 27.

be self-deceived. The rightness of people's actions are not meant to be measured solely according to their own consent but according to God's.

At the same time, the secular view touches upon a truth that a Christian perspective should uphold. While God's validation is the only sure criterion for goodness and authenticity, he has designed human beings to willingly agree with his judgments, knowing that the values God calls them to obey and internalize are for their good. In one sense, then, Harter and Winnicott are right to assert the necessary balance between "autonomy and connectedness." To experience psychological health, people need to depend on God to provide them the right values and to validate their true self, while also still being able to approve the values they are given and freely adopting them as their own. The congruence between self-validation and God's validation is essential to wellbeing.

The "Coerced, Socially-Implanted Self" Is Not the Primary Cause of the False Self—Sin Is

Because of their secular assumptions, Winnicott and Harter maintain that the false self develops ultimately because coercive and unsupportive social experiences impinge on self-development.

While Winnicott thinks the false self is ultimately maladaptive since it disables authenticity, he explains that it arises from the motive of self-preservation. Winnicott speaks of the false self having a double function: "hiding the true self and complying with the demands that the world makes from moment to moment."[186] The self needs to be confirmed or given legitimacy in order to exist, and if people cannot gain confidence in themselves in a way that is compatible with their authenticity, then they will attempt to get it another way, the false self.

Similarly, Harter says that ideally people will receive enough affirmation about their true self that it will flourish. If approval is contingent on meeting others' demands, however, then they may be forced to get it through false self behavior. Harter says the false self results from the rejection of a person's authentic or true self. If children's parents refuse to affirm the self they feel they actually are, then they will likely modify the self so that it does win affirmation. If parental approval and support are contingent on meeting up to unrealistic standards—that is, standards

---

186. Winnicott, "Group Influences and the Maladjusted Child," 216.

that the child is not able to fulfill in a natural and authentic way—then the child will try to adapt with false self behavior.

For Winnicott and Harter, people need to have their true or authentic self supported and affirmed, rather than be coerced into behaving and thinking in false ways in order to get their needs met. In both theorist's understanding the true self becomes hidden under compliant behavior to gain approval, and because it is concealed, one loses touch with who one really is. Living in the false self means showing up falsely with others as well as holding a false self-view. Self-development becomes pathological when people adopt a false understanding of self (i.e., a false Me-self) and a false way of acting in the world (i.e., a false I-self).

From a Christian vantage, however, the false self is more than the result of poor social experiences derailing normal psychological development. Granted, social influences do encourage false self understanding in the ways that Harter and Winnicott describe: coercion and contingent love are culprits in the loss of authenticity, especially for infants, children, and others who have not developed the ability to understand themselves as bearing moral responsibility. On the other hand, Christianity explains that the reason people coerce others into false self understanding and behavior is that they are sinners, and the reason people eventually adopt a life of self-deception is to conceal their own sin. Human beings are weak and sinful, due to the fall, leaving them both susceptible to the pressures of others who would have them become false, and also desirous to hide the shame of their moral and spiritual corruption. A secular view that posits a merely psychosocial explanation for the false self misidentifies its main efficient cause.

"The Facilitating Environment" That Downplays Moral Categories

Finally, because the interventions that Winnicott and Harter employ are steeped in secular presuppositions, the "wheat" in their therapy strategies must be separated from the "tares."

The secular goals of their interventions were very similar, though some of their interventions varied from each other because of their particular vocations: Winnicott was an analyst who worked with parents and patients and shared his clinical insights through academic papers and some popular books. Harter, however, has mainly focused on empirical research as a developmental psychologist. Yet, their therapeutic aims were very similar. Winnicott used psychoanalysis for the purpose of facilitating the competence of the patient's true self (i.e., building up ego-strength), in which "the patient begins to take for granted a feeling of existing in his or her own right."[187] Likewise, Harter is especially interested in interventions that aim to strengthen realistic self-perceptions, authenticity, and true self-esteem. For both theorists, one of the most crucial goals of therapy is to help patients become competent and authentic. It is not enough for clients to feel better about themselves; they should also sense that they are authentic (not false) and pursuing their own self-determined goals (not complying with others' demands).

While in themselves these aims have merit, they fall short of the final purpose of therapy from a Christian standpoint. Taking a Christian perspective on interventions requires confirming that the final goal of psychological healing is spiritual restoration. Therapists and patients should be working to resolve the inner conflicts of their souls, so that their souls can partake in eternal life with God. Developing greater authenticity and true self-understanding is a means to more than just feeling real, having more satisfying relationships, or enjoying life in the world. A Christian understanding of health must direct all interventions toward feeling real in God, partaking in loving fellowship with other people and God, and enjoying life *coram Deo*.

The secular goals of health advocated by Winnicott and Harter require them to shape their therapeutic strategies in ways that negate any positive value for interventions that explicitly foster moral or spiritual beliefs. Rather, their inventions avoid ethicospiritual overtones in a misguided effort to promote patients' autonomy. Both theorists agree that in order for people to develop well a certain kind of "facilitating environment" is needed: one that is non-coercive, highly supportive, and adaptive. In regard to non-coerciveness, Winnicott held that if people's true self is to be strengthened, then the therapist must work in accordance with patients' spontaneity and freedom and never seek to pressure them into change. A good-enough therapist fosters a patient's true self by becoming subject to it—and not the other way around. Harter demonstrates similar thinking in her recommendation that parents validate their children's viewpoint and perspective rather than asserting their own narrative or agenda. Her model of doll therapy also demonstrates a

---

187. Winnicott, "The Aims of Psycho-Analytic Treatment," 168.

gradual, indirect approach that allows the child patient to safely work out a solution in cooperation with the therapist.

As imitable as the non-coercive approach modeled by these theorists is, it is made impotent by its lack of ethicospiritual fervor. Winnicott said, "In the role of care-curers we are non-moralistic. It does not help a patient to tell him or her that he or she is wicked to be ill. Nor does it help a thief, or a . . . schizophrenic to be put in a moralistic category."[188] One reason he gave for this stance was that he thought people should be allowed to naturally develop their own moral convictions, with the influence of others, but without being made to believe certain tenets against their will. Children who are taught too soon or forcibly that they should act according to particular values lose the chance to internalize those values as their own:

> If in the case of moral teaching we . . . treat certain things as sinful, how far can we be sure that we are not robbing the growing child of the capacity *on his own* to come to a personal sense of right and wrong . . . out of his own development?[189]

There is some merit to this idea; for, Christians should agree it is possible for parents and others to harm children by placing overly burdensome moral expectations. Winnicott has a point in saying that "*moral education is no substitute for love.*"[190] However, it is equally true that Winnicott's idea of "love" is no substitute for appropriate moral interventions. Love, according to Christianity, requires moral education, since helping people move toward God is the most loving service they can perform.

Although the value that Winnicott and Harter place on supporting and validating individuals is worth retaining in a Christian perspective of interventions, their resistance (and sometimes antipathy) toward prescribing ethicospiritual beliefs and behaviors is a huge mistake. Maintaining the difference between right and wrong in therapeutic communication is appropriate and necessary for effective soul care with people of all ages, since human wellbeing entails being rightly, or morally, oriented toward God. Without moral education and guidance, people will go adrift from the source of life and psychological health into the morass of sin.

188. Winnicott, *Home Is Where We Start From*, 116.

189. Winnicott, *Home Is Where We Start From*, 149.

190. Winnicott, "Morals and Education," 97.

Conclusion

The contributions of Winnicott and Harter are clearly very valuable. Despite a significant lacuna in their theories pertaining to the ethical and spiritual orders of human life, the attention they have given to the developmental and social aspects of the self has yielded important insights which a substantial psychology of the self should not omit. In the next chapter, these insights will be synthesized into a more robust Christian psychology of the false self and true self.

5

A Christian Perspective

HERE I WANT TO provide a robust theory of the false self and true self, taking into consideration all the voices we have heard from Scripture, Christian teachers, and secular psychologists. As we have done before, we will answer four questions: (1) Why do people reflect on themselves? (2) Why do they understand themselves wrongly? (i.e., constructing a false self) (3) What does true self-understanding entail? And (4) What interventions can foster true self-understanding?

The Self

We are meant to reflect on ourselves, so that we will ground ourselves in God. Self-understanding is a means to realizing our creational dependency and calling to be God's children.

The Final Cause of the Self: Choosing to Be God's Children

Humans are made in the image of God, which uniquely equips them among all other creatures for an intimate kind of life with each other and with God. Made with psychological structures that resemble structures in God's own being, people are blessed with the unique status of being children of the Creator—not just his creatures—who can commune with him as their father and with each other as fellow brothers and sisters. One of the most important gifts God has shared with us is self-consciousness, which enables us to know ourselves, and thereby to know ourselves in relation to other spiritual beings, especially God.

The highest purpose of self-understanding, or its final cause, is to enable us to recognize and consent to who we are and what we were made for: we are children of God, made to depend upon him for life and well-being, to know and love him, to resemble him, and to freely consent to his calling.

The Formal Cause of the Self: Self-Consciousness

Self-consciousness is the ability to think about ourselves and form a mental representation, and it enables us to know ourselves accurately, so that we can ground ourselves in God. The mental construct we form using this ability is the self.[1]

As "spirit," we are equipped with the capacity to discern and judge our growth as individuals in relation to another (i.e., an outside criterion) who prompts us to reach our full potential.[2] God is our ultimate criterion, and the ability to reflect on ourselves allows us to consciously conceive of our relation to God, so that by virtue of resting in that relationship we can properly be what God created us to be.

Humans are designed so that we can turn towards our "inner self," or the intelligible realm of our minds, and thereby realize that nothing outside us (i.e., in creation) nor inside us (i.e., our minds) can serve as the source of our life and being. Rather, God, who exists above creation and above our minds as the Creator of all, is the one who constitutes us through his word and who calls us to willingly consent to be so constituted.

In summary, self-understanding is a special power and responsibility given to us: the power to perceive ourselves, so that we can consent to who we are as God's sons and daughters and as those who are called to participate with God in the particular and unique unfolding of our individual lives.

---

1. Depending upon a person's cognitive-developmental capacity, the self will be a more or less integrated self-portrait. By "self," then, I refer to any mental self-representation along the continuum from the least cognizant sense of self in infants to the most integrated and capacious self-portrait possible.

2. Kierkegaard, *The Sickness unto Death*.

The Efficient Causes of the Self: God, Self, and Others

Before we can ground ourselves in God, we must develop the capacity for self-understanding by gradually becoming aware of ourselves and the world around us. This development begins in the first weeks of life.

Early in infancy, a primitive sense of self begins to be established in the context of the infant-parent relationship. In their dependency upon parents who adequately provide for their needs, infants gain a sense of being, or "aliveness." As this sense is nourished by the parent's sensitive, reliable care, so is the infant's capacity for experiencing relations. Because of a secure "facilitating environment," infants are enabled to emerge from enmeshment with the environment into a burgeoning apprehension of "me" and "not-me."

An infant's movement towards self- and other-awareness is facilitated by the parents' "holding" as well as by their gradual de-adaptation to the infant, in which the highly sensitive attunement and preoccupation that first characterized their care decreases. Although a parent's care at this stage may seem fairly simple and monotonous, it supplies a secure base from which infants can eventually launch out and make the profound discovery that they and others exist.

Having learned from their experience in the infant-parent relationship, infants who eventually grow into toddlers, children, adolescents, and adults possess the skill needed to understand themselves and their world with increasing objectivity. We succeed in the task of "reality acceptance" by traversing the "transitional space" between our inner psychical world and the objective world outside us, bridging the gap with "identifications" we discern between them. Equipped with a sense of competence gained from prior experiences, when we meet novel, strange, and challenging experiences, we have the potential to adapt our understanding in light of new discoveries. This task of exploration and "reality acceptance" is designed by God to culminate in a larger and more accurate knowledge and enjoyment of him. Thus, the infant-parent relationship lays the foundation not just for mental health but also for experiencing God. As parents lovingly provide their baby with its basic needs, they are (knowingly or not) building up another human being's capacity to commune with his or her Divine Parent.

The capacity for communion and grounding in God is meant to be increasingly strengthened in every stage of growth through cognitive advances and supportive social experiences. Progress in each stage is characterized by certain cognitive advances that result in a richer and greater capacity in humans to be aware of themselves, leading to a more and more integrated self-understanding, provided that these advances are met with loving support from others.

For example, the cognitive abilities of very young children (ages 2–4) allow them to recognize concrete, observable attributes about themselves like physical skills, and while these attributes can be internalized as self-representations, they cannot be integrated. Thus, very young children often manifest "all-or-none thinking" and unrealistic, vaunted self-evaluations, e.g., "I can jump as high as the sky!"[3] Because their self-representations do not differentiate between what is ideal and what is actual about themselves, when children at this stage make extreme self-enhancing evaluations, they are speaking the truth as it seems to them, in their own limited fashion. Although it means that very young children are limited in how much accurate knowledge they can have about the world, this aspect of their cognition is actually just what they need, because it affords them the (over)confidence required to meet difficult but necessary challenges in their growth. God knows that little ones face daunting obstacles (e.g., learning to walk, climb, jump, communicate through language), and so he gives them the facility (i.e., an exaggerated sense of competence) to overcome them.

Besides this cognitive advance, God gives them support in the form of parents and other caregivers who validate their self-expressions. Recognizing that the inaccuracy of their self-evaluations does not usually equate with lying but with honesty, supportive parents will respond to their children's expressions of competence with approval.[4] By doing this, significant others support very young children's authenticity and sense of competence: authenticity, because the children are encouraged to express what they actually think or feel; competence, because by having their self-enhancing evaluations approved, their courage to keep meeting new challenges is bolstered.

I don't mean to suggest that parents should approve everything children do; on the contrary, for children to grow well, God gives them loving adults to teach them what is appropriate wholesome behavior and

3. As a three-year-old, my son illustrated this once by climbing to the top of a playhouse in the backyard and jumping to the ground without hesitation, being surprised by the jolt he received upon landing.

4. Thus, when after a wrestling victory with dad a child says, "I'm stronger than daddy," understanding parents will respond with validation: "You are strong!"

what is not. Some behaviors are to be rewarded because they are good for the child, and others result in discipline because they are harmful. God intends adults to place expectations on children that are within their ability to meet and for their own good, so that as they are appropriately directed towards certain behaviors and away from others, they will gradually internalize values about what is good and bad, about what can benefit them and what can harm them.

Very young children are meant to receive from parents and others a seamless combination of supportive moral instruction and validation. When children express their reactions to the benefits of right behavior (or the consequences of wrong behavior), parents and others are provided to validate their thoughts and feelings. By doing so, the parents affirm children's own authentic realization of what is intrinsically good (or bad) for them. When children engage in virtuous (or vicious) actions—perceiving the fuller meaning of the values imparted by parents and responding with thoughts and emotions—and then have this experience validated by another, they are being led to realize with greater and greater understanding and conviction that they have certain innate needs and that there is a right and wrong way for these needs to be met. This applies not only to preschoolers, but also to persons at every stage of development. God's design for human maturation is that, regardless of their particular cognitive abilities, people would have others who lovingly direct them to find wholeness and virtue and who encourage them onward by validating their experience.

Ultimately, God gives us parents, family members, teachers, and others who love us, so that we can see his image reflected in the validation and moral instruction they provide. In the stages of childhood and adolescence, our parents and other caregivers act as God's representatives, laying the groundwork for us to realize that God is the one who knows us completely (i.e., with perfect validation) and that he is the ultimate source of our wellbeing. As we embark into the world of adulthood, utilizing skills learned from prior experience and receiving validation and godly support from others, we are meant to learn and adapt our understanding of ourselves and the world more and more accurately to God's understanding, so that we come to consent to our identity as God's children and to his calling upon us.

The Content of the Self

The content of human beings' self-understanding consists in all that they know about themselves as unique individuals. The content of that knowledge would depend upon their capacity for self-understanding according to their stage of development, their particular experiences, memories of those experiences, and the informing perspective of others who know them. The further along people are in their development, the more they have experienced and may remember, and the more their self-knowledge is informed by others who know them, the more their understanding will approximate God's knowledge of them. Every individual's self-knowledge will be unique to them because their experiences are unique to them, but there are several aspects of their lives that they share with all other human beings by virtue of their shared human nature, and because they all go through the same basic stages of development, the kind of knowledge they can have about themselves in each particular stage is also held in common.[5]

Because all human beings share the same nature, there are certain biological, psychological, social, ethical, and spiritual aspects of life that we all share. Although it depends upon our current ability to access this knowledge (due to our cognitive-developmental stage, experiences, and education), all of us can eventually discover the same general facts about the bodies, souls, social relationships, ethical standards, and spiritual life that come with being human. Presumably, however, no matter how advanced our understanding of these things becomes, we will never understand all of them completely.[6] While all of these facts are worthy of knowing, only some are essential to know for wellbeing. The most important facts God intends us to know about ourselves are ethical and spiritual truths: we are God's children, our life depends upon God and his word, and we are called to love him and to become like him.

---

5. The seven stages of self-development are: very early childhood, early to middle childhood, middle to late childhood, early adolescence, middle adolescence, late adolescence, and emerging adulthood. The kinds of knowledge that characterize the capacity for self-understanding in each stage are explained in chapter five in the section "Harter on the Self." See also Harter, *The Construction of the Self*, chap. 2–4.

6. While it is possible (though difficult) to imagine that complete knowledge of the human body can be gained, it is impossible for people to completely understand their relationship with God, since though God is knowable he is not comprehendible.

Thesis One: The Divinely Created Self

Why do people reflect on themselves? God made us capable for self-understanding to enable us to ground ourselves in him, depending on him for all our needs, trusting him as our perfectly loving and understanding Father. Realizing our identity as children of God and consenting to trust him and resemble him is a process. It begins with parents and other caregivers who establish a solid base of support and build up a sense of competence, enabling children to successfully go out and discover more about the world and themselves. It continues through every stage of development, as children, adolescents, and adults cognitively construct an increasingly vivid and accurate understanding of reality in cooperation with God and others, who validate them and affirm their integration of virtuous, godly values, so that they continually experience a greater and more satisfying capacity to understand reality. In God's good creation, before sin entered, we were intended to grow to recognize ourselves as the people God always meant us to be, that is, as selves constructed not merely through our own self-representations and the support of others, but as selves created by God.

The False Self

We distort our self-understanding into a false self, so that we can hide from sublime and paradoxical dynamics in our hearts: the innate desire for wellbeing and the unavoidable despair over weakness and sin.

The Final Causes of the False Self

There are at least four respects in which false self-understanding is an activity intended to have certain effects: the false self is always intended by Satan (along with other demons) as a means to deceive and destroy humans; it can be intended by individuals as a means to coerce others into meeting their sinful desires; it can be intended by individuals as a means to legitimately protect themselves from harm; and it can be intended by individuals a means to hide from their moral and spiritual condition.[7]

7. In the latter three cases, by saying that false self-understanding is "intended," it is assumed that the intention may be more or less conscious. Thus, in the second case, wherein people coerce others into false self-understanding, they may be very aware that they are trying to make the other person act falsely, making their intent

First, Satan intends for false self-understanding to trap people in ignorance and separation from life with God. His province as "the prince of the power of the air" and "the spirit that is now at work in the sons of disobedience" is that of humanity's moral and spiritual misdirection and deception (Eph 2:1–3). As he tempted Eve (Gen 3:1–5) and Christ (Matt 4:1–11), so he and his minions tempt all human beings with false promises of freedom, truth, love, and power, in order to dissuade them from "the things of God" (Matt 16:23). His aims are to blind people from seeing "the light of the gospel of the glory of Christ," to destroy people's faith in God as "the tempter," and to "devour" souls (2 Cor 4:4; 1 Thess 3:5; 1 Pet 5:8–9;).

Second, in order to gratify sinful motives and (often unknowingly) in league with Satan, people may coerce others into false self-understanding. In this case, a person demands compliance from someone weaker, because doing so satisfies a wicked desire, such as a sense of power through domination or a sense of intimacy through validation. For example, a man who desires to feel respected may attempt to wrangle it from his children by making his affection contingent on them meeting unrealistic expectations. By pressuring them to put on a show of respect that exceeds their abilities, he is at the same time forcing them into a false mold and image of themselves. Whether such people are aware or not, by leveraging their power to drive another into the false self, they are acting in cooperation with the designs of the devil.

Third, vulnerable persons may engage in false self-understanding to protect themselves from real or perceived harm. In the previous example, the children pressured by their father would fit in this category. Without the inner psychological resources (i.e., "ego-strength") to resist coercion upon their will, people in this category fall prey to the domination of other people with greater agentic power. Among the four possible final causes for the false self, this one merits no condemnation. Being forced into false self-representations or behavior against one's will constitutes suffering, not sin. Being an instance of weakness, people who use false self-understanding solely to shield themselves from danger to their created needs (psychological or physical) deserve compassion and help from others to be healed from the evil done to them. In one sense, God can

---

malicious, or only partially aware, making their intent less so. In the third and fourth cases, wherein false understanding necessarily involves self-deception, the intention to hide the truth from oneself is *itself* part of the truth that one is attempting to hide, and thus the intent is subliminal to one degree or other.

be said to approve this use, since, as the defender of the weak, he desires to protect the innocent; furthermore, even more than the person who uses it, God intends this particular use, and because he wills to preserve such persons from worse evil than false self-understanding, he permits their self-understanding to be occluded. It should be observed that only in the context of a fallen world where evils threaten the weak would God approve false self-understanding as a means of protection. For, in itself, false self-understanding is an evil that attenuates one's sense of authenticity and diminishes psychological wellbeing.

Fourth, people allow themselves to be deceived in order to conceal their sin. This use of the false self supports the pretense that wellbeing can be had apart from God. Here, the motivation for false self-understanding is energized by the lie that a complete and satisfying life is possible outside of communion and trust in God. Having willingly entered into sin, human beings accept this lie and repress the truth, because the truth has become too offensive.[8] Although reason, conscience, experience, and God's revelation confirm the truth they know deep in their hearts, pride and the shame of their sin keep them from confessing it. Humans despair over their sinful existence, and because it is so despairing, they hide it from themselves with the false self. Why people consent to live in despair or sin in the first place cannot be fully explained by human reason; it seems that human minds are not privy to the ultimate explanation for sin.[9] Significantly more can be said about sin's workings and effects in false self-understanding.

We should observe that people who are motivated according to the fourth final cause are always also motivated according to the third final cause. That is to say, the sinful desire to conceal one's sin, while evil, is at the same time motivated by a deeper longing for one's own good. Sin works in us by misdirecting our desires for real goods that come from God to the mere appearance of goods; although sin can reorient us to seek our best in the wrong ways, it cannot change the fact that we are made to want what is best for us. By using the false self to hide from our

---

8. Only those who qualify as having "willingly entered into sin" belong in this category. To use the false self to conceal sin requires that one has come to "know sin" (see Rom 7:7). And so, individuals who lack the cognitive capacity for such knowledge, due to age or impairment, do not belong in this category.

9. After all, since Christians have difficulty explaining how God created everything out of nothing (*creatio ex nihilo*), it is unsurprising that they find it hard to explain sin, which is nothing out of creation (*nil ex creatione*).

nothingness, shame, and misery (i.e., the fourth final cause), we are using falsehood to shield ourselves from perceived suffering. While this is partially due to our sinful condition (i.e., prideful, fleshly self-sufficiency), it is also due to our weakness. We do not come out of the womb with a ready-made false self to cover our sin. Rather, we develop our false self out of a social context, in which stronger people (abetting Satan's intent) force us to construct a false self to one degree or another. In this state of coercion, our false self-understanding is a weakness not a sin. Once we have developed enough self-awareness to come to a knowledge of sin, however, we start to use self-deception as a means to perpetuate our sin, making the false self a culpable fault.[10]

The Formal Cause of the False Self

The false self is a mental construct consisting of any degree of distortion in self-understanding, and people use it to conceal and protect themselves.[11] God's design for self-understanding has been hindered by people's own moral and spiritual condition, as well as by psychological harm they have received from others. People no longer naturally grow to depend upon God as their Father, because their self-understanding is rendered false either by their enslavement to moral and epistemological self-sufficiency—variously referred to in Scripture as "foolishness," "hypocrisy," and "confidence in the flesh"—or by psychological damage they have suffered.

Thus, there are two ways in which people use the false self to conceal and protect. On the one hand, the false self can serve to defend oneself from real or perceived danger by concealing one's actual experience. In

10. The false self should be considered in the category of "fault." It is neither purely the result of sin, for which people are totally responsible and which deserves God's wrath, nor is it just a manifestation of weakness, for which people bear no responsibility and about which God compassionately cares. As a fault, the false self results both from sin and weakness: "Psychological fault refers to a biopsychosocial and ethico-spiritual disorder involving both weakness and sin—a deficient condition influenced by biological and social factors and woven into one's created nature, but having ethical and spiritual significance." Johnson, *God and Soul Care*, 286.

11. Here I am employing Winnicott's conception of the false self as any degree of distortion in one's sense of self. This conception stands in contrast to Harter's full-fledged idea of the false self as an inaccurate *global* self-portrait, and is more in line with what she means by inaccurate self-representations, which can include descriptions and evaluations of *aspects* of oneself and are not limited to the whole person.

persons who have not come to a knowledge of sin, this function is not in itself sinful. On the other hand, the false self can serve to defend oneself against feeling the wretchedness of one's sin (i.e., as a way to hide from the truth about their moral and spiritual condition). In this case, the former use is also implied, since false self-understanding is similarly being employed for protection from harm. However, unlike the former case, which in itself is not sinful, this case is sinful, since it is for the purpose of defending and perpetuating sin.

In summary, the formal cause of the false self, or what the false self is, is primarily moral, spiritual, and psychological in nature: the false self is a mental form of concealment, which is used to shield people from real or perceived the danger in a legitimate and innocent way (i.e., out of psychological weakness), or to shield people from the shame of their sin in an illegitimate way (i.e., out of sin and psychological weakness).

The Efficient Causes of the False Self: Self-Reflection, Other People, and the Individual Moral Agent

Three efficient causes cooperate in the construction of the false self: self-reflection, other people, and sin. First, self-reflection or self-understanding is the ability to form a mental representation of oneself, and when people use this ability to conceal actual facts about themselves, they construct a false self. Second, other people contribute to this construction by forcing the person to falsify his or her self-representations by making their love contingent on the person's compliance. Third, by directing people's desires away from God as their source of goodness and truth and into unconscious despair, sin motivates people as individual moral agents to conceal moral and epistemological truths about themselves and thus further misrepresent who they actually are. These three efficient causes abet the construction of the false self throughout people's lifetime.

Self-Reflection and Other People

Ideally, people would begin to develop coherent and authentic self-representations in infancy and childhood through sensitive, reliable, and loving care; but in the fallen world, the care little ones receive never matches this ideal, and so they will inevitably begin to develop some degree of false self-understanding. In infancy, the rudiments of false self-understanding can form when caregivers excessively require infants to comply with external demands that are not in their best interests. When infants are coerced like this over a sufficient period, they become trained or conformed into a way of acting that is motivated by fear. Thus, rather than being edified with a sense of competency that will propel them into the task of exploration and "reality acceptance," infants can internalize a self-protective stance, because their experience tells them that the world is an unsafe place, and that needs (especially agape love) do not come simply by asking and receiving but by paying a price (i.e., meeting conditions).[12] Specifically, in order to get what they need (e.g., psychologically, physically) they have to submit themselves to others' desires (i.e., through appeasement) who refuse to freely give them what they want, that is, who make love contingent. Because the real innate needs that little ones experience are often not validated by others except as they can be manipulated to serve the others' separate interests, infants and children eventually assimilate an extrinsically motivated schema that depends upon compliance and the falsification of their own will (i.e., their desire for agape love) in order to ensure their wellbeing. This schema could probably not be verbalized by most older children, and certainly not by any young ones. Nevertheless, at some point in their development—infancy, childhood, or perhaps as late as adolescence—people falsify their self-understanding, particularly as it concerns their need for love and how it is gotten, to deal with the coercion and invalidation they perceive from others.

In this learned state of false self-understanding, the task of exploration and "reality acceptance" that God intended for human beings is hindered. Instead of children being equipped by parents and others for the eternal pursuit of discovering and experiencing God, they are in some measure stymied. Social experiences that should have established people's capacity to commune with God have instead stunted that capacity, because those experiences misrepresented reality and served to instill the idea that love (and other needs) are contingent upon compliance and forfeiting one's authenticity. Rather than gaining a greater and more satisfying capacity to understand themselves, others, and God, they have been handed a mask and told to wear it if they want to move ahead in life like everyone else. The social world people are born and raised in is not what God designed, but a corrupted system that infects everyone within

---

12. By "agape love," I refer to gracious, unmerited love that is given freely and is not contingent on payment of any kind.

it by educating them to construct a self-image that is contrary to and misrepresentative of the image of God intrinsic to their nature.

The question then arises, who is to blame for the false self? Certainly, the corrupted system bears some fault. Also, as mentioned, Satan bears responsibility for people's delusions about themselves. What about the individual? Because self-reflection and the perception of others' coercion and invalidation happen in the individual, the formation of the false self is a personal cognitive construction as well a social construction.

The Individual Moral Agent

While the moral responsibility for the false self definitely lies to some degree with others (e.g., parents, caregivers, peers, Satan, demons), it may also lie with the individual. It *may*, but not always. Children and others with certain cognitive limitations who have not attained the capacity to willfully account for their actions are not morally responsible for constructing and using the false self. On the other hand, those who have reached the stage of moral accountability do bear some of the blame, because such persons have not only been coerced to form false self-representations but have consented to that coercion as morally aware agents. Individuals with moral agency are culpable for their false self, while individuals without moral agency are not.[13]

Applying the terminology of the Book of Proverbs, the class of individuals who are without moral agency overlaps with those described as "simple" (*peti*), sharing that category's qualities of moral ignorance and innocence. The class of individuals who are moral agents would be further divided into the morally smug (*keˢsîl*) and the incorrigibly wicked (*ewîl*). Having already described the formation of the false self in "the simple," I will now look at the efficient causes of the false self in moral agents (the smug and the wicked).

For people who have become willfully moral agents and can consent to the false self, the driving force motivating them to false self-understanding is no longer just protection from other people, but from the shame of their sin. When people become moral agents, they

13. By "moral agency," I refer to the ability to willfully decide between right and wrong actions, with right actions understood as behaviors that are motivated out of intrinsic love for God, and wrong actions understood as behaviors motivated by sinful desires, or desires that are misdirected toward goods in a way that unnaturally abstracts those goods from God.

become sinners like Adam and Eve and realize that due to their sin they are shameful. Also, like their primordial parents, sinners cover up their shame with "fig leaves." False self-understanding is an attempt that sinners make to conceal the truth that they have willfully chosen to forsake God as the source and ground of their wellbeing, and that because of this choice they are now wretched.

Sin is shameful because it has made people immoral and foolish. Sin has corrupted the motives behind behaviors and cordoned off a whole realm of thought. In their sinful condition, the desires of people's hearts are directed towards what is bad for them, while the considerations of their minds are limited to subjective standards of truth that are prejudiced against God's revelation. These two aspects of sin—moral and epistemological corruption—are reciprocally linked: sinners' misdirected desires motivate them to repress ethicospiritual truth and to consent to falsehood, and the lies they believe draw their desires away from God as the ultimate Good and Ground of their being. Immorality and foolishness go hand-in-hand: sinners have insufficient righteousness, because they smugly assume their moral center is in themselves, and sinners have insufficient knowledge, because their highest epistemological standard is likewise in themselves. How, specifically, is the false self-understanding of sinners immoral, and how is it foolish?

First, sinner's false self-understanding is immoral because it consists in stupidly and smugly misunderstanding the direction of one's will. In other words, people who live "according to the flesh" implicitly trust that the desires and values they hold in their hearts are steering them towards life and wellbeing, when actually their hearts are moving them to willingly pursue a life of misery and death.[14] The general process whereby people are lured away from desiring God, who is the true source of wellbeing, is called temptation: "But each person is tempted when he is lured and enticed by his own desire. This desire when it has conceived gives birth to sin, and sin when it is fully grown brings forth death" (Jas 1:14–15). People are tempted to seek their good apart from God, because they are deceived into believing it is expedient to do so. Although they may not necessarily consider themselves sinners, because they think the

---

14. Augustine explains that in sin humans willingly consent to their harm because they are deceived into thinking it is for their good: "For sin only takes place due to our willing either that things should go well for us or that they should go badly for us. Thus the falsehood is this: we sin so that things may go better for us, and instead the result is that they get worse." Augustine, *The City of God* (2013), 14.4.103.

good life can be gotten without God, people become willing and obedient "slaves" to their sin (Rom 6:16, 19b, 20). Their willing hankering
after sinful desires seems right, but in the end the only fruit it bears is
death (Rom 6:21, 23a). People are drawn to sin because they are deceived
into imagining that what they need for a good life is not from God, but
from another source. Indeed, they are deceived into believing that there
is another source apart from God. Caught in the "deceitfulness of sin,"
people's hearts are hardened against God, so that God appears evil and
sin appears good (Heb 3:12–13). Sin deceives people by seeming to provide them with authentic goods that they naturally desire, so that their
desires are misdirected toward goods in a way that unnaturally abstracts
those goods from God.[15] Because of this, people do not recognize their
sin as sin. In their morally false self-understanding, they cannot enjoy
real goods (e.g., sex, spirituality, friendship, food) as goods from God,
but only as twisted and corrupted pleasures that are actually forms of
moral and psychological pathology: "sexual immorality, impurity, sensuality, idolatry, sorcery, enmity, strife, jealousy, fits of anger, rivalries,
dissensions, divisions, envy, drunkenness, orgies, and things like these"
(Gal 5:19–20). The depraved state of the human heart, which blindly ex-
changes goodness and life in God for misery and death in sin, makes the
false self a moral evil.

Second, sinner's false self-understanding is foolish, because it consists in doubting God, the highest source of wisdom, and thereby living
in ignorance and pride. In sin, people refuse to receive God's instruction,
preferring instead to "lean on their own understanding" (Prov 3:5). By
doubting God and cordoning themselves off from his word, they keep
themselves ignorant of all that God has revealed to them, including their
identity as his children, their purpose in the world as his image-bearers,
their fall into sin, God's offer to reconcile them to himself through the
cross, and the inauguration of the new age in Jesus Christ, who is "on
the move" and bringing his heavenly kingdom to earth. Living in sin and
the flesh blinds people to their place in history and how Jesus' life relates
to theirs. This blindness is what separates non-believers from believers.
In one sense, the most distinguishing mark of the Christian is true self-
understanding, whereas the most distinguishing mark of the unbeliever
is false self-understanding. By the Holy Spirit's illumination, Christians
realize that they are among the many "who were made sinners" (Rom

15. See Lewis, *The Screwtape Letters*, 49.

5:19), but that in Christ's death and resurrection, God has reconciled them back to himself. Those who doubt God and live "according to the flesh," however, cannot comprehend "the things of the Spirit of God" (1 Cor 2:14), and thus they have a false self-understanding of their spiritual condition, repressing the truth that they are sinners separate from God and without hope outside of faith in Christ, and who instead in prideful self-reliance presume to find truth and wellbeing apart from God.

Depending upon the degree to which people have internalized and integrated the immoral values and foolish beliefs of sin, they will be more or less responsible and culpable for their false self, ranging from smug sinners ($k^e s\hat{\imath}l$) of the least aware and stupidest kind to incorrigibly wicked fools ($ew\hat{\imath}l$) of the most aware and intelligent kind. To be a morally culpable agent (i.e., sinner) of any degree, one must have willfully internalized sinful values. Values are "ways that the self goes about trying to grow and satisfy its needs."[16] People's values direct them to certain behaviors and away from others. To adopt *sinful values*, then, means that one has internalized or consented to ways of acting in the world that are aimed at achieving wellbeing apart from God. To have done so also means that one has also consented to sinful beliefs, specifically, the two "cover stories" that one is morally self-sufficient (i.e., righteous in myself) and epistemologically self-sufficient (i.e., able to attain righteousness). People who are least aware of having consented to these beliefs have thereby internalized sinful values the least. These would be the least aware of sinners and the least culpable. On the other hand, people who have consented to their moral and epistemological self-sufficiency with the greatest cognizance are the most culpable.

With these two extremes in mind, one final aspect of the efficient causes of the false self can be discerned. The greater a person's capacity has been built up for self-understanding, the greater the extent that he or she can use false self-understanding to conceal sin. People who are highly functional and competent, enjoying advantages like above-average intelligence and a non-coercive and validating social environment, yet who—when they become moral agents—refuse to ground themselves in God, construct the most efficient false selves. Therefore, for people with moral awareness, with the awareness of the difference between the actual way to life in God and the way of sin, the greatest determining factor—and, in fact, the ultimate one—in the construction of the false self is neither the

16. Kasser, "Sketches for a Self-Determination Theory of Values," 127.

integrity or capability of their psyche, nor the adequacy of the social context that nurtured their development, but whether they lean on their fleshly advantages (e.g., intelligence, upbringing, accomplishments) or on God.

The Content of the False Self

Although God designed people's self-understanding to continually grow in capacity and accuracy through cognitive-developmental advances, knowledge gained through experience, and education provided by others who know them, the accuracy of self-understanding has been hindered by human weakness and sin. While it is still possible to expand the content of the self through reason, experience, and outside authorities, the accuracy of that content will always be frustrated as long as a person remains in sin, refusing to depend upon God as his or her ultimate moral and epistemological authority.

Because sinners repress their awareness of God and his word, leaning instead on their own understanding, the content of their self-understanding will always be partitioned into two compartments: in the more consciously accessible compartment are self-representations that reinforce or validate my presumed self-sufficiency, and, in the other less consciously accessible compartment are actual facts about myself (particularly ethicospiritual facts) that upset my self-sufficiency. As long as this compartmentalization remains in a person, the content of his or her self-understanding will be false to some degree. More importantly, as long as sinners repress the ethical and spiritual facts about their need for God, they will be enslaved to sin and headed for death.

Thesis Two: The Self-Protecting False Self

Why do people understand themselves wrongly, or construct a false self? In its most basic sense, the false self is any degree of distortion in self-understanding that is used as a form of concealment and protection.

In people who have not reached the stage of moral accountability (e.g., children and others with certain cognitive limitations), the false self serves to protect them from harm, attenuates a sense of authenticity and so diminishes wellbeing, does not denote sinful motives, and is therefore an instance of weakness that makes them deserving of help and healing from the evil done to them. In this case, God intends the false self as a means to protect the innocent from worse harm.

In morally responsible agents, the false self serves to defend them from the shame of sin by concealing it, denotes both sinful motives and the deeper desire for life, and is therefore an instance of moral fault (i.e., sin combined with weakness). In this case, Satan intends the false self as a means of blinding moral agents to the gospel, so that they will be ultimately ruined and devoured by him. The ultimate determining factor in whether Satan's goal is realized, however, is not the extent of blindness that Satan causes, but the choice people make between consenting to be blind, so that they can hide from themselves and pretend to hide from God, or to be seeing, so that they can be exposed and transparent before themselves and God.

The True Self

Uncovering the true self is about people coming closer to the perfect knowledge that God has about them. While a daunting task for fallen human beings, it is possible through God's grace.

The Final Cause of the True Self: Choosing to Be God's Children

Despite humanity's fall into sin, humans are still made in the image of God and have the opportunity to ground themselves in God, because God still desires it, and, though they have hidden it from themselves, sinners also still desire it. Because God has not changed his will, neither has his final purpose for self-understanding: to enable human beings to understand themselves so that they can depend on him as their Divine Parent and the ultimate ground of their lives.

The Formal Cause of the True Self

The formal cause of the true self is the opposite of that of the false self: instead of being a form of concealment, it is a form of revelation. In contrast to the false self, the true self is a mental construct completely free from distortion, because instead of serving as a form of concealment used defensively to create distance from another perceived as harmful, it ultimately serves as a form of revelation used to close the distance between another whose communion is desirable.

The false self is a mental construct that represents *who people wrongly conceive themselves to be* based on the invalidation and coercion of others and also, in moral agents, on their presumption of moral and epistemological self-sufficiency: a self-portrait representing the damaging influence of sin and weakness on their self-understanding. The true self, however, is a mental construct that represents *who people actually are*, and it is based on accurate knowledge gained from self-reflection, experience, and outside authorities.

The true self may be more or less perceived by people, and it is reflected completely only in God's omniscient comprehension. While people may have access to many aspects of their true self, only God understands it completely, because of the subversion of human self-understanding. For this reason, the true self is not merely who people perceive themselves to be—which constitutes the false self—but who they actually are in God's understanding. Insofar as weak and sinful human beings are enabled to perceive what God perceives about them, their true self is revealed to them.

There are three outcomes that follow from the true self's revelation. First, as the true self is disclosed, people experience a greater sense of authenticity. Second, true self-understanding enhances one's fellowship with other human beings. Third, true self-understanding helps to restore one's communion with God (i.e., as a way to consent to the truth about their moral and spiritual need for God, who is the ultimate source of their wellbeing).

The Efficient Causes of the True Self

Three efficient causes cooperate to reveal the true self: self-reflection, other people, and God. First, when people use their capacity for reflection accurately, the true self is revealed to them in some degree. Second, the true self can be made known to a person by other people who invite the person to consent to his or her true self-representations by validating his or her self-expressions and affirming the internalization of godly values and beliefs that lead to wellbeing. Third, as the ultimate efficient cause for the true self, God reveals people's true selves by providing them with the other two efficient causes (their power of self-reflection and other people), and also by revealing universal truths about human beings through the wisdom of learned persons, the Bible, and Jesus Christ. These three efficient causes—individual self-reflection, other people, and God—work together to reveal the true self.

For individuals who have not reached moral agency, false self-understanding has not yet taken on an ethicospiritual dimension but pertains to the psychosocial aspects of one's self-understanding. As a result, the revelation of the true self occurs in much the same fashion as was described in the previous section on "The Efficient Causes of the Self." God provides little ones with other people (e.g., parents, other caregivers, peers) who lovingly help them to instill godly values and who validate their actual experience. Despite the fact that God's natural design for self-understanding in little ones has been thwarted by the presence of evil in their lives (e.g., unloving caregivers) forcing them to protect themselves with false self-understanding, that design continues to operate and controvert the false self whenever they receive compassion and help. These persons can be aided in their self-understanding by others who love them, for although the context of their development has certainly changed since the human race fell in Eden, the power of love has not changed.

That said, because God has revealed himself in progressive ways throughout salvation history, it is incumbent on loving parents to sensitively teach their children truths revealed about him in Scripture and particularly in Jesus Christ. God's plan for maturation in the context of the child-parent relationship is, after all, that people would grow up to realize that the loving guidance and validation they received from human parents was a reflection of God's divine parenthood. This realization can be nurtured along as human parents not only demonstrate God's care but teach their children about it, using stories from the Bible, psalms and songs, and other means that lay particular emphasis on Jesus, since he is the image of God. Although individuals can still be led to accurate self-understanding (and out of false self-understanding) through the loving training and validation of others, the revelation of God's love and its culmination in Christ need to be included in the education curriculum.

For morally responsible agents, who have placed their confidence in the flesh and over whom sin has become an enslaving power, the moral and spiritual dimensions of the true self can be effectively disclosed only through a personal encounter with God's Word, which uncovers the deepest aspects of the true self that sinners have repressed: "For the word of God is living and active . . . piercing to the division of soul and spirit, of joints and marrow, and discerning the thoughts and intentions of the heart. And no creature is hidden from his sight, but all are naked and exposed" (Heb 4:12–13; see John 16:7–9). God cuts through the concealment of the false self and reveals sin particularly by the word of the gospel.

The gospel subverts the false self by directing sinners' eyes to the cross where their sin is most clearly revealed. In Jesus' death, the wretchedness of humanity that the false self attempts to obscure is exposed. The purpose of the crucifixion was to make plain the shame and futility of sin by demonstrating that the just end of sin is death. By being made "to be sin" and accepting the judgment of death, Jesus showed that all human beings are cut off from their Creator and will inevitably lose whatever wellbeing they attained in this life when they die, since they are condemned by their Creator for their independence—a judgment revealed in Christ's shameful, excruciating death. Christ speaks the words of despair that all sinners would say if they were honest about their spiritual condition: "My God, my God, why have you forsaken me?" In the message of the cross, one's wretchedness and despair is brought into the light. To consent to this aspect of the true self is humbling, yet by subverting sinners' pride, the gospel allows them to understand another aspect of their true self that was even more concealed by their false self: that they need agape love.[17]

In his death, Jesus reveals the impotence of human fleshliness and iniquity, but he also reveals how much God loves human beings, since Christ died not on behalf of righteous people or people who had done much good, but for sinners: "For one will scarcely die for a righteous person—though perhaps for a good person one would dare even to die—but God shows his love for us in that while we were still sinners, Christ died for us" (Rom 5:7–8). Christ died for sinners so that they would be justified, reconciled with God, and given eternal life (Rom 5:9–11; John 3:16). Being justified through faith, the believer's sin is transferred to Christ and Christ's righteousness is imputed to him or her. This means that the shame and punishment of sin has been expiated and "the righteous requirement of the law" fulfilled for believers, with the result that God

---

17. Augustine believed that through humility sinners are saved and raised up. He writes, "And I dare say that it is beneficial for the proud, who had already fallen by being pleased with themselves, to fall into some open and obvious sin which might lead them to be displeased with themselves." He then quotes Psalm 83:16, "Fill their faces with shame, that they may seek your name, O Lord." Augustine, *The City of God* (2013), 14.14.121.

bears no condemnation towards them (Rom 8:1–4). The grace and love shown in Jesus Christ goes beyond anything sinners could have reasonably hoped to purchase for themselves, and at the same time it proves that they long to be so loved.

The gospel reveals the true self desire for grace and agape love, which human beings intrinsically need, but which they conceal with the false self. As creatures made by God and who receive every good gift from him, humans have nothing, not even their righteousness, with which they can repay him (Job 35:7; 41:11; Rom 11:35). Rather, God created humans to receive all their needs from him freely. In their turn to sin and self-sufficiency, people repressed that fundamental aspect of their nature and were hardened to grace by "the deceitfulness of sin" (see Heb 3:7–13). Sinners are prone to mistrust grace, but put great stock in their own powers, especially reason. Receiving the grace presented in the gospel takes faith, because it challenges human reason to the point of offense.[18] Sinners are more willing to pay for their lives than receive it freely; some will sacrifice themselves on wanton pleasures, while others devote themselves to the rigors of legalism. False self-understanding has made grace look suspicious.

Yet, the extraordinary grace demonstrated in Jesus so outshines all other gracious offers that it can actually transform people and draw their hearts back to dependence on God, even religious hypocrites: "Yes, to this day whenever Moses is read a veil lies over their hearts. But when one turns to the Lord the veil is removed. . . . And we all, with unveiled face, beholding the glory of the Lord, are being transformed into the same image" (2 Cor 3:15–18).

The realization of our true need for God's grace comes through an encounter with God in Jesus Christ, yet this encounter provokes us to make a choice whether to respond in faith or offense. The message of the cross makes this choice salient by presenting our true selves to us, giving us the chance to respond. Although refusing God's grace in this encounter results in further hardening our hearts, believing even in the smallest amount results in a radical shift: union with Christ. Whoever believes is

18. Recall Kierkegaard's story about the poor day laborer who is offered to become the son-in-law of the mightiest emperor who ever lived. The offer would seem so extraordinary so as to be incredible, raising the man's suspicions about its genuineness. Recall also Kierkegaard's differentiation between "religiousness A" and "religiousness B." The former is marked by trust in one's understanding, self-sufficiency, and self-determination, whereas the latter in one's trust in God. Kierkegaard, *The Essential Kierkegaard*, 84, 111.

immediately united with him in his death and receives the guarantee of being united with him in his resurrection (Rom 6:3–5). Furthermore, as believers continue "beholding the glory of the Lord" they are transformed and reconstituted into his likeness "from one degree of glory to another" (2 Cor 3:18).

God's grace in Christ as communicated by the gospel is internalized through the efficient causes of the true self: self-reflection, loving relationships with others, and encounters with God (e.g., through Scripture, wise teaching, prayer, sermons). For Christians the gospel has already begun to be internalized, and thus these channels of God's grace will be received with more willingness for them than they do with unbelievers. Regardless, experiences of the gospel through these forms are necessary for anyone to break out of sin's deception and find true ethicospiritual self-understanding. Self-reflection, loving relationships with others, and encounters with God work to *deconstruct* the old values and beliefs of the flesh and *internalize* the values and beliefs of the gospel.[19]

Until this work is completed, it will be difficult for Christians to the degree that sinful values and beliefs have become entrenched in their hearts. Internalizing gospel values and beliefs will often feel not only unpleasant, but phony and alien, since they conflict with our old ways of behaving and thinking. If, however, we come to trust that the values and beliefs being conveyed in gospel forms will eventually provide what we need, then we will be able to increasingly take a more active role in the work.

Attaining the new resurrection life (i.e., sanctification) is a gradual process. Healing from deep pathology—and sin is the deepest—requires work. The old values of life in the flesh must be worked through and discarded, and the new identity found in Christ must be worked in and integrated. Until this work is completed, true self-understanding and authentic behavior may be hoped for, and cultivated, but never presumed: "Not that I have already obtained this or am already perfect, but I press on to make it my own. . . . I do not consider that I have made it my own. But . . . I press on toward the goal for the prize of the upward call of God in Christ Jesus" (Phil 3:12–14). Discovering the true self is a task that will continue throughout Christians' lives. As it is revealed through self-reflection, other people, and God's revelation, more and more of the content of the true self will be understood.

19. I am here employing Johnson's schema of "deconstruction" and "internalization." Johnson, *Foundations for Soul Care.*

The Content of the True Self

The content of the true self consists in all that people can know about themselves as unique individuals. As the *actual* self, the content of the true self is only partially available to human beings. As long as people live in the fallen world, where harm comes to little ones forcing them to adopt the false self, and where sin inevitably corrupts human beings so that they turn their hearts away from God and lean on their own understanding, people's self-understanding will always be a mixture of true and false self-representations, to one degree or another. Furthermore, people who have reached a stage of moral agency and become sinners will be effectively blocked from certain ethicospiritual facts about themselves that they need to believe in order to be saved.

However, because the "light of the knowledge of the glory of God in the face of Jesus Christ" reorients sinners' hearts back to God, people who believe in Christ begin to experience a transformation of their minds that will eventually end in total freedom from the false self (2 Cor 4:6). Although, due to their remaining sin (i.e., their old, deeply embedded fleshly values and beliefs), they will continue to hold false self-representations, the trajectory of a Christian's psychological development is toward greater and greater true self-understanding. For believers, the true self may be fully explored—even though it may not be possible to fully comprehend—because consent to God's word enables them to accept the truth about themselves, warts and all.

The access that people have to the content of their true self depends upon many factors, particularly and most importantly the state of their hearts towards God. But because people's true selves are known completely to God, there is an objective, actual self that is discoverable. The content of the true self consists of who a person actually is, good and bad, conscious and unconscious, as God knows him or her to be. The true self is not necessarily the self reflected in people's consciousness but who they actually are in God's knowledge.[20] For those whose minds are being transformed by the gospel, their self-understanding has been enabled to steadily move toward a more accurate approximation of God's comprehensive perspective of them, including knowledge of their particular body, soul, social relationships, character, and personal narrative. Of

---

20. For the phrasing of this sentence, I am indebted to Lewis, who once wrote, "It is the self you really are and not its reflection in consciousness that matters most." Lewis, "Letter to Edith Gates," 617.

particular importance are the following ethicospiritual truths revealed about the true self in the gospel: that one is created by God for sonship, fallen from glory, loved by God in Christ, and incomplete.

Thesis Three: The Divinely Revealed Self

What does true self-understanding entail? To perceive the true self entails using one's self-reflection to accurately understand some measure of the person that God knows one to be. As the actual self, the true self is not wholly accessible to human beings because of weakness and sin, and to perceive it requires not just self-reflection, but the experience of agape love from others and especially from God in Christ. God's purpose in true self-understanding is that people would depend on him for all their needs. As the true self is revealed, people experience greater authenticity, enhanced fellowship with other human beings and the restoration of communion with God. The true self is ultimately a gift of God, revealed to his children for their benefit.

Interventions Fostering the True Self

Interventions that foster the true self are those strategies used by individuals, others, and God that deconstruct sinful values and beliefs and internalize godly values and beliefs that are affirmed and communicated by God's Word.

The Application of Interventions

Fostering the true self is fundamentally a task of forming and reforming individuals' values and beliefs. The values and beliefs that effectively promote true self-understanding are those that direct people toward what they truly need: life and wellbeing in God.

Human beings were created to desire their own good and to find their good in God. In other words, God willed that humanity would flourish and flower by willing to be grounded in him. To delight in the Lord for satisfaction is a value that is intrinsic to human nature, as basic to being human as breathing or eating (see Ps 37:4). In this perfect, uncorrupted economy, human beings' desire for their flourishing would have been totally compatible with God's will for them to depend upon and delight themselves in him. By seeking their true, natural needs from God, therefore, they would not feel in the least bit coerced or invalidated, as if they were being forced to subvert and falsify their wills, because they would be fulfilling their wills. Rather, by delightfully depending on God as the gracious giver of all good gifts, their true needs would be met and validated, and thus their true self affirmed.

Helping to promote individuals' true selves necessitates drawing them back to this *creational* value system, which was corrupted by the fall. In children and the young especially, it entails instilling the value of "delighting in the Lord" early in their development and teaching them about God's nature as the loving Father and gracious giver of all good things. In those who have become moral agents, and thus sinners, it especially entails deconstructing old sinful values and beliefs that contravene dependence on God.

The successful application of interventions will look different at various stages of the individual's development. From a moral and spiritual standpoint, there are two main stages of development: those who are becoming moral agents, and those who have become moral agents. In the former category belong infants, some children, and other persons who lack the cognitive-developmental capacity required for moral agency; this set of persons will be labeled as "the simple" (*peti*), whereas the other set will be labeled "moral agents." The key difference between the simple and moral agents is that the latter group has come to "the knowledge of sin" and become culpable sinners (Rom 3:20; 7:7–8).[21] For those who have become moral agents, the law has made sin known and given rise to actual sins. Because of this difference, interventions for the simple will focus less on deconstructing the sinful, fleshly aspects of their false self (since sinful values and beliefs have not yet become entrenched in them) and more on internalizing godly values and beliefs. Interventions for moral agents, on the other hand, will require equal focus on deconstruction and internalization. In both groups, the twin goals of intervention should always be the deconstruction of sinful beliefs or values and the internalization of godly beliefs and values. Wisdom and sensitivity to the individual's particular stage of development, however, should moderate the application of interventions.

Fostering the true self can occur through several different modes of interventions, but in order to be effective they must always be aimed

---

21. The one exception is Jesus, who became a moral agent without also becoming a sinner.

at conforming individuals' values and beliefs to those that God designed for humans to possess, that is, to those that reflect the intrinsic value of depending on God. Since this value has been obscured by sin and false self-understanding, a criterion for interventions that promote this value must be relied upon in addition to human reasoning and experience, so that interventions and their progress can be objectively evaluated. That criterion is God's revelation in Scripture, specifically the message of the gospel, which communicates God's grace in the most concentrated and effulgent form (i.e., the cross). Interventions must be "gospel interventions" that expose the false self, with its faulty system of sinful values and beliefs, and that internalize gospel values and beliefs. In what follows, several strategies will be suggested that typify such gospel interventions as they would be utilized by individuals and those attempting to help them (e.g., parents, counselors, and other caregivers).

Strategies for Individuals

Individuals can promote their own true self by practicing certain gospel interventions on themselves. Some such practices explicitly commended in Scripture include: doing good deeds (e.g., prayer) in secret, judging oneself before judging others, and meditating on certain objective truths about oneself. These interventions help individuals to re-constitute their system of values and beliefs so that it draws them toward dependence and delight in the Lord, or grounding themselves in God.

First, doing good deeds in secret helps individuals internalize the value of seeking delight or "reward" in God rather than other sources (Matt 6:1–18). To learn to delight in God and find fulfillment in him instead of the pleasures of sin requires seeking fulfillment in an environment where sinful pleasures are mitigated. One such pleasure is receiving applause from other people for one's good deeds, or practicing "righteousness before other people in order to be seen by them" (Matt 6:1). Getting satisfaction in this way builds up the false self value and belief that one's wellbeing comes from fleshly accomplishments, like earning people's praise through philanthropic acts. The antidote, Jesus says, is to refrain from doing good deeds in public "in order to be seen," and instead to do them in secret where only God sees, and where the main satisfaction to be had is delight in *his* seeing. Thus, when giving, individuals should give secretly; when praying, they should pray in a room with closed doors; and when fasting, they should hide the signs of fasting by anointing their head and washing their face. By practicing righteousness *coram deo*, individuals conform their values and beliefs to the truth that behaving in the ways that God esteems (and not merely other people) brings delight.

Second, by judging themselves before they judge others, individuals undermine their implicit and sinful assumption that they are righteous. As individuals internalize the value of Jesus' instruction to "first take the log out of your own eye," they will simultaneously be deconstructing the delusion that those who most need judging are other people, not one-self (Matt 7:3). Individuals promote their true self in this intervention, because they internalize the truth that they are prone to sin due to their fallen condition.

Third, individuals can promote their true self by meditating on certain objective truths, which are revealed about human beings in the Bible. This intervention focuses especially on the internalization of godly beliefs. The gospel reveals that humans are created by God as his sons and daughters; they are fallen from glory into weakness and sin; they are loved by God in Christ; and they are incomplete in mind, body, and spirit. As these beliefs are internalized, they explain and give rational support to godly behaviors. At the same time, they serve to contradict the lies of sin and Satan. Paul provides a clear model for this intervention in Philippians 3:1–15.

Individuals who wish to foster their true self must engage the task as active participants, trusting that God is their great Ally, working within them to eventually bring about the task's completion (Phil 2:12–13). Yet, God also gives them other human agents to help in the work: parents, teachers, friends, counselors, and other allies.

Strategies for Allies

Here I share strategies we can use to help other people. In this section, I will speak in terms of current commonly known therapy modalities (e.g., behavioral, cognitive, biomedical), because I want to help readers who are therapists or psychologists to make connections between what I've written and ideas they are already familiar with in their field. That's not to say that only therapists or psychologists will find this section useful;

though I'm using categories most commonly used by people in these fields, all my readers should be able to readily grasp and apply these ideas.

Johnson has identified the following modalities as those that have long been used by soul care providers (both secular and Christian) and that have proven to be effective: biomedical, behavioral, cognitive, relational, family and group, symbolic, narrative/dramatic, dynamic, experiential/emotion focused, spiritual direction, and character.[22] These interventions can be employed by soul-care allies to help individuals deconstruct the sinful values and beliefs of their false self and internalize godly ones, provided that they are intentionally directed toward promoting the true self as it is revealed by God. None of the following modalities should be employed as an end in itself: they are all merely different tools that may be more or less helpful depending upon the nature of individuals' biological and psychological condition.

The Biomedical Modality

In some cases, pharmaceutical medication should be used to foster true self-understanding.[23] Biochemical abnormalities can interfere with people's ability to reform their values and beliefs, and so medicine may be needed to offset interfering symptoms. For example, for persons immobilized by severe depression, anti-depressants may temporarily supply the physical and emotional stamina needed to attend to self-examination.

The Behavioral Modality

Behavior therapy is based on the principle that as people are trained to respond to external stimuli, either attractive reinforcements or aversive punishments, patterns of behavior are established. Changing one's behaviors without any parallel change in cognition (i.e., values and beliefs) is insufficient, in itself, to impact the accuracy of people's self-understanding. For example, training a person afraid of spiders to feel calm around them (systematic desensitization) does not automatically help him or her to internalize godly values or beliefs. Yet, such behavior-change can aid

22. These modalities are those identified and Christianly interpreted by Johnson. He defines modalities as "particular, irreducible and justifiable intervention pathways for soul care." Johnson, *Foundations for Soul Care*, 569.

23. Harter, "Authenticity," 392.

the application of other modalities. For example, if people with nicotine addictions have linked their excessive smoking with a certain ungodly belief or value (e.g., "I need to smoke to feel good"), treatments that help them interrupt or terminate their behavioral patterns can aid other modes of treatment that attack the cognitive side of the link. Many traditional spiritual practices that consist of behaviors (e.g., participation in routine congregational worship, exposure to the public reading of Scripture and preaching, taking the Lord's Supper) can be done to help inculcate Christian beliefs and values into people's hearts, provided that complementary modalities are also at work to help connect the practices with their Christian meaning.

The Cognitive Modality

Cognitive therapy is directly applicable to internalizing true self beliefs. "The cognitive therapist trains counselees to analyze their core beliefs, automatic thoughts and reasoning processes and to internalize more life-enhancing beliefs and reasoning procedures."[24] One use of the cognitive modality is to teach people how to judge themselves accurately in terms of the psychosocial and ethicospiritual orders. Another would be to train people how to assent to the true self revealed in Scripture (created by God, fallen, loved in Christ, and incomplete).[25] For example, believers can learn to identify false self core beliefs such as "I'm not cared for" and replace them with true ones like "I am a beloved child of God." Likewise, instruction in distinguishing right and wrong values and behaviors should be given, while making accommodations that accord with a person's stage of cognitive development.[26] Thus, the sages of Proverbs aimed

24. Johnson, *Foundations for Soul Care*, 578.

25. However, cognitive therapy would need to be complemented by carditive modalities in order to go beyond intellectual *assent* to the true self with willful and affective *consent*.

26. Here is an instance when the difference between persons at various developmental stages becomes salient: certain behaviors that are wrong for a mature adult might not be wrong for very young child. For example, a two-year-old who boasts about being able to "run forever" with utter earnestness should not be chided as if they were manifesting false self behavior. On the other hand, correction would be appropriate for an adult who cunningly employs *suggestio falsi* or *suppressio veri* to enhance his self-esteem. Moral instruction for children is a critical area for research in Christian psychology. To begin, a thorough review of Christian thought on this subject is needed. Of seminal importance is Kierkegaard's view of childhood innocence and

their instruction at "the simple person" (*petî*) and "the young" (*na'ar*) and presented it in a way that was especially suitable for them (e.g., short, memorable, and witty aphorisms).

The Relational Modality

By cultivating healthy adult relationships, relational therapy works to re-forge the representations of self and other that people have previously formed, and in this way it can help them experience a right and true relationship with God. Safety, support, genuine care, and confidentiality are requisite qualities of the relational counselor. Winnicott's approach as outlined in chapter four is a good model in many respects, despite its secular framing.[27] A Christian appropriation of the relational modality will aim at much more than enabling people to relate more adaptively to the therapist and other people:

> The development of a healthy human relationship with a ma-ture, loving soul caregiver can be a catalyst for a breakthrough in one's relationship with God, as one experiences—perhaps for the first time—a concrete, healing exemplification of God's love and holiness.[28]

As Johnson here shows, the most important relationship one needs to experience rightly is with God, and so he must eventually transcend the counselor as the explicit focus of one's relational work. The relational mo-dality can help validate individuals' true self need for communion with God and dependence on him.

The Family and Group Modalities

These modalities focus on persons' current close relationships, either in one's family or in a therapy group. The work done in family and group modalities is aimed at utilizing these relational contexts to facilitate

---

the development of self-consciousness and moral responsibility. See Come, *Kierkeg-aard as Theologian*, 155–89.

27. For example, Winnicott helpfully warns of the dangers of countertransference in the analyst-analysand relationship. The mature caregiver must remain objective, in order to facilitate the counselee's own maturing in objectivity. Winnicott, "The Aims of Psycho-Analytic Treatment."

28. Johnson, *Foundations for Soul Care*, 583.

change in both the individual and the other members. The family is regarded as a system in which the actions of individual members automatically impact the other members. Since the roots of the false self go back to the parent-child relationship, employing this modality can aid in the deconstruction of false values and beliefs that individuals learned from bad experiences with their parents. For example, memories can be reframed in light of the true/false self dichotomy in order to discern how false self-representations were formed and have been reinforced over the years, so as to better understand and address their current manifestations (e.g., through transference) in life now.[29] Caregivers working within the family modality should be alert for signs of parental coercion and invalidation that stifle the child's sense of authenticity and competence, and they should guide parents into how to build up their infant's ego-strength with "good-enough" parenting, and how to strengthen their children's true self-representations through listening, verbal validation of their self-expressions and autobiographical reflections, and agape support. Additionally, differences in moral stages of development among family members should be taken into account, so that appropriate standards are applied to each member.

The group modality has at least two distinct advantages for fostering the true self over other modalities, because it provides a *social* context for internalizing Christian values and beliefs. In groups, the therapeutic relationship encompasses more people than in typical one-on-one settings, so that one engages with a number of different kinds of persons, rather than just the counselor. The first advantage of this larger therapeutic setting is that it creates a greater potential for experiencing God's love in Christ. As one shares burdens and receives compassion, the other group members who are being transformed into the *imago Christi* (if Christians) or who at least bear the marred *imago Dei* (if non-Christians) will convey God's own love toward him or her. As members sense their relatedness to each other and to God who works through them, their trust and openness to authenticity will be boosted. Second, provided that the group has agreed to transparency and true self behavior as one of its goals, the group offers a unique opportunity for each member to practice "taking the log out of his or her own eye," because the members will continually be faced with how they should deal with the "speck" in their brothers' and sisters' eyes. Group leaders should remember Jesus' instruction and guide members

29. Plass and Cofield offer a helpful tool for such a reframing called "lifemapping." Plass and Cofield, *The Relational Soul*.

to become aware of the temptation to judge each other, so that they can learn to judge themselves first. As members' authenticity is strengthened within the group context, they can develop habits of authentic behavior and thinking and transfer them to other relationships in their life.

The Symbolic Modality

Among prominent modern psychologists, Carl Jung probably made the greatest use of the symbolic modality. Jung analyzed patients' dreams, fantasies, slips-of-the-tongue and other material arising from their unconscious in order to uncover their symbolic meaning. He believed these phenomena are "the natural reaction of a self-regulating psychic system" that tell people what needs to change in their psyche in order to achieve healing.[30] When people engage the symbols emanating from their unconscious, they can follow them as clues to solve internal conflicts and find wholeness. Christian soul care providers can also appreciate the importance of the symbolic associations of their counselees, and they can become skilled at discerning how symbols indicate the presence of truth and falsehood in the unconscious. Symbols in dreams, fantasies, and so on may signify values, beliefs, and identifications that belong to the true self or the false self.

Even as Jung valued the externalization of symbols that lie latent in people's psyche, he also appreciated that people may internalize symbols that come from outside. Thus, Jungian analysts are trained to help patients "incorporate new symbols and meaning" in their self-understanding.[31] When Christians appropriate the symbolic modality, they will also recognize that symbolic associations can powerfully alter people's grasp of themselves, others, and God.[32] The nourishment of the true self and authenticity is often derailed by overlooking or misinterpreting God-ordained symbols found in creation and Scripture.[33] On the other hand,

---

30. Jung, *Analytical Psychology*, 123.

31. Ryckman, *Theories of Personality*, 76.

32. Interestingly, and by Jung's own account, symbolism had a profound effect upon his relationship with Christ, leading him to reject Christianity as a worldview. Jung, *Memories, Dreams, Reflections*.

33. This seems to have been the case with Jung, who was drawn to the beauty and wonder he saw in the natural marvels of his homeland, e.g., the glowing snow-covered Alps in evening and Lake Constance stretching away into the distance. Instead of interpreting these as symbols meant to lead him to Christ, he doubted that connection:

realizing the meaning behind these symbols aid the internalization of godly values and beliefs, directly and indirectly. Three particularly vital and Christian internalizations of symbolic meaning occur in baptism, partaking of the Lord's Supper, and preaching that taps into the Christian imagination. Luther understood these practices as "images" that represent God's personal communication of his word; thus, they employ symbols meant to be experienced as God's own speech (e.g., preaching), Christ's presence (Lord's Supper), and identification with Christ (baptism).

The Narrative/Dramatic Modality

Story is a series of events, as told in oral, written, or enacted forms. As simple as story may seem, humans depend on it to see their life as meaningful.[34] From a Christian viewpoint, every story is an attempt to convey truth about reality; literary critics refer to the truths depicted in stories as "themes." No story can capture the full meaningfulness of human life, because ultimately humans are meant to experience reality not as a series of events—with past, present, and future—but as an eternal present: "In life and in art both, as it seems to me, we are always trying to catch in our net of successive moments something that is not successive."[35] Nevertheless, as Lewis believed, stories (even more than experience) are sometimes able to capture reality, if only in part. For this reason, good stories and stories with good elements can help people to more accurately understand how their lives fit into reality. Through the process of "emplotment" people's "identity and narrative can be altered" and reinterpreted in light of humanity's true story or drama, in which every individual plays a role.[36]

Using the narrative/dramatic modality to promote the true self and undermine the false self requires the internalization of those themes and stories that depict reality. One function of the Bible is to reveal the true story of humanity. Creation, fall, redemption in Christ, and the present

---

"I always hoped I might be able to find something—perhaps in nature—that would give me the clue and show me where or what the secret was. . . . I was constantly on the lookout for something mysterious. Consciously, I was religious in the Christian sense, though always with the reservation: 'But it is not so certain as all that!'" Jung, *Memories, Dreams, Reflections*, 22.

34. See Johnson, *Foundations for Soul Care*, chap. 9.

35. Lewis, "On Stories," 19.

36. Johnson, *Foundations for Soul Care*, 591; see Ricoeur, *Time and Narrative*; Vanhoozer, *The Drama of Doctrine*.

dawn of the new creation should be internalized as the drama within which one performs. Just as crucial is the internalization of the way of life of the principal actor in humanity's drama, Jesus Christ. By internalizing his authentic performance when he lived on earth into their own lives, believers become more integrated and authentic actors themselves.

The Dynamic Modality

Dynamic therapies in modern psychology originated with Freud. This modality focuses on dismantling the psychological defenses that people automatically construct to hide and protect themselves, so that unconscious conflicts in people's psyche can be brought to awareness and resolved. It was the main modality employed by Winnicott, who worked in the object relations school of Freudian psychoanalysis. More directly than any other kind of therapy, dynamic therapy aims to help people feel they are living their real lives, and not hiding from themselves and others the "skeletons in the closet." It seeks to accomplish this by skillfully helping people find relief from the guilt and shame within their psyche. Due to the disregard for an objective ethical order inherent in a secular perspective, a secular approach to dynamic therapy cannot effectively resolve the true shame and guilt that people experience due to their sin; rather it tends to build up new defensives, and further hardens people to their sin. Because only the gospel can deal with the heart's true problem, bondage to sin, a Christian use of the dynamic modality will employ the gospel as the fundamental "insight" into one's soul and the main framework for interpreting people's psychodynamic conflicts.

The disclosure of the heart, with its conscious and unconscious material, is ultimately only salutary if it is done before God. A secular approach that leaves God out can do more harm than good; the real "sin against the self" is not for the true self to be totally disclosed to another (as Winnicott thought), but for it *not to be disclosed to God*.[37] God already knows people perfectly, but people do not know themselves before God; they have hidden from him (Gen 3:8). For the good of their souls, people need to willingly let God "search" and "know" their heart, so that he may guide them "in the way everlasting" (Ps 139:23–24). The goal of dynamic therapy should be to help people to "unveil" and "rest transparently" in God.[38]

---

37. See Winnicott, "Communicating and Not Communicating," 187.

38. Lewis, *Letters to Malcolm*, 21; Kierkegaard, *The Sickness unto Death*, 82.

The Experiential/Emotion-Focused Modality

Describing non-Christian applications of this modality, Johnson writes:

> Current secular, experience-oriented therapies focus on the sub-
> jectivity of counselees to help them grow in self-understanding,
> through listening to and articulating their emotional experience,
> in order to further their ability to take responsibility for them-
> selves, become more honest and regulate their emotions better.[39]

When people's subjective reflection is held in tandem with the objective criterion of God's Word, the true self can be promoted. People must
engage in subjective reflection if godly values and beliefs are to be internalized. The experiential/emotion-focused modality should be used,
therefore, to help people disentangle their emotions from their false self
and understand how emotions can express the true self, as well as to help
them cultivate religious affections, or those that represent the values they
have internalized from the gospel.[40]

The Spiritual Direction Modality

Seen from a Christian standpoint, all therapeutic modalities are spiritual.
The name of this particular modality, therefore, does not set it apart as
if it alone pertains to the spiritual order, but because it tends to limit its
focus to this order. Risking stereotypical language, one might say spiritual direction is the province of monks and mystics. More precisely, it is
a modality especially fit for Christians who are already relatively psychologically and spiritually healthy and yet who want to experience greater
communion with God, freedom from remaining sin, effectiveness in
their vocation, and greater authenticity as Christians.

　　Spiritual direction fosters the true self most directly by training
Christians to practice the spiritual disciplines taught in Scripture: prayer
in secret (i.e., in silence and solitude), self-examination, confession
and receiving absolution, and consent to the true self (in prayer and

---

39. Johnson, *Foundations for Soul Care*, 596–97.

40. A recent secular model that distinguishes between adaptive emotions and in-
hibitory emotions might just as well have distinguished true emotions from false ones.
In a Christian perspective, the difference between true and false emotions is more
salient and meaningful because it posits an objective criterion. A promising task for
Christian psychology would be to reframe this secular model in light of a Christian
view of true/false self emotions. McCullough et al., *Treating Affect Phobia*.

meditation). The Enneagram has also been used to help directees undermine their false self.[41]

The Character Modality

Finally, character-formation entails exerting one's agency and reason, in dependence on the power of the Spirit, in order to develop, over time, Christ-like virtues. One such virtue is authenticity. In order to ingrain true self behaviors, so that they form into habits, daily actions can be taken to thoughtfully and consensually perform the activities demonstrated by Christ, as well as any that are commensurate with a Christian perspective. Such a daily and hourly pursuit of virtuous agency cannot be boiled down to any rule of behavior except Christ and his example of prayerful dependence on the Father. Character-formation must run parallel with Paul's command to "pray without ceasing" (1 Thess 5:17) and Merton's conception of prayer as "contemplation": "We should not look for a 'method' or 'system,' but cultivate an 'attitude,' and 'outlook': faith, openness, attention, reverence, expectation, supplication, trust, joy."[42]

Thesis Four: Gospel Interventions

What interventions can foster true self-understanding? Fostering the true self requires reconstructing individuals' values and beliefs according to God's Word. Interventions must be, therefore, gospel interventions. Those who wish to foster true self-understanding in themselves and others should bear in mind the three agents or efficient causes of the true self: the individual who utilizes self-reflection to reform their self-understanding, others who lovingly support and validate the individual, and God who reveals truth to the individual. By virtue of their power of self-reflection, individuals can promote their own true self-understanding through interventions such as: doing good deeds in secret, judging themselves before judging others, and meditating on certain objective truths about themselves. Others who serve as allies in the task can aid individuals through several therapeutic modalities. Ultimately, God is the final cause of successful interventions and the individual's greatest ally, because he utilizes his divine powers to support the work from all sides:

41. Rohr and Ebert, *The Enneagram*; Plass and Cofield, *The Relational Soul*.

42. Merton and Steere, *The Climate of Monastic Prayer*, 49.

equipping the individual from within, sending other people to help them from without, and providing his Word as a "living and active" revealer of people's hearts and as the criterion for progress.

Conclusion

Knowing our true self is essential for wellbeing. As Augustine affirmed, the soul is designed to gravitate towards God, and thus towards goodness and truth. As we grow in our true self-understanding, we withdraw further from the self-reliant life of falsity and move closer to a life marked by a radical dependence on God that stems from consenting to our true self, which is revealed in the gospel as *simul justus et peccator*. By discovering our true selves, we recover an authentic awareness of our spiritual poverty and filial dependence and can "rest transparently" in God."[43]

This is a process, however, and it involves a continual struggle of resisting "the flesh, its desires and its illusions, in order to strengthen and elevate us more and more, and open our eyes to the full meaning of our life in Christ."[44] Ultimately, the revelation of the true self depends not on individuals or their human allies, but on the power of the Holy Spirit. People living in the flesh are effectively deceived about their spiritual condition, and thus blinded to the spiritual (sinful, Satanic) influences that motivate their actions as well as God's role in the fulfillment of their needs. Uncovering the true self is immensely difficult, because both the solution and the problem are often misunderstood, as in a secular approach. Believers and non-believers alike are impeded from utilizing their capacity for self-reflection to its maximal potential.[45]

In conclusion, we should always hold the veracity of our self-representations with a healthy degree of suspicion, knowing that only in resurrected bodies can we know ourselves fully, even as God knows us (1 Cor 13:12). While self-reflection and the counsel of others can be helpful, we should remember that true self-understanding is a gift of God.[46] Discov-

43. Kierkegaard, *The Sickness unto Death*, 113.

44. Merton, *The New Man*, 157–58.

45. If full self-understanding were possible, it may actually be harmful, as Lewis says, "Have we any reason to suppose that total self-knowledge, if it were given us, would be for our good? Children and fools, we are told, should never look at half-done work; and we are not yet, I trust, even half-done." Lewis, *Letters to Malcolm*, 34.

46. Merton believed that true self-understanding is impossible from the side of a person's own effort to find it, because, unlike the false self, the true self is not one's own

ering the true self and differentiating it from the false self can become a
pursuit that is abstracted from God and devolve into a fleshly attempt to
justify our actions—that is, as a way to depend on ourself or others to feel
authentic, instead of depending upon God in Christ. Self-examination
without recourse to God's Word relies on subjective perception, and will
surely lead to false self-understanding.[47] While seeking the perfection of
our true self-understanding is a worthy goal, in the end there are more
urgent and important ones: "the only way we become perfect is by leaving
ourselves, and, in a certain sense, forgetting our own perfection, to follow
Christ."[48] In Christianity, more clearly contemplating our own image is
good, but to see our reflection in truth, we must gaze on the image of
Christ. In his face we find that his goodness, suffering, sonship, and glory
are our own.

---

to construct (through subjective reflection): "Contemplation is precisely the awareness that this 'I' is really 'not I' and the awakening of the unknown 'I' that is beyond
observation and reflection and is incapable of commenting upon itself." Merton, *New
Seeds of Contemplation*, 7.

47. This vulnerability is demonstrated in Augustine's emphasis on the inward turn
without sufficiently describing it as a turn towards Christ. Jenson comments: "the
problem is not so much that Augustine portrays an inner self cut off from the rest of
the world. It is that the exteriority at the heart of his interiority is yet an exteriority
uncomfortable with the flesh of Christ. He can affirm with characteristic brio the in-
dispensability of Christ as the way to God. . . . But in the end, Christ remains a glorious
via rather than the re-definition of Augustine's God. . . . He looks for the *imago Dei*
in himself without sufficient attention paid to Christ, who is himself the *imago Dei*."
Jenson, *The Gravity of Sin*, 42–43.

48. Merton, *The New Man*, 27.

Bibliography

Althaus, Paul. *The Theology of Martin Luther*. Philadelphia: Fortress, 1966.

Arnold, Matthieu. "Luther on Christ's Person and Work." In *The Oxford Handbook of Martin Luther's Theology*, edited by Robert Kolb et al., 1st ed., 274–93. Oxford Handbooks. New York: Oxford University Press, 2014.

Augustine. *The City of God*. Translated by Marcus Dods. New York: Modern Library, 1950.

———. *The City of God*. Edited by Boniface Ramsey. Translated by William S. Babcock. Vol. 11–22. Hyde Park, NY: New City, 2013.

———. *Confessions*. Edited by Michael P. Foley. Translated by F. J. Sheed. 2nd ed. Indianapolis: Hackett, 2006.

———. Confessions. In *The Complete Ante-Nicene & Nicene and Post-Nicene Church Fathers Collection*, edited by Philip Schaff. Catholic Way, 2014. Kindle Edition.

———. "Soliloquies." In *The Complete Ante-Nicene & Nicene and Post-Nicene Church Fathers Collection*, edited by Philip Schaff. Catholic Way, 2014. Kindle Edition.

———. *The Trinity*. Edited by John E. Rotelle. Translated by Edmund Hill. The Works of Saint Augustine: A Translation for the 21st Century 5. Brooklyn: New City, 1991.

Baldwin, James M. *Mental Development of the Child and the Race: Methods and Processes*. New York: Macmillan, 1895.

Barth, Karl. *The Christian Life: Church Dogmatics IV, 4: Lecture Fragments*. Translated by Geoffrey W. Bromily. Grand Rapids: Eerdmans, 1981.

Batka, L'ubomír. "Luther's Teaching on Sin and Evil." In *The Oxford Handbook of Martin Luther's Theology*, edited by Robert Kolb et al., 233–53. Oxford Handbooks. New York: Oxford University Press, 2014.

Bauckham, Richard. *Jesus and the Eyewitnesses: The Gospels as Eyewitness Testimony*. Grand Rapids: Eerdmans, 2006.

Bauer, Jack J., and Heidi A. Wayment. "How the Ego Quiets as It Grows: Ego Development, Growth Stories, and Eudaimonic Personality Development." In *Transcending Self-Interest: Psychological Explorations of the Quiet Ego*, edited by H.

A. Wayment and J. J. Bauer, 199–210. Washington, DC: American Psychological Association, 2008.

Baumeister, Roy F. "Should Schools Try to Boost Self-Esteem? Beware the Dark Side." *American Educator* 43 (1996) 14–19.

Baumeister, Roy F., et al. "Does High Self-Esteem Cause Better Performance, Interpersonal Success, Happiness, or Healthier Lifestyles?" *Psychological Sciences in the Public Interest* 4 (2003) 1–44.

Bayer, Oswald. *Martin Luther's Theology: A Contemporary Interpretation.* Translated by Thomas H. Trapp. Grand Rapids: Eerdmans, 2008.

Best, Ernest. *A Critical and Exegetical Commentary on Ephesians.* Edinburgh: T. & T. Clark, 1998.

Blomberg, Craig. *Matthew.* Nashville: Broadman, 1992.

Broyles, C. C. "Gospel (Good News)." In *Dictionary of Jesus and the Gospels,* edited by Joel B. Green, 2nd ed., 282–86. Downers Grove, IL: IVP Academic, 2013.

Bruce, F. F. *The Letter of Paul to the Romans: An Introduction and Commentary.* Grand Rapids: Eerdmans, 1985.

Bultmann, Rudolph. *Theology of the New Testament.* Vol. 1. New York: Scribner's, 1951.

Calvin, John. *Institutes of the Christian Religion.* Translated by Ford Lewis Battles. Grand Rapids: Eerdmans, 1995.

Campbell, Constantine R. *Paul and Union with Christ: An Exegetical and Theological Study.* Grand Rapids: Zondervan, 2012.

Carr, Anne E. *A Search for Wisdom and Spirit: Thomas Merton's Theology of the Self.* Notre Dame: University of Notre Dame Press, 1988.

Cary, Phillip. *Augustine's Invention of the Inner Self: The Legacy of a Christian Platonist.* New York: Oxford University Press, 2000.

———. *Inner Grace: Augustine in the Traditions of Plato and Paul.* New York: Oxford University Press, 2008.

———. *Outward Signs: The Powerlessness of External Things in Augustine's Thought.* New York: Oxford University Press, 2008.

Chamblin, J. K. "Psychology." In *Dictionary of Paul and His Letters,* edited by Gerald F. Hawthorne et al., 765–75. Downers Grove, IL: InterVarsity, 1993.

Come, Arnold B. *Kierkegaard as Theologian: Recovering My Self.* Montreal: McGill-Queen's University Press, 1997.

Cooley, C. H. *Human Nature and the Social Order.* New York: Scribner's Sons, 1902.

Cortez, Marc. *Theological Anthropology: A Guide for the Perplexed.* Guides for the Perplexed. London: T. & T. Clark, 2010.

Crites, Stephen. "The Aesthetics of Self-Deception." *Soundings* 62 (1979) 114–18.

Danker, Frank W., et al. *A Greek-English Lexicon of the New Testament and Other Early Christian Literature.* Chicago: University of Chicago Press, 2000.

Davies, W. D., and Dale C. Allison. *A Critical and Exegetical Commentary on the Gospel according to Saint Matthew.* Vol. 1. Edinburgh: T. & T. Clark, 1988.

———. *Matthew: A Shorter Commentary.* London: T. & T. Clark, 2004.

Deci, E. L., and R. M. Ryan. *Intrinsic Motivation and Self-Determination in Human Behavior.* New York: Plenum, 1985.

Demarest, Bruce A. *The Cross and Salvation: The Doctrine of Salvation.* Foundations of Evangelical Theology 1. Wheaton: Crossway, 1997.

Dockery, D. S. "New Nature and Old Nature." In *Dictionary of Paul and His Letters*, edited by Gerald F. Hawthorne et al., 628–29. Downers Grove, IL: InterVarsity, 1993.

Dryden, J. de Waal. "Romans 7: Sin, the Self, and Spiritual Formation." Paper presented at the 66th annual meeting of the Evangelical Theological Society, San Diego, November 20, 2014.

Dunn, James D. G. *Romans 1–8.* Word Biblical Commentary 38A. Dallas: Word, 1988.

Evans, C. Stephen. *Søren Kierkegaard's Christian Psychology: Insight for Counseling and Pastoral Care.* Vancouver, BC: Regent College, 1995.

Evans, Craig A. *Matthew.* New York: Cambridge University Press, 2012.

Faricy, Robert. "Thomas Merton: Solitude and the True Self." *Science et Esprit* 31.2 (1979) 191–98.

Fee, Gordon D. "Some Reflections on Pauline Spirituality." In *Alive to God: Studies in Spirituality Presented to James Houston*, edited by J. M. Houston et al., 96–107. Downers Grove, IL: InterVarsity, 1992.

Ferry, Patrick. "Martin Luther on Preaching: Promises and Problems of the Sermon as a Source of Reformation History and as an Instrument of the Reformation." *Concordia Theological Quarterly* 54.4 (1990) 265–80.

Fingarette, Herbert. *Self-Deception.* London: Routledge, 1977.

Fitzmyer, Joseph A. *Romans: A New Translation with Introduction and Commentary.* Anchor Bible 33. New York: Doubleday, 1993.

Fowl, Stephen E. *Ephesians: A Commentary.* Louisville: Westminster John Knox, 2012.

Fox, Michael V. *Proverbs 1–9: A New Translation with Introduction and Commentary.* Anchor Bible 18a. New York: Doubleday, 2000.

———. *Proverbs 10–31: A New Translation with Introduction and Commentary.* The Anchor Yale Bible 18b. New Haven: Yale University Press, 2009.

Garland, David E. *Reading Matthew: A Literary and Theological Commentary.* Reading the New Testament Series. Macon, GA: Smyth & Helwys, 2001.

Gesenius, H. F. W. *A Hebrew and English Lexicon of the Old Testament.* Edited by S. R. Driver et al. Translated by Edward Robinson. New York: Oxford University Press, 1952.

Gibbs, Jeffrey A. *Matthew 1:1—11:1.* St. Louis: Concordia, 2006.

Gilovich, T., et al. "Shallow Thoughts about the Self: The Automatic Components in Self-Assessment." In *The Self in Social Judgment*, edited by M. D. Alicke et al., 67–84. New York: Psychology, 2005.

Greenwald, A. G. "The Totalitarian Ego: Fabrication and Revision of Personal History." *American Psychologist* 7 (1980) 603–18.

Grenz, Stanley. *The Social God and the Relational Self: A Trinitarian Theology of the Imago Dei.* Louisville: Westminster John Knox, 2007.

Gustafson, Hans. "Place, Spiritual Anthropology and Sacramentality in Thomas Merton's Later Years." *Merton Annual* 25 (2012) 74–90.

Guthrie, D., and R. P. Martin. "God." In *Dictionary of Paul and His Letters*, edited by Gerald F. Hawthorne et al., 354–69. Downers Grove, IL: InterVarsity, 1993.

Hagner, Donald A. *Matthew 1–13.* Word Biblical Commentary 33A. Dallas: Word, 1995.

Harter, Susan. "Authenticity." In *Handbook of Positive Psychology*, edited by C. R. Snyder and Shane J. Lopez, 382–94. New York: Oxford University Press, 2002.

———. "Cognitive-Developmental Considerations in the Conduct of Play Therapy." In *Handbook of Play Therapy*, edited by Charles E. Schaefer and Kevin J. O'Connor, 95–127. New York: Wiley, 1983.

———. *The Construction of the Self: Developmental and Sociocultural Foundations*. 2nd ed. New York: Guilford, 2012.

———. "Development of Self-Representations during Childhood and Adolescence." In *Handbook of Self and Identity*, edited by Mark R. Leary and June Price Tangney, 610–42. New York: Guilford, 2003.

———. "Developmental Perspectives on the Self-System." In *Socialization, Personality, and Social Development*, edited by E. Mavis Hetherington, 275–385. New York: Wiley, 1983.

———. "Self and Identity Development." In *At the Threshold: The Developing Adolescent*, edited by S. Shirley Feldman and Glen R. Elliott, 352–87. Cambridge: Harvard University Press, 1990.

Harter, Susan, and Donna B. Marold. "A Model of the Effects of Perceived Parent and Peer Support on Adolescent False Self Behavior." *Child Development* 67.2 (1996) 360–74.

Harter, Susan, et al. "Lack of Voice as a Manifestation of False Self-Behavior among Adolescents: The School Setting as a Stage upon Which the Drama of Authenticity is Enacted." *Educational Psychologist* 32.3 (1997) 153–73.

Hauerwas, Stanley. *Matthew*. Grand Rapids: Brazos, 2006.

Hodges, B., et al. "Difficulties in Recognizing One's Own Incompetence: Novice Physicians Who Are Unskilled and Unaware of It." *Academic Medicine* 76 (2001) 87–89.

Hoffman, Marie. "From Enemy Combatant to Strange Bedfellow: The Role of Religious Narratives in the Work of W. R. D. Fairbairn and D. W. Winnicott." *Psychoanalytic Dialogues* 14.6 (2004): 769–804.

———. "On Christianity, Psychoanalysis, and the Hope of Eternal Return." *Journal of Psychology and Christianity* 29.2 (2010).

Horan, Daniel P. "Thomas Merton the 'Dunce': Identity, Incarnation, and the Not-so-Subtle Influence of John Duns Scotus." *Cistercian Studies Quarterly* 47.2 (2012) 149–75.

Hurtado, L. W. "Son of God." In *Dictionary of Paul and His Letters*, edited by Gerald F. Hawthorne et al., 900–906. Downers Grove, IL: InterVarsity, 1993.

Jacobs, Alan. *How to Think: A Survival Guide for a World at Odds*. Currency: New York, 2017.

James, William. *The Principles of Psychology*. 2 vols. New York: Holt, 1890.

Janzen, J. G. "The Claim of the Shema." *Encounter* 59.1 (1998) 243–57.

Jenson, Matt. *The Gravity of Sin: Augustine, Luther, and Barth on* Homo Incurvatus in Se. London: T. & T. Clark, 2006.

Johnson, Eric L. *Foundations for Soul Care: A Christian Psychology Proposal*. Downers Grove, IL: IVP Academic, 2007.

———. *God and Soul Care: The Therapeutic Resources of the Christian Faith*. Downers Grove, IL: InterVarsity, 2017.

———, ed. *Psychology and Christianity: Five Views*. 2nd ed. Downers Grove, IL: IVP Academic, 2010.

Jones, Stanton L., and Richard E. Butman. *Modern Psychotherapies: A Comprehensive Christian Appraisal*. 2nd ed. Downers Grove, IL: IVP Academic, 2011.

Jowers, Dennis W. "Divine Unity and the Economy of Salvation in the *De Trinitate* of Augustine." *Reformed Theological Review* 60.2 (2001) 68–84.

Jung, Carl. G. *Analytical Psychology: Its Theory and Practice*. New York: Random House, 1968.

———. *Memories, Dreams, Reflections*. Edited by Aniela Jaffe. Translated by Clara Winston and Richard Winston. Rev. ed. New York: Vintage, 1989.

Kasser, Richard M. "Sketches for a Self-Determination Theory of Values." In *Handbook of Self-Determination Research*, edited by Edward L. Deci and Richard M. Ryan, 123–40. Rochester: University of Rochester Press, 2002.

Keener, Craig S. *Romans: A New Covenant Commentary*. Eugene: Cascade, 2009.

Keller, Timothy J. *Center Church: Doing Balanced, Gospel-Centered Ministry in Your City*. Grand Rapids: Zondervan, 2012.

Kernis, M. H., et al. "Master of One's Psychological Domain? Not Likely If One's Self-Esteem Is Unstable." *Personality and Social Psychology Bulletin* 26 (2000) 1297–305.

Kierkegaard, Søren. *The Concept of Anxiety: A Simple Psychologically Orienting Deliberation on the Dogmatic Issue of Hereditary Sin*. Translated by Reidar Thomte and Albert Anderson. Princeton: Princeton University Press, 1980.

———. *The Essential Kierkegaard*. Edited by Howard V. Hong and Edna H. Hong. Princeton: Princeton University Press, 2000.

———. *The Sickness unto Death: A Christian Psychological Exposition for Upbuilding and Awakening*. Translated by H. V. Hong and E. H. Hong. Princeton: Princeton University Press, 1983.

Kolb, Robert. "Luther on the Theology of the Cross." In *The Pastoral Luther: Essays on Martin Luther's Practical Theology*, edited by Timothy J. Wengert, 33–56. Lutheran Quarterly Books. Grand Rapids: Eerdmans, 2009.

Kolb, Robert, et al. *The Book of Concord: The Confessions of the Evangelical Lutheran Church*. Minneapolis: Fortress, 2000.

Kramer, Victor A. "Forgetting in Order to Find: The Self in Thomas Merton's Poetry." *Cross Currents* 43.3 (1993) 375–88.

Krueger, J., and D. Dunning. "Unskilled and Unaware of It: How Difficulty in Recognizing One's Own Incompetence Lead to Inflated Self-Assessments." *Journal of Personality and Social Psychology* 77 (1999) 1121–34.

Labrie, Ross. "Wholeness in Thomas Merton's Poetry." *Merton Annual* 22 (2009) 41–60.

Leary, M. R. *The Curse of the Self: Self-Awareness, Egotism, and the Quality of Human Life*. New York: Oxford University Press, 2004.

Lerner, Harriet Goldhor. *The Dance of Deception: Pretending and Truth-Telling in Women's Lives*. New York: HarperCollins, 1993.

Letham, Robert. *Union with Christ: In Scripture, History, and Theology*. Phillipsburg: P & R, 2011.

Lewis, C. S. "Letter to Edith Gates, Magdalen College, Oxford, May 23rd 1944." In *The Collected Letters of C. S. Lewis*. Vol. 2, *Books, Broadcasts, and the War, 1931–1949*, edited by Walter Hooper, 616–17. San Francisco: HarperSanFrancisco, 2004.

———. *Letters to Malcolm: Chiefly on Prayer*. 1st American ed. New York: Harcourt, Brace & World, 1964.

———. "On Stories." In *On Stories and Other Essays on Literature*, 3–20. Orlando: Harcourt, 1982.

———. *The Screwtape Letters*. New York: Macmillan, 1943.

Lincoln, Andrew T. *Ephesians*. Word Biblical Commentary 42. Dallas: Word, 1990.

Lipsey, Roger. "The Monk's Chief Service: Thomas Merton's Late Writings on Contemplation." *Cistercian Studies Quarterly* 45.2 (2010) 169–98.

Luter, A. B., Jr. "Gospel." In *Dictionary of Paul and His Letters*, edited by Gerald F. Hawthorne et al., 369–72. Downers Grove, IL: InterVarsity, 1993.

Luther, Martin. "First Sunday in Advent, Math. 21, 1–9: Christ Enters Jerusalem: Or Faith; Good Works; and the Spiritual Meaning of This Gospel." In *The Complete Sermons of Martin Luther*, edited and translated by J. N. Lenker, 1:17–58. Grand Rapids: Baker, 2000.

———. *Luther's Works*. Edited by Jaroslav Pelikan et al. 55 vols. St. Louis: Concordia, 1955.

Mannermaa, Tuomo. *Christ Present in Faith: Luther's View of Justification*. 1st ed. Minneapolis: Fortress, 2005.

Marshall, I. Howard. "Who Is a Hypocrite?" *Bibliotheca Sacra* 159 (2002) 131–50.

Masterson, James F. *The Search for the Real Self: Unmasking the Personality Disorders of Our Age*. New York: Free, 1988.

Matera, Frank J. *Romans*. Grand Rapids: Baker Academic, 2010.

Mattes, Mark. "Luther on Justification as Forensic and Effective." In *The Oxford Handbook of Martin Luther's Theology*, edited by Robert Kolb et al., 1st ed., 264–73. Oxford Handbooks. New York: Oxford University Press, 2014.

McAdams, D. P. "Generativity, the Redemptive Self, and the Problem of a Noisy Ego in American Life." In *Transcending Self-Interest: Psychological Explorations of the Quiet Ego*, edited by H. A. Wayment and J. J. Bauer, 235–42. Washington, DC: American Psychological Association, 2008.

McCullough, Leigh, et al. *Treating Affect Phobia: A Manual for Short-Term Dynamic Psychotherapy*. New York: Guilford, 2003.

McLaughlin, Brian P., and Amélie O. Rorty, eds. *Perspectives on Self-Deception*. Berkeley: University of California Press, 1988.

Mead, George Herbert. *Mind, Self & Society from the Standpoint of a Social Behaviorist*. Chicago: University of Chicago Press, 1934.

Merton, Thomas. *Conjectures of a Guilty Bystander*. Garden City, NY: Doubleday, 1966.

———. *Contemplative Prayer*. New York: Herder and Herder, 1969.

———. *Life and Holiness*. New York: Herder and Herder, 1963.

———. *The New Man*. New York: Farrar, Straus & Cudahy, 1961.

———. *New Seeds of Contemplation*. New York: New Directions, 2007.

———. *The Silent Life*. New York: Farrar, Straus & Cudahy, 1957.

Merton, Thomas, and Lawrence Cunningham. *Thomas Merton, Spiritual Master: The Essential Writings*. New York: Paulist, 1992.

Merton, Thomas, and Robert E. Daggy. *Dancing in the Water of Life: Seeking Peace in the Hermitage*. San Francisco: HarperSanFrancisco, 1997.

Merton, Thomas, and Douglas V. Steere. *The Climate of Monastic Prayer*. Spencer, MA: Cistercian, 1969.

Meye, R. P. "Spirituality." In *Dictionary of Paul and His Letters*, edited by Gerald F. Hawthorne et al., 906–16. Downers Grove, IL: InterVarsity, 1993.

Moo, Douglas J. "'Flesh' in Romans: A Challenge for the Translator." In *The Challenge of Bible Translation: Communicating God's Word to the World: Essays in Honor of Ronald F. Youngblood*, edited by Glen G. Scorgie et al., 365–80. Grand Rapids: Zondervan, 2003.

Morris, L. "Sin, Guilt." In *Dictionary of Paul and His Letters*, edited by Gerald F. Hawthorne et al., 877–81. Downers Grove, IL: InterVarsity, 1993.

Murray, John. *Principles of Conduct: Aspects of Biblical Ethics*. London: Tyndale, 1957.

Neff, Kristen D. "Self-Compassion: Moving Beyond the Pitfalls of a Separate Self-Concept." In *Transcending Self-Interest: Psychological Explorations of the Quiet Ego*, edited by H. A. Wayment and J. J. Bauer, 95–106. Washington, DC: American Psychological Association, 2008.

Nolland, John. *The Gospel of Matthew: A Commentary on the Greek Text*. Grand Rapids: Eerdmans, 2005.

Nygren, Anders. *Commentary on Romans*. Philadelphia: Muhlenberg, 1949.

Parker, Stephen E. *Winnicott and Religion*. Lanham, MD: Aronson, 2011.

Pemberton, Glenn D. "It's a Fool's Life: The Deformation of Character in Proverbs." *Restoration Quarterly* 50 (2008) 213–24.

Pennington, Jonathan T. *Reading the Gospels Wisely: A Narrative and Theological Introduction*. Grand Rapids: Baker Academic, 2012.

Perrin, Nicholas. "Gospels." In *Dictionary for Theological Interpretation of the Bible*, edited by Kevin J. Vanhoozer et al., 264–68. Grand Rapids: Baker Academic, 2005.

Plass, Richard, and James Cofield. *The Relational Soul: Moving from False Self to Deep Connection*. Downers Grove, IL: InterVarsity, 2014.

Ricoeur, Paul. *Time and Narrative*. Vols. 1–3. Translated by Kathleen Blamey and David Pellauer. Chicago: University of Chicago Press, 1984.

Ridderbos, Herman. *Paul: An Outline of His Theology*. Translated by John Richard de Witt. Grand Rapids: Eerdmans, 1975.

Rittgers, Ronald K. "Luther on Private Confession." *Lutheran Quarterly* 19.3 (2005) 312–31.

Rodman, F. Robert. *Winnicott: Life and Work*. Cambridge, MA: Perseus, 2003.

Rogers, Carl R. *Client-Centered Therapy: Its Current Practice, Implications, and Theory*. Boston: Houghton Mifflin, 1951.

Rohr, Richard, and Andreas Ebert. *The Enneagram: A Christian Perspective*. New York: Crossroad, 2001.

Rosenthal, David M. "XV—Unity of Consciousness and the Self." *Proceedings of the Aristotelian Society* 103.1 (2003) 325–52.

Ryan, Richard M., and Kirk W. Brown. "What Is Optimal Self-Esteem? The Cultivation and Consequences of Contingent vs. True Self-Esteem as Viewed from the Self-Determination Theory Perspective." In *Self-Esteem: Issues and Answers*, edited by M. H. Kernis, 120–31. New York: Psychology, 2006.

Ryckman, Richard M. *Theories of Personality*. New York: Nostrand, 1978.

Sæbø, M. "Ḥkm." In *Theological Lexicon of the Old Testament*, edited by E. Jenni and C. Westermann, 1:418–24. Peabody, MA: Hendrickson, 1997.

Schreiner, Thomas R. "Baptism in the Epistles: An Initiation Rite for Believers." In *Believer's Baptism: Sign of the New Covenant in Christ*, edited by Thomas R. Schreiner and Shawn D. Wright, 67–96. Nashville: B&H, 2006.

———. *Romans*. Grand Rapids: Baker, 1998.

Schwanke, Johannes. "Luther's Theology of Creation." In *The Oxford Handbook of Martin Luther's Theology*, edited by Robert Kolb et al., 201–11. Oxford Handbooks. New York: Oxford University Press, 2014.

Schwarz, Reinhard. "The Last Supper: The Testament of Jesus." In *The Pastoral Luther: Essays on Martin Luther's Practical Theology*, edited by Timothy J. Wengert, 198–210. Lutheran Quarterly Books. Grand Rapids: Eerdmans, 2009.

Seifrid, Mark A. "Romans 7: The Voice of the Law." In *Perspectives on Our Struggle with Sin: 3 Views of Romans 7*, edited by Terry L. Wilder, 111–65. Nashville: B&H Academic, 2011.

Silcock, Jeffrey. "Luther on the Holy Spirit and His Use of God's Word." In *The Oxford Handbook of Martin Luther's Theology*, edited by Robert Kolb et al., 294–309. Oxford Handbooks. New York: Oxford University Press, 2014.

Sliva, Moisés. *Philippians*. 2nd ed. Grand Rapids: Baker Academic, 2005.

Slenczka, Notger. "Luther's Anthropology." In *The Oxford Handbook of Martin Luther's Theology*, edited by Robert Kolb et al., 212–32. Oxford Handbooks. New York: Oxford University Press, 2014.

Snyder, C. R., and Raymond L. Higgins. "Reality Negotiation: Governing One's Self and Being Governed by Others." *General Psychology Review* 4 (1997) 336–50.

Stacey, W. David. *The Pauline View of Man: In Relation to Its Judaic and Hellenistic Background*. New York: Macmillan, 1956.

Steindl-Rast, David. "Recollections of Thomas Merton's Last Days in the West." *Monastic Studies* 7 (1969) 2–3.

Strohl, Jane E. "Luther's Spiritual Journey." In *The Cambridge Companion to Martin Luther*, edited by Donald K. McKim, 149–64. New York: Cambridge University Press, 2003.

Tangney, June Price. "Humility." In *Oxford Handbook of Positive Psychology*, edited by S. J. Lopez and C. R. Snyder, 2nd ed., 483–90. New York: Oxford University Press, 2009.

Taylor, Charles. *Sources of the Self: The Making of the Modern Identity*. Cambridge: Harvard University Press, 1989.

Taylor, Shelley E., and Jonathan D. Brown. "Illusion and Well-Being: A Social Psychological Perspective on Mental Health." In *The Self in Social Psychology*, edited by R. F. Baumeister, 43–66. Cleveland: Taylor and Francis, 1999.

Thielman, Frank. *Ephesians*. Baker Exegetical Commentary on the New Testament. Grand Rapids: Baker Academic, 2010.

Torrance, Thomas F. *Atonement: The Person and Work of Christ*. Edited by Robert T. Walker. Downers Grove, IL: IVP Academic, 2009.

———. *Incarnation: The Person and Life of Christ*. Edited by Robert T. Walker. Downers Grove, IL: IVP Academic, 2008.

Trigg, Jonathan. "Luther on Baptism and Penance." In *The Oxford Handbook of Martin Luther's Theology*, edited by Robert Kolb et al., 310–21. Oxford Handbooks. New York: Oxford University Press, 2014.

Tuber, Steven. *Attachment, Play, and Authenticity: A Winnicott Primer*. Lanham, MD: Aronson, 2008.

Turner, David L. *Matthew*. Baker Exegetical Commentary on the New Testament. Grand Rapids: Baker Academic, 2008.

Vanhoozer, Kevin J. *The Drama of Doctrine: A Canonical-Linguistic Approach to Christian Theology*. Louisville: Westminster John Knox, 2005.

Via, Dan O. *Self-Deception and Wholeness in Paul and Matthew*. Minneapolis: Fortress, 1990.

Waltke, Bruce K. *The Book of Proverbs*. Grand Rapids: Eerdmans, 2004.

Wannenwetsch, Bernd. "Luther's Moral Theology." In *The Cambridge Companion to Martin Luther*, edited by Donald K. McKim, 120–35. New York: Cambridge University Press, 2003.

Williamson, Peter S., and Mary Healy. *Ephesians*. Catholic Commentary on Sacred Scripture. Grand Rapids: Baker Academic, 2009.

Wilson, Henry S. "Luther on Preaching as God Speaking." *Lutheran Quarterly* 19.1 (2005) 63–76.

Wingren, Gustaf. *The Living Word: A Theological Study of Preaching and the Church*. Philadelphia: Muhlenberg, 1960.

Winnicott, D. W. "Advising Parents." In *The Family and Individual Development*, 165–75. New York: Routledge, 2006.

———. "Appetite and Emotional Disorder." In *Through Paediatrics to Psycho-Analysis*, 33–51. New York: Basic, 1975.

———. *Babies and Their Mothers*. Edited by Clare Winnicott et al.. 1st U.S. ed. Reading, MA: Addison-Wesley, 1987.

———. "Child Analysis in the Latency Period." In *The Maturational Processes and the Facilitating Environment: Studies in the Theory of Emotional Development*, 115–23. New York: International Universities Press, 1965.

———. "Classification: Is There a Psycho-Analytic Contribution to Psychiatric Classification?" In *The Maturational Processes and the Facilitating Environment: Studies in the Theory of Emotional Development*, 124–39. New York: International Universities Press, 1965.

———. "Communicating and Not Communicating Leading to a Study of Certain Opposites." In *The Maturational Processes and the Facilitating Environment: Studies in the Theory of Emotional Development*, 179–92. New York: International Universities Press, 1965.

———. "Counter-Transference." In *The Maturational Processes and the Facilitating Environment: Studies in the Theory of Emotional Development*, 158–65. New York: International Universities Press, 1965.

———. "Ego Distortion in Terms of True and False Self." In *The Maturational Processes and the Facilitating Environment: Studies in the Theory of Emotional Development*, 140–52. New York: International Universities Press, 1965.

———. "Ego Integration in Child Development." In *The Maturational Processes and the Facilitating Environment: Studies in the Theory of Emotional Development*, 56–63. New York: International Universities Press, 1965.

———. "From Dependence towards Independence in the Development of the Individual." In *The Maturational Processes and the Facilitating Environment: Studies in the Theory of Emotional Development*, 83–92. New York: International Universities Press, 1965.

———. "Group Influences and the Maladjusted Child: The School Aspect." In *The Family and Individual Development*, 214–27. New York: Routledge, 2006.

———. *Home Is Where We Start From: Essays by a Psychoanalyst*. Edited by Clare Winnicott et al. New York: Norton, 1986.

———. *Human Nature*. 1st American ed. New York: Schocken, 1988.

———. "Mind and Its Relation to the Psyche-Soma." In *Through Paediatrics to Psycho-Analysis*, 243–54. New York: Basic, 1975.

———. "Morals and Education." In *The Maturational Processes and the Facilitating Environment: Studies in the Theory of Emotional Development*, 93–105. New York: International Universities Press, 1965.

———. "Ocular Psychoneuroses of Childhood." In *Through Paediatrics to Psycho-Analysis*, 85–90. New York: Basic, 1975.

———. "Primary Maternal Preoccupation." In *Through Paediatrics to Psycho-Analysis*, 300–305. New York: Basic, 1975.

———. "Primitive Emotional Development." In *Through Paediatrics to Psycho-Analysis*, 145–56. New York: Basic, 1975.

———. "The Aims of Psycho-Analytic Treatment." In *The Maturational Processes and the Facilitating Environment: Studies in the Theory of Emotional Development*, 166–70. New York: International Universities Press, 1965.

———. *The Child, the Family, and the Outside World*. Reading, MA: Addison-Wesley, 1987.

———. "The Development of the Capacity for Concern." In *The Maturational Processes and the Facilitating Environment: Studies in the Theory of Emotional Development*, 73–82. New York: International Universities Press, 1965.

———. *The Maturational Processes and the Facilitating Environment: Studies in the Theory of Emotional Development*. London: Karnac, 1990.

———. *The Spontaneous Gesture: Selected Letters of D. W. Winnicott*. Edited by F. Robert Rodman. Cambridge: Harvard University Press, 1987.

———. "The Theory of the Parent-Infant Relationship." In *The Maturational Processes and the Facilitating Environment: Studies in the Theory of Emotional Development*, 37–55. New York: International Universities Press, 1965.

———. *Thinking about Children*. Edited by Jennifer Johns et al. Reading, MA: Addison-Wesley, 1996.

———. "Transitional Objects and Transitional Phenomena." In *Through Paediatrics to Psycho-Analysis*, 229–42. New York: Basic, 1975.

Witherington, Ben, III. *Jesus the Sage: The Pilgrimage of Wisdom*. Minneapolis: Fortress Press, 2000.

Subject Index

Scripture Index